STEFAN GEORGE
THE HOMOSEXUAL IMAGINARY

LEGENDA

LEGENDA is the Modern Humanities Research Association's book imprint for new research in the Humanities. Founded in 1995 by Malcolm Bowie and others within the University of Oxford, Legenda has always been a collaborative publishing enterprise, directly governed by scholars. The Modern Humanities Research Association (MHRA) joined this collaboration in 1998, became half-owner in 2004, in partnership with Maney Publishing and then Routledge, and has since 2016 been sole owner. Titles range from medieval texts to contemporary cinema and form a widely comparative view of the modern humanities, including works on Arabic, Catalan, English, French, German, Greek, Italian, Portuguese, Russian, Spanish, and Yiddish literature. Editorial boards and committees of more than 60 leading academic specialists work in collaboration with bodies such as the Society for French Studies, the British Comparative Literature Association and the Association of Hispanists of Great Britain & Ireland.

The MHRA encourages and promotes advanced study and research in the field of the modern humanities, especially modern European languages and literature, including English, and also cinema. It aims to break down the barriers between scholars working in different disciplines and to maintain the unity of humanistic scholarship. The Association fulfils this purpose through the publication of journals, bibliographies, monographs, critical editions, and the MHRA Style Guide, and by making grants in support of research. Membership is open to all who work in the Humanities, whether independent or in a University post, and the participation of younger colleagues entering the field is especially welcomed.

ALSO PUBLISHED BY THE ASSOCIATION

Critical Texts
Tudor and Stuart Translations • *New Translations* • *European Translations*
MHRA Library of Medieval Welsh Literature

MHRA Bibliographies
Publications of the Modern Humanities Research Association

The Annual Bibliography of English Language & Literature
Austrian Studies
Modern Language Review
Portuguese Studies
The Slavonic and East European Review
Working Papers in the Humanities
The Yearbook of English Studies

www.mhra.org.uk
www.legendabooks.com

GERMANIC LITERATURES

Germanic Literatures includes monographs and essay collections on literature originally written not only in German, but also in Dutch and the Scandinavian languages. Within the German-speaking area, it seeks also to publish studies of other national literatures such as those of Austria and Switzerland. The chronological scope of the series extends from the early Middle Ages down to the present day.

APPEARING IN THIS SERIES

11. *E.T.A. Hoffmann's Orient*, by Joanna Neilly
12. *Structures of Subjugation in Dutch Literature*, by Judit Gera
13. *Isak Dinesen Reading Søren Kierkegaard: On Christianity, Seduction, Gender, and Repetition*, by Mads Bunch
14. *Yvan Goll: The Thwarted Pursuit of the Whole*, by Robert Vilain
15. *Foreign Parts: German and Austrian Actors on the British Stage 1933–1960*, by Richard Dove
16. *Paul Celan's Unfinished Poetics*, by Thomas C. Connolly
17. *Encounters with Albion: Britain and the British in Texts by Jewish Refugees from Nazism*, by Anthony Grenville
18. *The Law of Poetry: Studies in Hölderlin's Poetics*, by Charles Lewis
19. *Georg Hermann: A Writer's Life*, by John Craig-Sharples
20. *Alfred Döblin: Monsters, Cyborgs and Berliners 1900–1933*, by Robert Craig
21. *Confrontational Readings: Literary Neo-Avant-Gardes in Dutch and German*, edited by Inge Arteel, Lars Bernaerts and Olivier Couder
22. *Poetry, Painting, Park: Goethe and Claude Lorrain*, by Franz R. Kempf
23. *Childhood, Memory, and the Nation: Young Lives under Nazism in Contemporary German Culture*, by Alexandra Lloyd

Managing Editor
Dr Graham Nelson, 41 Wellington Square, Oxford OX1 2JF, UK
www.legendabooks.com

Stefan George

The Homosexual Imaginary

PETER MORGAN

LEGENDA
Germanic Literatures 30
Modern Humanities Research Association
2024

Published by Legenda
an imprint of the Modern Humanities Research Association
Salisbury House, Station Road, Cambridge CB1 2LA

ISBN 978-1-83954-229-9

First published 2024

Copy-Editor: Dr Nigel Hope

CONTENTS

Dedication and Acknowledgements   ix
George's Works   x

Introduction   1

    Methodology and Terminology   8

1 Stefan George's Germany   17

    Male Homosexual Identity in Nineteenth-Century Germany   17
    George's Life   26
    The George Circle   28
    George's Notoriety   31
    Homosexuality in George's Poems   38
    George's Lyric *Vita*   40

2 Discovering the Homosexual Imaginary   51

    Finding a Beginning   51
    A Path to the Self: *Algabal*   63
    Valorizing Male Eros in the *Bücher*   66
    George's Inclusive Imaginary   74
    Homosexual Love in *Das Jahr der Seele*   77
    A New Sense of Self: *Der Teppich des Lebens*   94

3 Damaged Narcissus   115

    Coming to Terms with the Self: *Der siebente Ring*   115
    Art versus Life: Maximin   123
    Group Identity and Self-Realization in *Die Aufnahme in den Orden*   131
    The Conflicted Self of *Der Stern des Bundes*   134
    Apostle of Narcissus   142

4 The Healing of Narcissus   147

    War and Crisis   147
    Friendship, Love and Self-Acceptance: *Das Neue Reich*   150
    The Healing of Narcissus   163
    George's Homosexual Imaginary   175

Bibliography   181
Index   193

DEDICATION AND ACKNOWLEDGEMENTS

Friends and colleagues far and near have offered helpful advice, criticism, and support for the completion of this book. Professor David Roberts encouraged me early and provided astute and insightful comments on the first version. The Legenda team, Professor Ritchie Robertson, Series Editor for Germanic Literatures, Managing Editor Dr Graham Nelson, and copy-editor Dr Nigel Hope have given invaluable editorial and production advice. Ritchie in particular was unstinting in his commitment to the finalization of a unified and focused manuscript. Dr Danica Jenkins read and critically commented on the penultimate version. I take this opportunity to thank you for your generous and constructive input.

Writing this book has made me think about the people who have helped me shape my life as a gay man. My parents, both long since deceased, loved and accepted me early as I am. Among the living, I thank my partner and companion Dimitry, for forty-six years of love and caring; my older brother, Adrian, who offered support at a time when such support was rare; and more recently but no less loved, Christian along with his cherished mate, Nouggs. I dedicate this book to you.

Here, too, I acknowledge the memory of the late Professor Emeritus Philip Thomson, an inspiring teacher during my early university years and gratefully remembered by me and generations of Australian students of German language and literature.

P.M., Sydney, September 2023

GEORGE'S WORKS

Original Title	Date	English Translation
Hymnen	1890	*Hymns*
Pilgerfahrten	1891	*Pilgrim Journeys*
Algabal	1892	*Heliogabalus*
Die Bücher der Hirten- und Preisgedichte der Sagen und Sänge und der hängenden Gärten	1895	*The Books of Eclogues and Eulogies, of Legends and Lays, and of the Hanging Gardens*
Das Jahr der Seele	1897	*The Year of the Soul*
Der Teppich des Lebens und die Lieder von Traum und Tod. Mit einem Vorspiel	1899/1900	*The Tapestry of Life and the Songs of Dream and Death. With a Prelude*
Die Fibel	1901	*The Primer*
Tage und Taten	1903	*Days and Works*
Der siebente Ring	1907	*The Seventh Ring*
Der Stern des Bundes	1914	*The Star of the Covenant*
Drei Gesänge	1921	*Three Songs*
Das Neue Reich	1928	*The New Empire*

The edition of George's works used for citations is *Sämtliche Werke in 18 Bänden*, ed. by Georg Peter Landmann and Ute Oelmann under the auspices of the Stefan George-Stiftung (Stuttgart: Klett-Cotta, 1981–2012) (*SW*).

In citing George's poems in English I have made free use of the 1949 version by Ernst Morwitz and Olga Marx, *The Works of Stefan George*. However this work, like all translations reflects the point of view of the translator. In this case Ernst Morwitz's personal relationship with George influences the overall tenor of the work as well as the particular details (see Jaeger, 'The Works of Stefan George', pp. 391–98). Moreover, George drew on the fullest resources of the German language. His employment of archaic and dialect expressions as well as the extraordinary syntactic and semantic consequences of the cancellation of capitalization of nouns, permitted ambiguities and implications well beyond the possibilities of standard written German. In order to convey an adequately literal translation of certain lines, I have been obliged in many cases to adapt Morwitz's version for literal readings: in these cases, an asterisk is used ('*Morwitz'). Unless otherwise noted, all unattributed translations are my own.

INTRODUCTION

Browsing through some volumes of poetry in a Marburg bookshop as a teenager, Hans-Georg Gadamer came across poems by Stefan George and was captivated by their originality.[1] Born in 1900, Gadamer belonged to the generation most influenced by George. Writing many years later in 1968, the eminent philosopher of hermeneutics returns to these memories in order to describe the ongoing influence of this poet on his life. Unlike Gadamer I did not read George as a student. That came later. While teaching German studies and catching up on names known but unread, I also was struck by the extraordinary strength and beauty of this poetry. Yet there is also something dated and no longer accessible about George both in the language of many poems and in the reports of so many of his disciples, friends and followers about the man himself. Gadamer felt it. Hence his late advocacy of this poet who had accompanied him through a lifetime. He was not alone. Other towering figures such as Georg Lukács, Walter Benjamin and Theodor Adorno were similarly engaged by George's oeuvre, seeking at various points in their lives to come to terms with its contradictions.

George was a controversial figure on account of his reactionary attitudes and his homosexuality. The former — the sense of the prophetic, the charismatic and the cultic — seems scarcely comprehensible after a century in which ideologies were tested and found wanting. Yet it reflects the experience of an era of crisis, upheaval and confusion. At the same time it liberated a poetic voice that continues to enthral a century later. Noting the unique intensity of George's poetry several decades ago, influential German literary critic Frank Schirrmacher challenged commentators and interpreters to free it finally from the controversies of the writer's life and recognize its timelessness.[2]

My study of George came about as the result of cognitive dissonance, as a way of negotiating the extremes of beauty, inculcation and commandment in his body of verse. The persona and the phenomenon of George remained alien to me while the poetry moved me profoundly. After long reflection I have come to see George differently from most, a reflection, perhaps, of my own life experiences, just as earlier commentators no doubt found something of their lives reflected in this spellbinding body of verse. In my case it was the recognition of a homosexual man's journey through life in a period before a gay male or queer identity existed. I belong to a generation which can still look back on a childhood in which the word homosexual or any of its synonyms was never used, in which sex was not discussed, in which the word belonged in specialist medical manuals, and in which no telephone directory, let alone internet address, provided access to help, services or companions. Life changed dramatically as even suburban Australia began to feel the consequences of gay liberation and the sexual revolution of the 1970s. For Stefan George, too, the world had changed dramatically and profoundly. The term 'homosexuality' came into use around the time of George's birth in 1868 and male homosexuality began to find a social existence in Germany at this time, albeit in ways that we today may find problematic. In this book I use the neutral term 'male homosexual' rather than later terms such as 'gay' or 'queer' in recognition of the differences over time and place in the self-understanding and self-representation of homosexual men.

I do not read George's poetry under the dominant academic rubrics of aesthetic fundamentalism, psychological narcissism, reactionary anti-modernism or political fascism, although these all play a part. I read it as the literary representation of a homosexual man's life from adolescence to old age, a carefully choreographed lyric biography covering the years from the late 1880s until 1928. In Gadamer's words it is 'the shift inwards of the poet's life-consciousness' into an inner narrative, in an environment where the inner and the outer worlds of the male homosexual could not yet be coordinated, where self-fulfilment and social convention did not yet intersect.[3] Each era and interpreter reads the poems differently, laying emphasis differently, selecting different poems, seeing different aspects. I cannot focus on 'secret Germany', the adoration of the ideal youth Maximin, or the prophetic and cultic aspects of George's work. For me, other, more meaningful qualities predominate in this body of verse: the ongoing encounter with self and the exploration of the possibility of existential happiness for a homosexual man.

This study represents a contribution to scholarship and analysis of George, but is not intended as a comprehensive overview of his life and works. It presents George as a homosexual writer at an early stage of modern male homosexual consciousness, for whom sexual orientation is a defining and determining aspect of identity. The term 'homosexual' was coined in 1869 by Austro-Hungarian journalist Karl Maria Kertbeny. It was a formal term of ascription for use in legal, medical and social contexts, not merely a term of derision or of in-group identification. At first the word was applied by a dominant group to a minority group. Soon, however the term came to be embraced by those seeking a language of self-ascription in order to articulate the dawning potentiality of their homosexual lives as trajectories of personal development including love, companionship and fulfilment, not merely self-loathing and social alienation.

With Paragraph 175 of the legal code, which outlawed homosexual acts, powerfully enforced in the wake of the Eulenburg affair in the upper echelons of Wilhelminian society in 1907, the danger of legal prosecution was high in Germany for anyone daring to publicize, proselytize or otherwise draw attention to homosexual behaviour or intentions.[4] George avoided public avowal of his homosexuality, given the dangers posed by Paragraph 175, but it was openly recognized and acknowledged by those closest to him. In 1914, the homosexual journalist, essayist and writer Peter Hamecher (1879–1938) contributed an article on 'masculine eros' in George's work to Magnus Hirschfeld's journal, *Jahrbuch für sexuelle Zwischenstufen*

(*Yearbook for Intermediate Sexual Types*), using George's own deliberately ambiguous terminology of 'suprasexual love' to draw attention to the homoeroticism inherent in the poet's work. Histories of gay literature since this time have claimed George as one of their own.[5] This is not to say, however, that George was a self-consciously or self-identifying homosexual poet in any contemporary sense. He eschewed the terminology of homosexuality of his era which had been claimed in the name of science and medicine. George preferred to understand himself and his disciples in terms of a fluid dynamic of male–male love and bonding which was nevertheless identified by his peers at the time as homosexual in nature.

From his earliest volumes of poetry George created a lyric persona purged of private and individual characteristics, but at the same time reflecting the attraction to men and imbued with a strong sense of masculine identity. Together these volumes implied an autobiographical trajectory, a single voice developing over time. This voice spoke eloquently and influentially to generations of young men at a time of social upheaval and youth disaffection with the disciplinarian, patriarchal structures of late Wilhelminian Germany. George's poetry brought together the physical aspects of homoerotic friendship with the spiritual aspects of love and affection. This represented a liberation from platonic models of earlier writers and from the pederastic-paternalistic models of the late nineteenth century. George's 'suprasexual love' no longer eschews the physical in the manner of earlier platonic love: it represents a love in which the body is appreciated as part of a greater whole. George wrote to his childhood friend Carl Rouge: 'Do you imagine that we love [...] the body less than the soul [...] its spiritual qualities? [...] I think of the body first [...] physical beauty alone inflames us.'[6]

The lyric voice spoke to the homosexual reader in such a way as to enable a sense of lived continuum of past, present and future, rather than merely evoking an elegiac sense of ancient heroic grandeur or pederastic sentimentality as earlier writers had done. This lyric life, despite — or perhaps because of — its detours, accorded with the experiences and wishes of homosexual men, and thereby contributed to the emergence of a homosexual *imaginary*, a sense of what it might be like to live a full life as a homosexual man. George's homosexual imaginary is an 'imagined social existence' in philosopher Charles Taylor's sense, in which he and the homosexual men who read his work could begin to understand and value their sense of 'how they fit together with others, how things go on between them and their fellows, the expectations that are normally met, and the deeper normative notions and images that underlie these expectations'.[7] George's *social imaginary* enabled homosexual men to begin to move from subjective to objective identity, to the creation of a sense of belonging to a community like themselves, and thence to construct an identity lived and experienced in social groups, rather than in isolation and alienation. While George's journey towards homosexual self-understanding took detours that proved illusory, it was the journey itself and the processes of coming to self-understanding and to self-validation that proved so powerful at the time. Through his poetry George provided a text which enabled homosexual men to embark on their own journeys of discovery — of self and others. George embodied many of the contradictions of his time but he came to a point of recognition of the truth of homosexual attraction that transcended the perspectives of his era.

> Du gabst genug mir welten zu bewegen:
> Den fussbreit festen grund worauf ich stehe. (VIII, 104)[8]

> [You gave me enough to change the course of planets:
> The single foot of solid ground I stand on.] (Morwitz 275)

Part of the difficulty of discussing George lies in the problematic relationship of life and art for this poet, who, influenced by French symbolist poet Stéphane Mallarmé and German philosopher Friedrich Nietzsche, styled himself a leader and prophet, and who exemplified Max Weber's sociological concept of modern *charisma*.[9] This study concerns itself with the poetry, not the man. Despite the difficulties of maintaining the separation, especially given the influence of his disciples during the 1930s and after the war, my thesis is that the poetry gives expression to aspects of George's inner life that the public persona did not. George certainly adopted stances and made judgements that allied him with reactionary currents of his time: in this he was no different from others of his generation. Unlike Thomas Mann he did not openly change his views in response to the recognition of the dangers of rising German nationalism. However, while he continued his hold over the imaginations of his disciples both near and far in Germany during the second and third decades of the century, he was not an antisemite, nor did he support Nazism. While George shared the susceptibilities of many of his generation to the attractions of authoritarianism, he remained critical and aloof, distancing himself early from the war enthusiasm of August 1914 and from Nazism throughout the post-war period and until his death in exile in Switzerland in 1933.[10] My argument focuses on aspects of the poetry that have been overlooked in the preoccupation with the intellectual and social history of the George phenomenon that is the focus of much recent literature. The reception of George from the beginnings of the student movement in the mid-1960s to the ending of the post-war era in the early 1990s was over-determined by his perceived role as a precursor of German nationalism and the rise of Nazism, obscuring his homosexuality as a significant aspect of his writing, not merely of his biography.

Over the past century George's homosexuality has been denied, lamented, condemned, equated with paedophilia, reviled as an element of fascism and, more recently, accepted as just another aspect of biography, of limited relevance to his literary voice. Jens Rieckmann and Marita Keilson-Lauritz have both written extensively on George's homosexuality in biographical terms and with reference to the poems. Most other commentators pay little attention to his sexuality in anything other than biographical terms. Some still talk in terms of bi- or heterosexuality.[11] They do not view the oeuvre as a whole in terms of a trajectory of discovery and exploration or the creation of a homosexual *imaginary*, a place in which other homosexual men could understand themselves as part of an affirmative lifeworld for the first time. For Rieckmann, himself homosexual, the poetry remains tainted by its context of homoeroticism in the youth movement and the *Männerbund* in the early decades of the century.[12] But this need not be the case. Over a century later we do not and cannot read the poetry in the same way. George discovered a specifically homosexual voice for his own time, expressing its problems and difficulties alongside its joys and its tribulations. His evocation of a homosexual imaginary embracing masculine identity, companionship, love and affection reverberates powerfully even today, long after the historical details or persons and places have passed into obscurity.

Homosexual attraction of course has existed for as long as human beings have. Sociological research since the late 1960s has shown us how homosexual men and others began to engage with and even take control of the emerging new scientific, legal and medical categories of sexuality from the 1860s onward, refusing simply to acquiesce to objectification in these fields. This represented the emergence of a homosexual identity, a sense of self as defined by sexual attraction over the duration of a life. Much of this history focused on the vocabulary of reference, the medical, legal and other definitions and conceptualizations, and the social and political struggles of homosexual men (and women) against the labels of sinfulness, immorality, criminality and deviance. The present study focuses on a different aspect of this consolidation of identity. While self-acceptance as an integral person was the first hurdle in the emergence of identity, the next stage involved the acknowledgement, acceptance and love in other men of that which was so problematic in oneself. The hatred of the self-in-the-other accompanied homosexual men until well into the twentieth century. The besetting issue here was loneliness, self-hatred, and the inability to form an attachment to anyone identified as similar to themselves.

Radclyffe Hall's 1928 novel *The Well of Loneliness* identified something common to homosexuals of both sexes, namely the sense of absolute isolation, of plummeting downward from the warmth and light of childhood to the cold dark loneliness of adulthood, for many to suicide. Loneliness was perhaps the earliest defining attibute of the modern homosexual, whether in the form of the alienated aestheticism of Oscar Wilde's Dorian Gray, the paedophile fantasies of John Henry Mackay's Fenny Skaller or Thomas Mann's Gustav von Aschenbach in the 1912 novella, *Der Tod in Venedig* (*Death in Venice*), or the protected isolation of Erich Ebermayer's and Albert Rausch's middle-class protagonists.[13] Earlier generations of homosexual men had romanticized ancient Greek and chivalric cultures in which male–male attraction was tacitly or explicitly accepted. However these were idealizations, torn from their past contexts and defined and determined by their impossibility in the present. Platonic love was, by definition, past, chaste and unfulfilled love. It had little to do with the realities of physical attraction and concrete affection in a modern world. The ability to love, the capacity for object love and the ability to accept other homosexual men without projecting self-hatred would remain a central theme of male homosexual literature until well into the twentieth century in classic works ranging from Gore Vidal's *The City and the Pillar* (1946) and James Baldwin's *Giovanni's Room* (1956), to Matt Crowley's *The Boys in the Band* (1968).[14] It was a major achievement to extend to fellow homosexuals the embraces of recognition, respect, friendship and love, but it depended on the development of an identity which included a sense of connectedness to each other as homosexuals as well as a shared set of ideas and behaviours. George's poetry came to offer both to homosexual men of his time.

The greatest of early twentieth-century German poets, Stefan George imaginatively explored and articulated the inner world of homosexual identity. On his journey he discovered the alienation and the divided sense of self; he rejoiced at the freedom, light and space that his breakthrough to self-acceptance enabled. The journey was not without its travails, crises and tragedies as we shall see in the years of narcissistic grandiosity shortly before the war that culminated in the volume, *Der Stern des Bundes* (*The Star of the Covenant*). But he moved through the narcissistic fixation of the Bund, experiencing love and loss during the war. Over the following chapters I analyse the progression from self-abnegation through narcissistic self-love to the recognition of a sense of community and the experience of object love in George's poetry from the youthful works of *Die Fibel* (*The Primer*) through to the abandonment of the community in favour of the individual at the end of the final volume, *Das Neue Reich* (*The New Empire*).

George's homosexual imaginary emerged in the context of the Wilhelminian Second Reich, an environment of accelerated socio-economic change unsettled by a pervasive sense of crisis. Laws against homosexual behaviour had been passed at the time of Unification in 1871, and in the 1890s and early years of the new century controversial texts such as Max Nordau's *Entartung* (*Degeneration*, 1892–93) and Otto Weininger's *Geschlecht und Charakter* (*Sex and Character*, 1903) appeared. This was an era of normative, even militant masculinity in educational establishments, in which in Weininger's terms, 'the true man [...] leads a balanced life free from the hysteria associated [...] with women, Jews, and homosexuals'.[15] And yet the term 'homosexual' itself was a new term giving expression to the emergence of a new category of modern man. George's imaginary is in Taylor's term, the imagined social existence of himself as a homosexual man among others, sharing a mutually validated and validating horizon of ideas, images, desires and behaviours.

The homosexual imaginary is born of the tension between self and world for a young man beginning to engage with his same-sex attractions. This imaginary represented the search for self-understanding at the point where modern homosexual men in Germany began to experience themselves as social identities and to explore the possibilities of self-presentation and self-representation in public language and in the public sphere. Intrinsic to such an imaginary are both the understanding of the self as an identity over time, a lifetime or *vita*, and the need for a sense of others as members of a community.

The dynamic tension between truth to self and the creation of a social space for the possibility of a homosexual communal identity in poetry unfolded over three overlapping stages in George's life: the beginnings in the late 1880s up to *Das Jahr der Seele* (*The Year of the Soul*, 1897) and *Der Teppich des Lebens* (*The Tapestry of Life*, 1899–1900); the period of the Bund (George's league or circle of disciples and associates) from the early years of the new century until 1914; the final long phase from the First World War until the publication of *Das Neue Reich* in 1928.[16]

In the first stage, from the late 1880s until the beginning of the new century, the poet regards himself in historical and imaginative guises that at once mask and confess his search for identity. The photographs of this era show a man obsessed with self-stylization and disguise, dressing up as a means of both revealing and concealing the truth in the self-reflecting lens of the camera and in the eyes of his admirers. The early volumes of poetry, *Pilgerfahrten* (*Pilgrim Journeys*, 1891), *Algabal* (*Heliogabalus*, 1892) and the *Bücher der Hirten- und Preisgedichte der Sagen und Sänge und der hängenden Gärten* (*The Books of Eclogues and Eulogies, of Legends and Lays, and of the Hanging Gardens*, 1895), mirror this process of exploration of lyric voices in the disguises of the wanderer and traveller, merging himself into the youthful Roman emperor notorious for his perversions and excesses, or into the pilgrim and traveller to imaginative lands associated with the homoerotic imagination. In *Das Jahr der Seele*, arguably George's greatest work, the lyric persona returns to a grey normality, sadder but wiser; but in *Der Teppich des Lebens* the metaphoric carpet of the title is at once the weave of life and the flying carpet that transports him to the longed-for shores of homosexual community in 'Hellas ewig unsre liebe' (v, 16, 'Hellas eternally our love').

The second, most notorious stage is that of the Bund, the grouping of young male disciples around the poet as charismatic leader. George's Bund is one of many bohemian subcultures of the period which formed creative refuges without crossing the threshold of self-selection to social inclusion. Throughout the poetry of this period a tension exists in the creation of a self-validating public space and the inward-turned nature of that space, constituted through a process of selection and exclusion, rendering it a place of refuge rather than engagement. It is to an extent a continuation of the previous stage of seeking a group identity. The public role-playing remains a strategy of self-concealment but its contradictions emerge in the two figurations of the self as the 'wounded youth' Narcissus and the idealized group alter ego, Maximin. For the disciples, inclusion involves subordination to the charismatic leader, leading to suspension of development and projections of an imagined future in 'secret Germany' rather than individuation and development. The homosexual self exists with others in shared fantasies of future chosenness and being, in unchecked dreams of self-validation. But its place in the wider society is still unexplored.

The third stage is the moment of tragic truth for George. The war brought crisis and fragmentation to the Bund as the disciples went their various ways. The Wilhelminian world that had provided the historical moment and the social conditions for George's poetic journey disappeared, and with it his public role collapsed. The lifelong mission to be a charismatic leader of young men had failed. The narcissist fantasy of Greek warriors and chivalric knights in the Bund had resulted in the deaths of beloved disciples in modern mechanized war. Yet at the point of recognition of failure of the Bund with its mission of redemption of the private and the public self of the homosexual imaginary, the poet speaks most clearly with his own voice.

In the wake of the war George recognized the extent to which he had sacrificed his search for self-realization to the public persona of the leader and had sacrificed other men like himself to his narcissism. His homosexual imaginary was defined by tragic loss in the grief and mourning of the war. In the final poems, the wounded Narcissus discovers love for someone other than himself. At that moment George discovered and represented homosexual love in poetry in such a way as to realize his own homosexual imaginary: a world in which one man can love another. The paradox of this third stage lies in the recognition of his own voice at the moment of failure of the public self. The tragedy lay in the fact that object love and liberation from the role of narcissistic group-ego came about only after the deaths of friends and disciples such as Bernhard von Uxkull-Gyllenband, Adalbert Cohrs and the many others remembered in the 'Sprüche an die Toten' ('Verses for the Dead') in *Das Neue Reich*.[17] George died at sixty-five, already an old, sick and lonely man. His homosexual imaginary died with him, a product of Wilhelminian Germany with little to sustain it during the Weimar era.

During the 1920s the homosexual imaginary took on new and different forms associated primarily with a younger generation and with the post-war cabaret culture of the Weimar Republic. The world had moved on and the homosexual imaginary was finding its new home in the Weimar of writers such as Erich Ebermayer, Friedrich Radszuweit and Klaus Mann even as George faded from the public imagination, a dying remnant of the pre-war era.[18]

Methodology and Terminology

Sexuality and Gender Identity

The primary methodologies of this study are literary analysis and historical sociology. Since the late 1960s essentialist views of sexuality and gender have been examined in relation to both scientific evidence and socio-cultural construction with the consequence that the language of sex, sexuality and gender is now viewed in terms of social and cultural as well as scientific and psychological approaches. In current Western environments, categories of sex, sexuality and gender no longer take the form of binaries. Post-structural analysis has drawn attention to the indeterminacies underpinning the terminology of sex and gender. Stefan George did not identify himself using terms such as 'homosexual', 'schwul' or other terms of the era. He eschewed the language of groups such as the *Gemeinschaft der Eigenen* around Adolf Brand, who favoured the term 'Freundesliebe', or Magnus Hirschfeld, who used the term 'Homosexualität' in the context of his work with the Scientific-Humanitarian Committee.[19] All these terms were loaded with associations that were anathema to George's emerging sense of sexuality and self. 'Queer' in its contemporary usage denotes various types of heteronormativity, including behaviours and beliefs that gain meaning only through the tension they create in relation to the allegedly normal. As such, it seems inappropriate for George and his circle. The application of the language of queer theory to this historical task would require a different articulation of the task of this study, which is to understand how George came to understand himself as a man and a homosexual in his own context, not as we might understand him in terms of contemporary gender expectations. For these reasons I have chosen not to apply this vocabulary to George and his circle.[20]

The critique of sex, sexuality and gender that has come about in the wake of Judith Butler's considerations regarding women and feminism in *Gender Trouble* (1999) requires a 'radical rethinking of the ontological constructions of identity' that would involve not merely a reappraisal of George's performance of masculinity as forms of homoeroticism and homosexual identity during his time, but a critique of the performance of masculinity and hence of sexual and gender roles *per se*.[21] Moreover, queer theory is divided in itself regarding particular readings of gender relationships and is contested in the broader contemporary discussion of sex and sexuality. Nor do I apply related theoretical constructions popularized in Eve Kosofsky Sedgwick's formulation of male homosocial desire in the 1990s.[22] The term 'homosociality' predates Kosofsky Sedgwick of course, having been used in relation to the work of figures such as historian of the youth movement, Hans Blüher, whose speculations on homosociality and male bonding in the *Wandervogel* movement are based on the work of anthropologist, Heinrich Schurtz a decade earlier at the turn of the century.

George came to understand himself in terms of referents of sex, gender and, ultimately, sexuality that belonged to his time as the outcomes of Nietzschean philosophy, French aestheticism and the German youth movement. Rather than Butler's intellectualized existential gambit of refusal of normativity, they sought collective norms in order to underwrite their homosexual existence, not the freedoms to celebrate the marginal. Butler's articulation of queer theory as 'collective contestation' would have found little comprehension among George's circle.[23] Their short-lived covenant as members of the homoerotic Bund was a desperate attempt at a form of belonging; it was anything but the self-possessed deviation that became possible in Western environments at the end of the twentieth century, which is celebrated in queer theory. Queer theory focuses on forms of heteronormativity which may exist in some contemporary Western spaces but not in George's Germany. For this reason I have avoided terminologies which imply strong ideological preferences in the understanding of sex and gender. This is in line with recent studies of homosexuality in Wilhelminian and Weimar Germany that avoid this language in favour of less loaded terminology.

Homosexuality

In 1976 Michel Foucault questioned the different norms for behaviour and desire along with the fundamental concepts and categories of sexuality, summarizing the change in attitude from homosexual behaviour to homosexual identity in Carl Westphal's early article on 'contrary sexual sensations'.[24] However earlier sociologists had already identified the emergence of the modern homosexual albeit without Foucault's ideational framework of power and knowledge. In fact social constructionist approaches had been applied since the mid-1960s to the concept of homosexual identity or self-concept. Studies of homosexuality from this time already began to distinguish between homosexual *behaviour* as documented throughout history and the emergence of a genre of *the homosexual* whose sexuality is the key identifying factor for a multi-dimensional modern life.[25] According to Mary McIntosh the creation of a 'specialized, despised and punished' homosexual role functioned as a means of controlling the behaviour of the broader society, much as 'the similar treatment of some kinds of criminals helps keep the rest of society law-abiding'. Once labelled, people become fixed in the 'deviant' behaviours with which they have been identified.[26] Within this latter framework the emergence of the modern homosexual of the late nineteenth century is a product of less clearly defined forces than in Foucault's reading and is capable of forms of self-definition and of self-liberation, as has been documented in Klaus Müller's important early study of male homosexual pathographies.[27] Hence the present study, while referencing Foucault as a pioneer in the reading of sexuality in terms of specific frameworks of representation, does not adopt a Foucauldian or post-Foucauldian, or queer studies approach.

Social Imaginary

The concept of the 'imaginary' in the title refers to the combination of beliefs, values, and symbols which enables a group of individuals to imagine themselves in their interconnectedness as a (potential) social whole. John Thompson in *Studies in the Theory of Ideology* draws on earlier social theorists, Cornelius Castoriadis, Jürgen Habermas and Charles Taylor, to define the social imaginary as 'the creative and symbolic dimension of the social world, the dimension through which human beings create their ways of living together and their ways of representing their collective life'.[28] Castoriadis had popularized the term in *The Imaginary Institution of Society*, using the metaphor of interlacing significations which give coherence and definition to a society or group. German sociologist Jürgen Habermas refers to the common backdrop of an intersubjectively shared lifeworld that creates the possibility for consensus and thus community. For Charles Taylor the concept functions as a means of representing changes in the norm systems of modernity. Here the modern social imaginary is not a single (traditional) sphere, but rather a series of interconnecting spheres, each with its particular normative ideals. Benedict Anderson's concept of an imagined community is also relevant to this set of ideas, in which the nation as a political community is the result of imagined points of linkage among groups of individuals whose geographical or social reality may not otherwise intersect.[29]

Habitus, Sociogenesis and wir-Gefühl

Social fragmentation and the sense of crisis after the First World War alerted the Breslau-based sociologist, Norbert Elias (1897–1990) to the inadequacy of the classical theory of Durkheim, Weber and Tönnies to describe the dynamics of individual and social development. Elias aimed to 'close the gap that opens up when we think about individual and society' through a structural approach in which human beings in society are defined by their relationships and interdependences with each other.[30]

He developed a dynamic theory of individual-social interrelationships in which the stages of formation of 'ego identity' and 'group consciousness' or *wir-Gefühl* are closely dependent on each other.

> [I]t is often forgotten that each person's striving for gratification is directed towards other people from the very outset. Nor is gratification itself derived entirely from one's own body — it depends a great deal on other people too. Indeed this is one of the universal interdependencies which bind people together.[31]

With 'figurational' or 'process sociology' Elias denoted the study of human society as groupings of integrated processes involving habitus development or the development of shared dispositions and behaviours. Essential to the idea of habitus is the nature of ingrained learned habits and unselfconscious or un-self-reflexive behaviours and attitudes. Elias focused on the interrelations or interdependencies of human individuals with each other in their social relations or networks. For him the individual did not exist in any autonomous way in interaction with society; rather the human individual exists in and through relations with others. 'We are social to our very core, and only exist in and through our relations with others, developing a socially constructed "habitus" or "second nature".'[32] Thus 'psychogenesis' and 'sociogenesis' are linked in a dynamic developmental process, with psychological development and change in personality structure or habitus occurring alongside social transformation.

Earlier US sociologist, Charles Horton Cooley (1864–1929) had coined the term 'we-ness' in *Human Nature and the Social Order* (1902) to problematize classical formulations of group identity such as Durkheim's 'collective consciousness' and Tönnies's *Gemeinschaft*. For Cooley society and individual are different aspects of the same thing, not separable phenomena. 'The notion addresses the "we-ness" of a group, stressing the similarities or shared attributes around which group members coalesce.'[33] Intersubjectivity is central to Cooley's understanding of social life: in his shared awareness we live in the minds of others and vice versa. 'Individuals, as well as being separate units, may also be joined together as components of larger units, such as pairs, threesomes, and still larger groups.'[34] Cooley's dynamic view of the interrelations of the I and the we preceded Norbert Elias' more detailed account of the dynamic interactions of psychogenesis and sociogenesis in the creation of modern social identities.[35]

For Elias, *wir-Gefühl* (literally 'we-feeling', or 'we-identity') lies at the core of individual social habitus. The term identifies the sense of commonality with the social and environmental forces that determine our sense of self. Where in earlier societies this *wir-Identität* or *wir-Gefühl* was stronger and existed in a more stable balance with the ego-ideal (*Ich-Ideal*), modernity has brought about changes both in dynamics and balance of the *ich–wir* relationship.[36] As a result of this increased complexity of social relationships, individuals are obliged to reflect on their identifications, to subject themselves and their relationships to examination and potentially to make choices.[37]

While modernity involved increasing individualization, it did so in an environment of social spaces that enable a level of 'choice regarding the construction of individual identity, derived from the peculiarity of how the individual interprets the social roles and lives in them'.[38] Elias focuses his discussion of this aspect of identity formation in terms of the development of I–you relationships and of individual and group habitus. Using the personal pronouns as a figurational model for the European context, Elias elaborates the formation of different types of habitus, in which the 'I' is 'irrevocably embedded' in the 'we' in order to explain it as a 'permanent feature' of human social life.[39]

For homosexual men at this time, issues of *wir-Gefühl* and sociogenesis became critical.[40] Sexuality is the strongest and most demonstrative manifestation of the individual's need for other members of the species. While Elias does not consider the new potential formations brought about by same-sex relationships, he includes changes to sexual and generational relations in the spectrum of increased change-ability of human relationships.[41] The individual homosexual's 'sense of fundamental directedness' towards other homosexual men, including the variations in the nature of that directedness in terms of both quality and degree — as sexual attraction, sympathy with the other man's existential experiences, etc — is what makes up the individual's *wir-Gefühl* or sense of commonality and connectedness. For those men who had begun to see themselves in terms of their homosexual orientation in the final decades of the nineteenth century, the question of social existence comes to the fore by the turn of the century in this context of changing 'ich–wir' balance, and fragmentation and multiplicity of individual and social habitus.

The concept of the 'wirloses Ich', the 'kollektivlose Individualität' the self without a sense of commonality with others around him, becomes one of the main concerns of those writers who confront the emergence of a homosexual identity in literature from the turn of the century. The desire for emotional warmth and companionship with another man is accompanied by the recognition of the existence of a potential 'wir' of other men in similar situations from which the imagined lover will appear.

The recourse to Charles Taylor's concept of the social imaginary enables explanation of the ways in which Elias's *wir-Gefühl* manifests itself in the shared intersubjective space of group existence. *Wir-Gefühl* is, as the term implies, a *feeling*; it is not a content. In the social imaginary a poet such as George could construct from the social environment of the emerging homosexual a forward-looking imaginative space as a dynamic and changing component of shared identity, ultimately of group identity. That the social imaginary might become a dangerous space in terms of the articulation of shared dreams as ideals and potential realities scarcely needs to be pointed out in relation to the Weimar years. Nevertheless, it performed the necessary function of establishing the imagined worlds that would enable the formation of a modern group identity for male homosexuals in Germany at the time.

The Anti-Modern Reaction

Various terms have been used to identify the mixture of anti-modernist ideology and modernist technological, social and even cultural practice characteristic of the German intellectual scene in the decades preceding Nazism. Moeller van den Bruck coined the term 'conservative revolution' during the 1920s in order to express the sense of *völkisch*-chthonic reaction against an imported and superficial modernity. In 1962 Kurt Sontheimer coined 'antidemokratisches Denken' in order to identify the particular progression of German political thought between the end of the First World War and the beginning of the Nazi period in 1933.[42] Neither of these terms, however, articulates the uniqueness of the combination of technological and social modernity with backward-looking, fundamentalist and reactionary politics of this era. Jeffrey Herf coined the term 'reactionary modernism' in reference to figures such as Ernst Jünger, Oswald Spengler and Carl Schmitt, who combined romantic idealization of the past with forward-looking technological modernity. And while these figures' concrete political, social and cultural ideals were different from George's, the explosive dynamics of incongruity is common to all of them. Terms such as Herf's highlight the tensions in ways that 'anti-democratic thinking' or 'Romantic anti-modernism' do not. At the core of George's idealized politics is the charismatic figure of the poet as leader borrowing the pre-modern imageries of masculinity and warfare. In reference to George, Gert Mattenklott coined the expression 'aesthetic anti-modernism' and Stefan Breuer 'aesthetic fundamentalism', both of which identify the two essential elements of the aesthetic modernist and the backward-looking political idealist. Throughout this study I use the term 'anti-modernism' to refer broadly to George's social and political attitudes.

The crisis of accelerated modernization, the loss of traditional lifeworlds and the absence of alternatives based in liberal-democratic political traditions led to nostalgia for past securities. Herf identifies a range of ideational constructs expressing desire for social 're-enchantment' through the creation of backward-looking forms of organic *Gemeinschaft* (community) in conjunction with, rather than opposition to, technical and other aspects of modernization.[43] The turn-of-the century youth movements fulfilled this desire among young people of the generations born from the mid-1880s onward.

Notes to the Introduction

1. Gadamer, 'Der Dichter Stefan George', pp. 19, 23.
2. Schirrmacher, 'Dies ist der Pfeil des Meisters'.
3. Gadamer, 'Der Dichter Stefan George', p. 33.
4. Socialist journalist Maximilian Harden accused high-ranking aristocrats and military figures close to the Kaiser, Prince Philipp zu Eulenburg (1847–1921), Count Kuno von Moltke (1847–1923) and Chancellor Bernhard von Bülow (1849–1929), of involvement in homosexual behaviour during the years 1907–09. This led to trials and convictions of those involved (including Adolf Brand, founder of the *Gemeinschaft der Eigenen*, which led to the latter's subsequent imprisonment) and generated public awareness and discussion of homosexuality comparable to the Oscar Wilde trials in England a decade earlier. See Norton, *Secret Germany*, pp. 122–23, 451.
5. Rieckmann, *George und Hofmannsthal*, p. 207.
6. Cited in Boehringer, *Mein Bild von Stefan George*, p. 27.

7. Taylor, *Modern Social Imaginaries*, p. 23.
8. References to George's works are to the eighteen-volume Klett-Cotta *Sämtliche Werke* by volume number (Latin) and page number (Arabic); translations are by Morwitz with some modification by me where more literal rendition is required.
9. On Weber and George, see Turner, *The Religious and the Political*, pp. 40–41; also Lepenies, *Die drei Kulturen*, p. 314.
10. Aurnhammer and others, *Stefan George und sein Kreis*, p. 1093. See also Robertson, 'George, Nietzsche and Nazism', passim; Petrow, *Der Dichter als Führer*, pp. 483–532; and Fricker, *Stefan George*, pp. 311–18.
11. As late as 1993 Klieneberger claimed that George's relationship with Ida Coblenz rendered him 'bisexual rather than exclusively homosexual' (Klieneberger, *Rilke, Hofmannsthal and the Romantic Tradition*, p. 13). The jury seems still to be out for various contributors to the recent compendia by Aurnhammer and Egyptien.
12. The German expression, *Männerbund*, is used in anthropological studies in the absence in English of a workable expression for an 'association', 'league' or 'band of men' meaning a body of men bound together in friendship and service to the state or to a conception of the state. The terms 'communion', or 'covenant' used by Morwitz, to translate the title of George's late work, *Der Stern des Bundes*, add the religious or mystical associations that have come to attend some German usages of Bund which are missing in the usual English translations.-For a detailed analysis of etymology and usage of the word Bund in German, see Hetherington, 'The Contemporary Significance of Schmalenbach's Concept of the Bund', pp. 3–4.
13. **John Henry Mackay** (1864–1933) was a German writer of dual British-German descent who wrote a sequence of works under the pseudonym Sagitta, dealing with male homosexual love in the early years of the century, including the novel *Fenny Skaller: Ein Leben der namenlosen Liebe (Fenny Skaller: A Life of Love without a Name)*.

   Erich Ebermayer (1900–1970) gained prominence with the early collection of novellas about homosexual men, *Dr. Angelo* (1922), as well as novels and dramas during the Weimar Republic. He remained in 'inner exile' during the war, and while most of his novels were banned, he was utilized by the German film industry as a talented scriptwriter.

   Albert Rausch (aka Henry Bernath, 1882–1949) established himself as a writer of classically tinged homoerotic and aestheticist prose works and essays including *Jonathan/Patroklos* (1916), *Die Träume von Siena* (*The Dreams of Siena*, 1920) and *Ephebische Trilogie* (1924). Independently wealthy, he was able to spend the war years (both First World War and Second World War) in Italy, producing historical novels after 1933 under the pseudonym Henry Benrath that were acceptable to the Nazi government and readership.
14. Altman, *Homosexual Oppression and Liberation*, pp. 229–30.
15. Mosse, *The Image of Man*, p. 70.
16. The title *Der Teppich des Lebens* was translated by Morwitz as *The Tapestry of Life*. While a more usual translation of 'Teppich' might be 'rug' or 'carpet', 'tapestry' better brings out the associations of artistry, colour, and weaving of the original, and can in fact be used in reference to a wall covering (e.g. 'Wandteppich').
17. The name Uxkull-Gyllenband seems to have several forms, including Üxküll and Uexkull; I have retained the spelling that George used for Bernhard Count Uxkull, who is commemorated in the final poem of *Das Neue Reich*.
18. Friedrich Radszuweit (1876–1932) was an activist, writer and publisher, whose popular novel, *Männer zu verkaufen* (*Men for Sale*, 1930) documents the different groupings of homosexual men that had emerged in the Berlin of the late Weimar Republic. Klaus Mann (1906–49), the gifted but tragic son of Thomas Mann, gained early notoriety with his novel *Der fromme Tanz* (*The Pious Dance*, 1926), as well as with his essays and other writings. In a range of novels through the 1920s and 1930s he engaged more or less directly with aspects of male homosexuality, especially *Alexander, Roman der Utopie* (*Alexander, Novel of Utopia*, 1929), *Symphonie Pathétique* (1935) and *Der Vulkan* (*The Volcano*, 1939).
19. The name of Brand's organization is curious in German and difficult to translate into English. Roper translates it as 'society of the self-determined'. Other possible translations would be

'society of individuals' or of 'individual selves'. See Roper, 'Die Gemeinschaft der Eigenen', p. vi. 'Gemeinschaft' means 'community' rather than 'society' in English.

20. The use of non-historical terminology and contextualizations can lead to misinterpretations. Infante's recent discussion of George as an influence on the poets of the 'Berkeley Renaissance', for example, fails to address contextual issues of reactionary modernism and homosexuality in George's *vita*, focusing solely on his alleged articulation of 'a space for the emergence and expression of a desire to overcome a heteronormative outside that prohibited and oppressed that same creative drive in its full and open manifestation'. Infante futher alleges that 'the harsh treatment of homosexuals in George's lifetime recalled the Americans' situation' (Infante, *The Transfer and Circulation of Modern Poetics*, p. 90). This may be the case, but it tells us little of George's intellectual environment or creative aspirations, despite Infante's heavy reliance on Norton's biography. Infante futher argues that George found in the practice of poetry and the other activities of the Bund 'the only place where his sexual orientation and desires could be displayed truthfully and publicly out-side the punitive heteronormative constraints imposed by German law and society' (ibid., p. 91). That this is a serious simplification is evident even from Norton's biographical overview. Moreover Infante's evaluation of 'the cult of Maximin' as the poetic manifestation of sexual love at the core of George's overall project can hardly be maintained with reference to the poetry or the life.

21. Butler, *Gender Trouble*, p. 8.

22. In particular Sedgwick, *Between Men*, passim; see also Stein and Plummer, '"I Can't Even Think Straight"', pp. 133–34; Epstein, 'A Queer Encounter', pp. 154–55.

23. Butler, *Bodies That Matter*, p. 228; see also Kornak, 'Judith Butler's Queer Conceptual Politics'.

24. Foucault, *The History of Sexuality*, I, 43; see Butler, *Gender Trouble*, p. 23.

25. Using 'labelling' or 'social construction' theories of deviance, historical sociologists such as Mary McIntosh and Kenneth Plummer argued that a major reconceptualization of homosexuality took place in the late nineteenth century, in which the homosexual was 'invented'. See McIntosh, 'The Homosexual Role'; Weeks, 'The Construction of Homosexuality'; Plummer, *The Making of the Modern Homosexual*.

26. McIntosh, 'The Homosexual Role', p. 184.

27. Müller, *Aber in meinem Herzen sprach eine Stimme*, passim.

28. Thompson, *Studies in the Theory of Ideology*, p. 6.

29. Anderson, *Imagined Communities*, esp. 1–8.

30. Elias, *Die Gesellschaft der Individuen*, p. 34.

31. Elias, *What is Sociology?*, pp. 134–35.

32. Van Krieken, *Norbert Elias*, p. 6.

33. Cerulo, 'Identity Construction', p. 386.

34. Sheff, 'Looking-Glass Self', p. 165.

35. Mann, *Understanding Society*, p. 183.

36. Elias, *Die Gesellschaft der Individuen*, p. 211.

37. Ibid., p. 245.

38. Leonardi, 'Changes in the We–I Balance', p. 169.

39. Elias, *Die Gesellschaft der Individuen*, pp. 92–93.

40. See Cooley, *Human Nature and the Social Order*; Scheff, 'Looking-Glass Self'; Cerulo, 'Identity Construction'; Leonardi, 'Changes in the We–I Balance'.

41. Elias, *Die Gesellschaft der Individuen*, pp. 271–72.

42. Sontheimer, *Antidemokratisches Denken in der Weimarer Republik*, passim.

43. Herf, *Reactionary Modernism*, pp. 1–17.

CHAPTER 1

Stefan George's Germany

Male Homosexual Identity in Nineteenth-Century Germany

Homosexual identity gained a name and a social profile in the last decades of the nineteenth century. Before then, of course, men had been attracted to and practised sex with each other. Some societies have created social categories for inclusion of such men. But in Europe this was not the case. Homosexuality existed as a range of feelings and desires, but scarcely as an identity. Coteries of homosexual men existed in some large cities in Germany as throughout parts of Europe, but their existence was secretive and the terms used to identify them, if at all, were derogatory. Educated homosexual men had long found solace and inspiration in the works of pre-Christian antiquity. This material was drawn in the first instance from ancient Greek texts such as Plato's *Symposium* and *Phaedrus* idealizing ancient pederasty and from historical sources such as Plutarch's *Lives*. Art historian Johann Joachim Winckelmann's (1717–68) rediscovery of ancient sculpture introduced ideas of classical masculine beauty to German audiences and contributed to the idealization of male–male relationships. Karl Philipp Moritz (1756–93) discussed male homosexuality in the *Magazin für Erfahrungsseelenkunde* (*Magazine for Empirical Psychology*), Johann Wolfgang Goethe (1749–1832) evoked male homosexuality in his poem 'Ganymed' and in his essay on Winckelmann makes enlightened reference to the latter's homosexuality, and late Romantic poet and dramatist August von Platen (1796–1835) evoked homosexual love in his works. Friedrich II left behind an ambiguous legacy of homosexuality and Prussian militarism, represented by aristocratic soldiers such as Johann Wilhelm Ludwig Gleim (1719–1803), Ewald Christian von Kleist (1715–59) and his troubled distant relation, Heinrich von Kleist (1777–1811), and in works such as the Prussian Alexander Freiherr von Ungern-Sternberg's (1806–69) novel, *Jena und Leipzig* (1844). The dominant sources of inspiration were the warrior traditions of the Homeric epics and the Greek city states of the Archaic and Classical periods and the heroic reciprocal loyalties of leader and follower in the Germanic *comitatus* or the 'band of brothers' evoked by Shakespeare's Henry V. Famous warrior pairs such as Achilles and Patroclus, Harmodius and Aristogeiton, and the heroes of the Theban Band brought homosexual love to the defence of society and the state, thereby demonstrating their masculinity and their civic virtue.[1]

Those men who became aware of their sexual orientation at this time confronted immense social pressures and prohibitory forces. Each came to discover his own life to be predetermined in social terms by the languages of psychiatric perversion and criminal law, as well as by religious disapproval, social prejudice and hostility.[2] There was little for the individual to rely on other than the strength of his own personality in order to survive. And the options were limited: to acquiesce to the dominant clinical descriptions, to act as if sexual identity could be denied and disguised, or to defy social stereotyping and strike out alone.

In terms of the law, various German states had begun adopting codes that exempted same-sex acts from criminal prosecution from 1812 onward.[3] Bavaria was the first (with the exception of cases involving force or children under twelve years of age) and Württemberg, Baden, Hanover and Brunswick followed over the following decades. Prussia and Saxony maintained sodomy as a punishable criminal act. The Prussian state revised its penal code in 1851, reducing the penalty but retaining the criminal charge. After the unification of the German states into the German Empire in May 1871 the earlier Prussian criminal code became Paragraph 175 of the new Imperial Criminal Code, thereby recriminalizing sodomy across the Empire. Homosexual acts between males became a crime (along with underage sexual abuse) throughout Germany.

In 1864 lawyer and pioneering advocate Karl Heinrich Ulrichs (1825–95) had begun tackling the legal prohibitions on homosexuality with the publication of his first study calling for legal equality of 'Uranians' (Urninge), the term he coined in the absence of the later term 'homosexual'. Ulrichs would fight for law change until 1880 when he gave up defeated and left Germany. But by then there was an emergent homosexual rights movement and by the late 1890s Paragraph 175 was under attack from a range of activists such as physician and advocate Magnus Hirschfeld, founder of the homosexual emancipation organization, *Wissenschaftlich-humanitäres Komitee* (Scientific-humanitarian Committee), along with publisher Max Spohr, writer and journalist Adolf Brand, and wealthy advocate and scholar Benedict Friedlaender. The SPD (Social Democratic Party) under August Bebel supported abolition of paragraph 175 but did not achieve it in the Reichstag. A further attempt was made towards the end of the Weimar Republic in 1929 but the newly powerful NSDAP stalled the repeal process.[4]

Psychiatrist Richard von Krafft-Ebing (1840–1902) had pioneered the psychology of sex with the foundational work *Psychopathia Sexualis* (1886). A line of more or less enlightened medical and psychiatric figures followed in his path. However the attention given to homosexuality in the burgeoning sciences of psychiatry and criminology generated counter-responses from various circles.[5] For Magnus Hirschfeld, male homosexuals represented a 'third sex', characterized by a female psyche in a male body. Hirschfeld made a normative claim regarding homosexuality and the rights of homosexuals on the basis of scientific and biological demonstrations of homosexuality as a naturally occuring condition in the human and animal worlds. Yet for many homosexual men, this 'third sex' theory held little appeal. They did not feel themselves to be hybrid male-female identities. Grouped around

Adolf Brand's *Gemeinschaft der Eigenen*, and drawing on cultural sources since antiquity, these men challenged the 'third sex' model with one which increasingly would look to cultural values of masculinity to justify their existence. The new term 'homosexuality' was generally avoided in favour of the less specifically sexual concept of 'friendship' or 'Freundesliebe' which had a long tradition in Germany, as demonstrated in Alexander von Gleichen-Rußwurm's influential study, *Freundschaft* (*Friendship*, 1912).

The accelerated economic and industrial development of the foundation years or *Gründerzeit*, the problems of 'belated' nationhood (Helmuth Plessner), the weakness of democratic and civic traditions, and Wilhelminian bellicosity generated a sense of impending crisis expressed in increasing inter-generational tension at the turn of the century.[6] This environment broadly defined and determined the ways in which young homosexual men sought self-determination and emancipation. New social forms of modernity created conditions for the emergence of a homosexual *wir-Gefühl* or sense of group identity in Germany that was quite different to the situation in Britain or France at the time.

Pederasty and Homosexuality

Before this time the social imaginary *of* — as opposed to *about* — homosexual men, was tied to an idealized vision of ancient Greece, and was largely the preserve of the educated middle classes. Pederastic love between an older, more mature man or *erastes* and a youth or *eromenos*, with its classical pedigree, provided one of the few positive points of cultural reference for homosexual men in Germany and Europe since Winckelmann. Socrates and Alcibiades enjoyed a chaste pederastic relationship according to legend, and Plato's Phaedrus remarks in the *Symposium*:

> I know not any greater blessing to a young man who is beginning in life than a virtuous lover, or to a lover than a beloved youth. For the principle, I say, neither kindred, nor honour, nor wealth, nor any motive is able to implant so well as love. Of what am I speaking? Of the sense of honour and dishonour, without which neither states nor individuals ever do any good or great work ... And if there were only some way of contriving that a state or an army should be made up of lovers and their loves, they would be the very best governors of their own city, abstaining from all dishonour and emulating one another in honour; and it is scarcely an exaggeration to say that when fighting at each other's side, although a mere handful, they would overcome the world.[7]

Pausanias in Plato's text extols the political value of pederastic love in the example of the legendary Athenian lovers Harmodius and Aristogeiton who overthrew the tyrant Hippias in order to establish democracy. (They feature in George's late poem, 'Goethes lezte Nacht in Italien'/'Goethe's last Night in Italy'.)

Elevated to a spiritual rather than physical relationship, pederasty came to serve as a basis for the emergent valorization of homosexuality as a generative and society-building force of civic society in the youth groups. Educators and youth leaders such as Wilhelm Jansen, Benedict Friedlaender and Gustav Wyneken, whose interest was explicitly homoerotic, advocated ideals of male leadership and mentoring based on this revered idea of the education and leadership of young men.[8] They blended elements of ancient pederasty and warrior traditions, educative mentoring and induction into civic-cultural values (i.e. the *paideia*) in a seductive ideal of intergenerational homoerotic friendship for adolescent boys. This is a more or less radical version of the Greek idea of *paideia* as education with the ideal of perfection as its aim, laid out in Werner Jaeger's three-volume *magnum opus* from the early 1930s.[9] It was an imaginative construct in which a link was posited between the private and the public spheres, as a means of reintegrating male homosexuality into broader patterns of contemporary socialization. What had been an intimate, private and solitary urge and a social crime or perversion might contribute towards the regeneration of civic values. There was thus a social component in the construction of a sense of community which was a liberating moment of connection and social validation for these men. Homosexuality would be valorized by its socially accepted position as an educating, formative and generative force in classical Greece, a cultural environment which the German *Bildungsbürgertum* held in greatest respect. As pederasty understood in the Greek sense, this relationship adhered to the idea of education and leadership between an older and a younger man and hence represented a form of generativity at least in theory; in practice the attempted realization in the youth movement opened up the way for the sexual misuse of minors.[10] Thomas Mann's Aschenbach is indicative of the mixture of *Bildung* and repressed sexuality in the idealization of Greek pederasty. Contemporary theatre critic and essayist, Alfred Kerr targetted this confusion in his acid comment that the novella 'made pederasty acceptable to the educated middle classes'.[11] Taken out of its ancient context, its attempted realization in the youth movement opened up the way for the sexual misuse of minors, even at this time when the law was unclear on the definition of a male minor.[12]

Youth Movement, Männerbund and National Renewal

The German youth movements have attracted attention among historians and sociologists as a powerful new historical force in German society at the end of the nineteenth century, as an expression of a radical modernist conception of adolescence, and as the formative environment for the new social formation of the Bund. Groups such as the *Wandervogel* movement expressed emergent social needs born of the tension of the previous decades of accelerated change. School environments had been reformed in the wake of German Unification to inculcate military values and to prepare young men for lives of discipline and commitment. The *Wandervögel* by contrast expressed themselves in terms of romantic anti-capitalist self-liberation. Country hikes and overnight stays in barns and lofts, with guitars, folk-songs and candles supplied the mise-en-scène for folk revival, German nationalism and the advocacy of Teutonic values along with more open attitudes towards mixing of the sexes and even, as the movement developed, sexuality. These groups did not emerge from existing scholastic or other social forms, and they operated through word-of-mouth, selection and co-option. Leaders were chosen, not imposed from outside. As a result, the locus of German adolescent sexuality moved outdoors into the informalized, self-directing and non-institutional settings of the various youth movements.

Writer Ludwig Renn spoke of 'the all-encompassing dishonesty of the nineteenth century' to express the sense among young people of the falseness of the lifeworld into which they had been plunged.[13] The *Wandervögel* and other youth groups became centres of rebellion against the authority of schools and parents, offering a sense of community to youth of both sexes by the beginning of the century. But they also provided an environment for charismatic teachers, leaders and extremists to influence young minds.[14] This proved powerful and even intoxicating for young men whose experiences hitherto had been characterized by the types of private humiliation, loneliness and exclusion represented in stories such as Hermann Hesse's *Unterm Rad* (*Beneath the Wheel*, 1906). In Franz Wedekind's drama *Frühlingserwachen* (*Spring Awakening*, 1891) a youthful homosexual friendship is one of the few relatively positive emotional experiences in an otherwise bleak environment. The absence of socio-psychological structures of libidinal investment and control for an emergent sexual orientation with little by way of social identity or profile rendered homosexual youths and men susceptible to these influences. A sub- and counter-culture of homosexuality developed, characterized by the broader alternative structures of the youth movement: rejection of paternal authority and familial hierarchies for small groups under the leadership of father-surrogates.[15]

Young people sought to recreate the sense of authentic organic existence in freely chosen unions in opposition to what many saw as the alienating individualism of modernity and the failure of their fathers to achieve a sense of genuine group belonging in the wake of national unification. In the words of historian George Mosse, the ideal of unity of 'soul, body and spirit as the prime law [...] was to be attained through shared eros'.[16] Those young men, for whom homosexuality was becoming a determining aspect of their sense of identity, did not merely seek others for sexual purposes; they were looking for like-mindedness and a sense of community that was increasingly underpinned by their awareness of their homosexual proclivity.

In the wake of these developments sociologist and Stefan George follower Hermann Schmalenbach introduced the concept of the Bund into sociology in 1922 as a third significant form of human socialization alongside the *Gemeinschaft* and the *Gesellschaft* models posited by Tönnies several decades earlier and adopted by Max Weber.[17] For Schmalenbach the Bund is a form of 'horizontally' selected *Gemeinschaft*, offering an organic sense of belonging (*Gemeinschaft*) as well as non-traditional, deliberative aspects of *Gesellschaft*.[18] Yet at the same time it offers neither the organic integrity of *Gemeinschaft*, nor the civic rationality of *Gesellschaft*. Sitting between the two conceptually, it offered its members the sense of group belonging without the 'vertical' components of traditional structures. It broke with traditional models in creating new 'horizontal' rules for socialization and group identity, but it did not at the same time dismantle group identity into a society of individuals on the one hand, or a formless mass society on the other. It is thus not traditional, organic and compulsory in form, nor is it contract-based, elective and alienated. Rather it is elective, spontaneous and enthusiastic, regaining the closeness of community, rooted in friendship and unified under a leadership principle.[19] Romantic small-group communion regains a place amidst the spiritlessness of the modern society. In his 1912 doctoral thesis, *Männerbund und Jünglingsbund*, historical sociologist Hans Fraenkel documents the emergence of the *Männerbünde* in the context of German nationalist groups after the Wars of Liberation. In Fraenkel's historical account the *Männerbund* is a product of the secretive nationalist movements that emerged in the German states from the 1820s until 1848 in response to the French Revolution. The formation of the Bund as described by Schmalenbach, Fraenkel and others facilitated the needs of the various groupings within the youth movement. It represented a 'horizontal' bonding phenomenon typically around a charismatic leadership figure, for example a progressively modern or even rebellious teacher. Stefan George would become one such leader.

According to early Frankfurt School sociologist, Franz Borkenau, writing under the pseudonym of Fritz Jungmann for the Frankfurt Institute of Social Research, this new social formation answered the particular needs of the generations born from around 1885 onward. The attraction of the Bund in the form of the youth movement was the absence of the rationalization that characterized modernity, the rejection of the rigid authoritarianism of the *bürgerlich* family, and the substitution of the father through the *Wandervogel* leader. It also led to a freeing up of homoerotic energies.[20]

> The boys henceforth accepted the strict sexual prohibitions that their parental home had not been able to force upon them, since they were compensated with a relationship with an older leader which, to be sure was muted and sublimated, but nevertheless non-authoritarian and hence unpaternal.[21]

For Jungmann the *Wandervogel* phenomenon led to sublimation rather than promotion of homosexual desires.

> Occasionally as a natural expression of the freeing up of tenderness towards the older man, the sensual component would break through powerfully, but only in a small minority of cases, to be sure. Here the most diverse types were found side by side: the real homosexual with an otherwise intact male habitus, the soft youth in protracted puberty clinging to schoolboy companionship out of fear of women, the progressive trainee teacher who sought authority-free contact with young people along the lines of modern pedagogical thinking.[22]

Homosexuality in the Bund: Bachofen, Schurtz and Blüher

The dangers of homoeroticism and homosexuality in these youth environments featured large in the context of popular unease at the emergence and public visibility of homosexuals during the Wilhelminian period.[23] This phenomenon seemed to be a corrupting influence on healthy sexuality, social stability and legitimate order, with homosexual scandals such as the Eulenburg affair suggesting that the highest echelons of Wihelminian society were being affected.[24] A weakening of the national fabric was feared as a result of increasing effeminacy and loss of masculinity among young men. To counter this suspicion, outspoken homosexual figures such as Adolf Brand rejected Hirschfeld's theory of an intermediate sex in order to advocate a radical opposition between the effeminized men of modernity and the true masculinity of earlier times. Homosexuality as such was not the problem, they argued, but rather the 'femininization' of men in general in contemporary society, which becomes confused with homosexuality *per se*. Homosexual men could be just as masculine as heterosexual men. Indeed homosexual men, undistracted by sexual attraction to women and family roles, could become leaders of men, more masculine, in fact, than their heterosexual counterparts. This was, of course, an implicit argument for the functionalizing and normalization of homosexuality, by providing it with a social role and a civic responsibility, but at the cost of excluding 'effeminate' homosexuals whose existence corrupts social order and stability, alongside women who are restricted to the traditional sphere of the family.

In the first decade of the new century ideas such as these were circulating in an environment of intense, radical openness to rearticulations of human sexual identity primarily among sections of the youth movement. Indeed German anthropologists and philologists since the 1860s had toyed with radical and speculative theories based on classical sources to explain sexual and gender roles in social development. Johann Jacob Bachofen's *Das Mutterrecht* (*Mother Right*, 1861) was a radical re-reading of antiquity, predating Nietzsche's *Die Geburt der Tragödie* (*Birth of Tragedy*, 1872) by a decade.[25]

In Bachofen's scheme, human history has been driven by conflict between the sexes since an original, hypothetical earth-bound matriarchy based on natural principles of life-giving and harmony. This order was replaced by a patriarchy representing the spiritual, rational and purposive aspects of human consciousness. Physical reproduction was the realm of the female, and social generativity belonged to the male realm. This male generativity took place via the *paideia*, the process of cultivation of the unformed boy into the formed youth prepared to enter manhood and equipped to undertake the roles and responsibilities of adult masculinity. The adult male's role in physical reproduction was merely mechanical; his constructive role commenced with the training and inculcation of young men into the roles and responsibilities of masculine adulthood. The male principle of generativity could express itself in terms of the social components of leading, teaching, and inculcating social and cultural values broadly in addition to the physical requirements of insemination and parenting as fathers and patriarchs. Essential to this process was a quality of love that was elevated, and non-physical, which Bachofen attributed particularly to the Greeks. Plato and Socrates manifested 'platonic love' as a force of attraction among men which superseded sex and which represented the essence of the patriarchal generative principle.[26] As homoeroticism, a building-block of human societies, male-male sexual attraction or libido led to studies of pederasty and the formation of social structure among a range of more or less influential thinkers from the late nineteenth century onward.

Bachofen's model of patriarchy as the outcome of generic conflict between the sexes after the overthrow of the original matriarchal order was taken up and embellished by writers Karl Wolfskehl and Ludwig Klages, for example, both members of Stefan George's innermost circle in the 1890s. Freud and others applied these ideas in metapsychological writings from the first decade of the twentieth century, and they entered the German popular consciousness through the work of historian and philosopher Hans Blüher shortly before the First World War. After the defeat of 1918, surcharged with bitterness and resentment, the political atmosphere of the *Männerbünde* moved to the far right, taking many of those homosexuals from the youth movement with it.

Ethnologist Heinrich Schurtz's idea of the *Männerbund*, developed in his 1902 work, *Altersklassen und Männerbünde (Age-classes and Male Bands)*, had its origins in nineteenth-century nationalist imaginings of elite compact bodies of men bound by patriotism to the service of the state. Schurtz formalized this idea into a social theory in which 'men, even married men, were always driven beyond the family toward a higher social association with other men'. This male bonding generated 'the creative spirit that shaped the main institutions of public life and the state'. Women by contrast are motivated 'solely by sacrifice for their family (a bulwark in the fabric of society)'.[27]

In the second decade of the new century historian Hans Blüher became the main spokesman for this line of masculinist argument. In his 1912 study, *Die Wandervogelbewegung als erotisches Phänomen (The Wandervogel Movement as Erotic Phenomenon)*, Blüher drew on Schurtz's terminology of the *Männerbund* to develop the idea that male eros was the binding force in all social configurations. For Blüher, the ideals of male leadership and mentoring were based on more or less explicit homoerotic ties.[28] Homosexual men thus gained a social function as leaders, in the context of male groups or bands based on an ethos of loyalty and service in contrast to the family group, and homoerotic libido was justified as a productive force in the context of the youth movement.[29] Blüher explicitly identified homoerotic *Männerbund* energies as the binding force of the *Wandervogel* groups. Homosexual leaders, dedicating themselves to the furtherment of their young charges, represented essential and irreplaceable constructive forces in modern German society for Blüher. In the strength of the *Wandervögel* lay the strength of the future Germany, and it was held together by charismatic homosexual leaders through the pedagogical manipulation and instrumentalization of adolescent male homoeroticism.

Blüher's *Männerbund* was the constitutive force of society, and the 'Vollinvertierte' or fully homosexual male was a natural leader in this environment, bringing men together around him, leading and devoting his life to the maintenance of the group. The task of procreation was left to the followers and to women. In Blüher's model, physical attraction, release or fulfilment were proscribed: the homoerotic driving force of a resurgent Germany depended as a social force on the suppression and redirection of homoerotic energies. It did not advocate physical love between adult males as the outcome of homoerotic energies. These are idealized political communities based on suppressed homoerotic desire. Nevertheless this validation of male generativity served the interests of homosexual men of the time, and also functioned more widely in an environment of concern, even panic, about changing sexual roles and perceived loss of male prestige.

Blüher later extended this reading in *Die Rolle der Erotik in der männlichen Gesellschaft: Eine Theorie der menschlichen Staatsbildung nach Wesen und Wert (The Role of Eroticism in Male Society: A Theory of State-Formation in its Nature and Value,*

1917/19), creating a conceptual bridge between the *Wandervögel* and later fascist political *Männerbund* groupings. The Bund of the youth movement liberated homoerotic energies which contributed to the regeneration of male supremacy.[30] This would provide the bridge between the earlier conceptualizations of the Bund and the later *Männerbünde*, which represented a politicized formation of the embittered post-war generations. The liberation of sexual energies in the youth movement created the opportunity for the manipulation and misuse of youthful enthusiasm and sexual inexperience in the environment of crisis and change in the first decade of the century, leading up to the First World War. In its origins, however, early in the century, this sociological phenomenon answered the needs of large numbers of young people, mainly young middle-class males, providing a common shared imaginary, erotically charged with neo-romantic images of organic community and anti-authoritarian leaders.

By the end of the nineteenth century, then, the concept of male homosexuality was established and increasingly large numbers of men were identifying in terms of a sexual orientation that nevertheless continued to generate guilt, attract social condemnation and opprobrium, and be associated with criminality, deviance, perversion and pathological states of mind. During the first decade of the twentieth century, however, this situation began to change. A new generation of young men in Germany, seeking self-affirmation, individual authenticity and group identity in the new youth movements of the early twentieth century, discovered their homo-sexuality as a liberation from the moribund social models of their parents. This involved the creation of narratives in which the individual and the group came together under the mantle of anti-egalitarian masculinist formations in natural hierarchies.[31] By the turn of the century Stefan George, a major new force on the German literary scene, would transform homosexual attraction, friendship, and the *Männerbund* into a poetic-mystical image of the redemptive *comitatus*, influencing profoundly those young men who came under his sway. George would take on a powerful role as leader and mouthpiece for the love that still may not have dared to speak its name, but was beginning to manifest itself under increasingly identifiable aliases.

George's writings for the most part predated the influential figures in the youth movement such as Gustav Wyneken and Hans Blüher. In his later (1920) auto-biography Blüher considered George the epitome of the homosexual male leader, writing, 'my concept of *eros* matched [him] exactly'.[32] For sociologist Schmalenbach, himself an acolyte of George who theorized the Bund as a fundamental new social formation, George's poetry spoke to a homoerotic element in the youth movement, as well as to other marginalized groups and individuals. It showed them a way forward by offering the promise of resolution of a problematic sense of personal identity into an idealized group identity. For male homosexuals it offered images of companionship in the group, and to some extent the freely flowing homoeroticism — as opposed to the homosexual object choice — of the Bund opened the door to the first glimmerings of a possibility: of participation in this group, of a *life* shared with similarly constituted men, and of mutual respect, admiration, love and friendship among men. The muted, even sublimated nature of this homoeroticism rendered it even more attractive to those for whom the idea of a homosexual life was already stretching the bounds of the imagination. The idea of George's Bund, at one level at least, could represent a positive phase in the process of self-recognition and self-emancipation of male homosexuals in Germany at this time. George represented through the poetic voice of his consecutive verse volumes a man coming to recognize and accept his attraction to other men despite the negativity of the society around him. Trespassing into forbidden or proscribed places, this verse rejected the traditional poetic vocabulary of love for a new vocabulary of other shores, blue skies, sunny climates and other men living freely in physical intimacy with each other, occupying a poetic-imaginary realm of homosexuality in a new way. In this sense the Bund must be considered a partial and historically evolving phase of homosexual emancipation and identity formation. George thus brought an early, unique voice to the ideas of leadership and collectivity among young homosexual men.[33] Ironically, George's homoerotic verse and the social imaginary it envisaged prepared the way for homosexual men to become involved in socio-political structures that would become increasingly homophobic as they were brought into line ('gleichgeschaltet') under Nazism by the late 1920s.

George's Life

Born into a Catholic family in the town of Bingen in the Rheinland-Pfalz in 1868, Stefan George demonstrated his poetic and linguistic gifts early, producing original compositions and translations from a variety of languages that he proceeded to teach himself, most notably French, English and Italian. His earliest poems date from the late 1880s while he was still a school student in Darmstadt and were retrospectively collected into *Die Fibel* in 1901.

After leaving school in 1888 he travelled to London, Vienna and Paris where he mixed in the circle of symbolist poet Mallarmé whose aestheticist doctrine of *l'art pour l'art* influenced him deeply, turning him further against the dominant poetic schools of realism and naturalism currently in vogue in Germany. He began studying Romance languages at the Friedrich-Wilhelms-University in Berlin but broke off after three semesters and for the rest of his life pursued a peripatetic existence, living with friends and supporters as well as in the parental home for long periods. The family owned a successful wine business and George was relieved of the need to work for a living thanks to a substantial inheritance. He could devote himself to the life of a writer and translator from an early age, working and networking with others to introduce symbolism and aestheticism to Germany but also moving on and out to develop his own distinctive poetic voice by the early 1890s. In 1892 he co-founded with Carl August Klein the magazine *Blätter für die Kunst* (*Pages for Art*) as a vehicle for the new doctrine of art for art's sake oriented towards a select circle of readers, which would only cease production after the war in 1919. George's own first volume, *Hymnen*, appeared in 1890, followed by *Pilgerfahrten* and *Algabal* in quick succession. While he was an adept manipulator of his unique image and used his charisma to further his poetic mission, from the beginning he aimed to speak only to a select few, whether reciting his work in small groups of disciples and followers, or supervising the production of exquisitely designed and illustrated volumes by artist Melchior Lechter for limited production and distribution. *Das Jahr der Seele* (1897) and *Der Teppich des Lebens* (1899/1900) sealed George's success, the former remaining his consistently most highly praised work. The collection and publication of selected early poems from adolescence and early adulthood in *Die Fibel* marked a change in perception of the sequence of volumes from the historical to the symbolic. *Die Fibel* marked the origins of a life recounted through verse. Over the early years of the new century George built up his circle of gifted disciples and acolytes with figures who would later achieve prominence as scholars such as Friedrich Gundolf (1880–1931), Ernst Morwitz (1887–1971), Ernst Kantorowicz (1895–1963) and Max Kommerell (1902–44), and as poets and thinkers in their own right such as Karl Wolfskehl (1869–1948) and Ludwig Klages (1872–1956). Claus von Stauffenberg (1907–44), later implicated in the plot against Hitler, belonged to the last generation of disciples, along with his brothers Alexander and Bernhard.

From late 1904 the figure of Maximin begins to figure in George's poetry, an idealized image of the young Maximilian Kronberger (1888–1904). George noticed the adolescent boy in passing in 1902.[34] In early 1903 he befriended the young man and budding poet, introducing him to the circle associated with his literary journal, *Blätter für die Kunst*. Despite his infatuation, George remained physically distant as well as imperious and demanding in his dealings with Maximilian. The sudden death of Kronberger in April 1904, shortly after his sixteenth birthday and after only a year of acquaintance, caused George deep distress, leading to the creation of an idealized poetic image, Maximin, who would feature as the focal point of the circle during the following years. A change in consciousness and poetic mission announced itself in *Der siebente Ring* (1907) in which Maximin appears as the mystical leader of the Bund or *comitatus*.

The high point of George's popularity and influence was reached in the years before the First World War with the increasingly hieratic tone of the 1914 volume, *Der Stern des Bundes*, in the wake of which George published only one further volume, *Das Neue Reich* in 1928 after an interval of fourteen years and before his death at the age of 65 in 1933. His rejection of the nationalism of the Wilhelminian Reich that led to war and catastrophe for Germany by 1918, his distress as beloved disciples enlisted and were lost, and his increasing physical frailty by his early fifties caused him to withdraw from public life as Germany moved towards Nazism in the late 1920s. In the end he moved to Minusio in Switzerland, neutral territory, in which he was sheltered from the attentions of the new NSDAP government's Minister for Culture, Bernhard Rust, who sought George's endorsement by offering him membership of the Prussian Academy after the resignation of figures such as Thomas Mann, Alfred Döblin and Ricarda Huch.[35]

Regarding George's political views as precursors of Nazism, Robertson writes that 'George's fantasies have nothing to do with the Third Reich as an economic and political entity, but they are not wholly removed from its imaginative and even religious dimensions'. It must be added, however, that religiously charged, even apocalyptic fantasies of national rebirth and restitution of the Reich were ubiquitous in German anti-modernism, and that George was hardly unique in this respect.[36] However we must also beware of what Robertson himself, following Bernstein, refers to as 'backshadowing'. namely using retrospective knowledge to judge participants in historical processes as though they knew what would follow.[37] George's foregrounding of Nazi ideology extended to a sympathy with the aims of national rebirth; he rejected the politics and the thuggery and did not envisage or welcome in any way the concrete victimization of Jews and others under Nazism. Moreover he rejected Rust's advances, using his (Jewish) protegé Ernst Morwitz as his spokesman.[38]

For all his radical rejection of Wilhelminian Germany, George was a product of his time. He found inspiration in aspects of contemporary Germany, transforming them into his poetic world: the sociability of the youth movement, the attraction to all-male environments, in which homoerotic energies underpinned the cohesion of the whole, the renewed late romantic interest in the poetic-mythological worlds of antiquity, chivalry and the Germanic middle ages. Suggestions of sexual liberation attended all of these, and indeed the crisis of Wilhelminian *Bürgertum* provided the backdrop for sexual experimentation and self-discovery that took many detours during the three decades of relative freedom from the turn of the century to the end of the Weimar Republic.

The George Circle

George had gathered a loose grouping of young men around him in the early 1890s, particularly after the foundation of the journal, *Blätter für die Kunst* in 1892. Carl August Klein worked on the journal with him from the beginning and remained a close associate over the following decades. Early collaborators included friends such as the Belgian Paul Gérardy, the Pole Wacław Rolicz-Lieder, the Dutchman Albert Verwey (to whom George addressed *Preisgedichte in Das Buch der Hirten- und Preisgedichte* of 1895), and later in the 1890s Karl Wolfskehl and Richard Perls. The Munich intellectuals and so-called 'cosmic circle' members Alfred Schuler and Ludwig Klages also joined the circle by the late 1890s. With the accession of the young Friedrich Gundolf in 1899, George found an intimate friend as well as admirer. They later worked together on translations of Shakespeare's sonnets and Gundolf would go on to write an important monograph on the English dramatist along with studies of George himself and Goethe, and become an influential academic in the literary humanities. George broke from Gundolf after the latter's marriage to pianist Agathe Mallachow. Attractive young men like Gundolf featured in the circle, handsome, intelligent and adoring of the Master. Some refused to be drawn in, such as the young Hugo von Hofmannsthal, who nevertheless maintained a distanced relationship with George until the early years of the new century. Others, such as writer Albert Rausch were courted but refused. Later members included Roderich Huch, a cousin of the writer Ricarda Huch, the jurist Ernst Morwitz, and Robert Boehringer who would act as George's literary executor. But it was the young Maximilian Kronberger who, during his brief life, became the image of the *Knabe Lenker*, the youth as promise of a future new order in Goethe's *Faust II* who symbolized the young men of George's *Kreis* or Bund.[39] Later significant figures included the historian Ernst Kantorowicz and the Stauffenberg brothers (Alexander, Berthold and Claus).

These younger men sought George's approval, guidance and leadership. He offered patronage and affection, and looked after their interests as long as they continued to coincide with his own. Breuer speaks of him as a mother-figure, and Dörr writes of his 'protective and nourishing effect', fending off foreign and hostile forces and merged in an almost symbiotic way with his creatures.[40] The disciples competed for George's approval and yet there is little sign of jealousy among them. This suggests that the need for identity, self-validation and belonging was the primary emotional tie in this homoerotic environment. These young men who were drawn to and gathered around George received the attention and in many cases the affection that they craved — for whatever reason.[41] That so many of them were homosexuals is remarkable only insofar as it indicates that this group was particularly susceptible to George's poetry and charismatic personality. George, unlike other heterosexual leadership figures, embodied and communicated aspects of life and lifespan experience with which they could identify. While many moved on as they matured, a more or less stable group had formed by the turn of the century, which referred to themselves as a *Kreis* or circle, with the charismatic poet at its centre playing the role of leader and 'Meister'. Many of these young men came from educated backgrounds and would exercise influence in intellectual and cultural spheres in later life.

The formation and structure of the *Kreis* remained unwritten, but everything was choreographed and every member selected by George himself. Meetings of the circle had the character of the aesthetic-ritualistic *Männerbund* evoked in the dramatic poem, 'Aufnahme in den Orden' ('Admission into the Order'). The First World War represented a major break for the *Kreis* with the loss of six disciples, remembered in the 'Sprüche an die Toten' ('Verses to the Dead') of *Das Neue Reich*. In the wake of the death of Maximilian Kronberger and idealization of the figure of Maximin, the expression, 'Geheimes Deutschland' ('secret Germany'), gained currency for the Bund as the imaginative-poetic construct of a new transfigured Germany.[42]

In the popular imagination of the time, George's circle and the later, more formally constituted Bund were viewed with suspicion in the context of the homosexual scandals of the first decade of the century. As early as 1909, poet Rudolf Borchardt had hinted that George's homosexuality was a danger to the nation's youth, and in his 1936 essay, 'Aufzeichnung Stefan George betreffend', Borchardt excoriated George's damaged and dangerous homosexuality.[43] Blüher wrote in 1920, 'No-one can know for sure [...] whether George engaged in sexual activity with his favourites. But without doubt, boys were the object of his *erotic* interest.'[44] In his biography, Norton notes the extent to which George's fear of persecution as a homosexual determined his cult of privacy, and suggests that George had sexual relations with Ernst Glöckner.[45] However the evidence is indirect for this one allegation and overall no evidence exists of George having attempted physical relations with any of his youthful followers after the devastating Hofmannsthal affair. Moreover the disciples were generally in late adolescence or in their twenties when they were associating with George. With others, such as Maximilian Kronberger, he kept his distance and there is little even to suggest sexual interest in his correspondence. Like Mann's Aschenbach, George appears to have kept his fantasies to his imagination, whether they involved underage boys or not.[46]

In terms of his own language of self-reference, George dismissed the *Gemeinschaft der Eigenen* and refused to identify in terms of any current definition of homosexuality, including Hirschfeld's 'third sex'. His idea of 'suprasexual love' seems deliberately ambiguous, playing on Bachofen's original idea of a male eros that sought to escape the carnality that was associated with heterosexual love and 'tended toward ever increasing degrees of abstraction and immateriality'.[47] But as Keilson-Lauritz shows, this conceptualization of male–male love provided an alibi for levels of physical intimacy, enabling men in George's poems to kiss, hold hands, lie together and embrace in the service of a love that was physical, but also included affection.[48] Moreover the implied accusation of sexual misuse of minors that has accompanied George since the formation of the Bund is undeserved. It was a way of discrediting this controversial and difficult figure who refused to be drawn by or to identify with any political grouping, including the nationalist and later Nazi parties. George's preferred imagery was not drawn from Plato and the apologists for pederasty in the manner of Mackay, and as imagined by Mann's Aschenbach. George drew his inspiration from the bands of brothers of classical and feudal male communities of monks, soldiers, knights. He did not sentimentalize pubescent boys on the verge of adolescence and discovery of their homosexual otherness in the way that other writers of this period do. He increasingly imagined a homosexual community of young men viewed as enjoying their physicality in and for themselves. Indeed it lacks the voyeurism, sentimentality and prurience of so much of the homosexual men's writing of this time. In its place he revived a body of images and ideas that had both become a faded and bloodless ideal of classical antiquity and dated alibi for homosexuals in Germany and Western Europe from the 1860s onward, typified in J. A. Symonds's wan evocation of the Theban Band in 'Song of Love and Death'.[49] In these images of Hellenic masculinity George revitalized a faded dream of sundrenched landscapes, and male community untarnished by Christian prohibitions. The Theban Band and other legendary or historical *Männerbund* groups are reimagined as like-minded young men unified in homoerotic love, national unity and loyalty to their leaders, later idealized as Maximin. George's recasting of this symbolic imaginary revived an idea of symbolic community, generating a sense of *wir-Gefühl* and manifesting a sense of shared generativity.

George's Notoriety

Even now, a century after his influence began to wane, Stefan George polarizes readers. His name provokes associations of homosexuality, underage boys, pederasty, charismatic elitism, reactionary politics, even Nazism, but few who read his poetry are left unmoved. Few writers have experienced the vicissitudes of celebrity and notoriety that George has since his death in Switzerland in 1933.

During his lifetime George achieved cult status, reaching its peak around the time of the First World War. But his star had begun to fall as the post-war environment gave birth to the new Germany of Weimar culture and as Nazism loomed by the end of the decade. George's self-stylization as the leader of a group of younger men led to accusations of homosexuality, corruption of young men, and later of preparing the way for Nazism. George's cult of himself as master and prophet, and of his ego-ideal, Maximin, the idealized German youth and hero, quickly came to overshadow his writings.

While he was an undoubtedly charismatic and influential figure for the men who adored him, there is no evidence of sexual harassment against those close to him. Moreover he was hardly alone in this role as mentor. This was the era of the first modern youth movement, in which young people were seeking — and finding in figures such as George — alternative father-figures and leadership models to those of the traditional German family.[50] Later, when major German writers and intellectuals supported the German war-effort in 1914, George distanced himself in a series of poems whose rejection of the bellicose populism of the era represented more than a passing political statement.[51] For the Nazis he was too much the sovereign aristocrat; he rejected them, and by the mid-1930s his questionable sexuality had rendered him unfit for inclusion in the Nazi canon in any case.

The criticisms of George's conservative-revolutionary values tends to overlook the extent to which this poet was *not* responsible for fascism, masculinist militarism, or even authoritarian-charismatic leadership in Germany. In his study of the apocalyptic and visionary currents of this era, Braune notes that the George Circle 'was far from being the only circle of this type'.[52] And as Braungart himself notes, it has become difficult to define which of the intellectuals of this era of crisis the rubric of conservative revolution does *not* fit.[53] George was certainly charismatic as a figure, but he exercised this power over only a small group of men and some women in his immediate vicinity. His readership was primarily among young men born during the 1890s and reached its peak in the years from 1910 to 1914, primarily through the youth movement. It cannot be discounted but it can be exaggerated. The war marked the end of George's wider following.

If George's poetry were notable simply for its reactionary aesthetic-political positions, the poet would have disappeared from view or at best would occupy a minor niche in the history of reactionary modernism. Yet continuing academic interest demonstrates that George remains a poet to be reckoned with regardless of his political views. Even Gert Mattenklott recognizes the power of George's poetic language and the value of individual poems while excoriating the political significance.[54] Scholar and literary critic for the *Frankfurter Allgemeine Zeitung*, Frank

Schirrmacher, reviewing Breuer's study of George, *Ästhetischer Fundamentalismus* in 1995 noted the failure of critics to account for the enduring quality of George's poems: 'Some of his poems have a beauty and intensity even today — one is tempted to say for today and ever more — that few others can bear comparison with.' Schirrmacher argues that we can no longer simply read the poems as documents of their time. In a different world we can — and indeed must — read them differently, 'freed from the task of tracing out the biography of this singular human being'.[55]

George may have gained a place in literary history for having introduced aestheticism to late nineteenth-century German poetry, but this does not explain the power of the poetry itself. Nor does his importance lie in his influence on other poets. Like Rilke, Hofmannsthal, Borchardt and others, he represents an end point and was largely ignored by the following generations. Many of these late poems remain deeply moving even for those who are repelled by the anti-modernist and reactionary aspects of George's beliefs. The focus on the political content of selected poems fails to explain what *is* important about his work as literature.

Lukács, Benjamin and Adorno on George

Seminal early figures such as Georg Lukács (1885–1971), Walter Benjamin (1892–1940) and Theodor Adorno (1903–69) engaged with George throughout their lives, unable either to condemn or to approve the oeuvre as a whole. All three are significant as members of the intellectual and philosophical left, born 1885, 1892 and 1903 respectively, who like their contemporaries were powerfully influenced in their youth by George's poetry and who engaged with it early and positively in their writing. Reading George in the light of the development of German and European fascism, however, they were obliged to come to terms with their early and even ongoing admiration of at least parts of the oeuvre. None was able to consign George simply to the ranks of reactionary anti-modernists and precursors of German Nazism. All three identify a break between George's early and late work, locating the separation biographically around the time of the death of Maximilian Kronberger and aesthetically in the changed direction of the poetry from *Der siebente Ring* (1907) onwards.

Georg Lukács (1885–1971) wrote admiringly of George in his early 1907 essay in *Soul and Form*, well before the war and the crises of German society that led to his conversion to Marxism. But even in the later, polemical *Kurze Skizze einer Geschichte der neueren deutschen Literatur* (*Short Sketch of a History of Modern German Literature*), written during the last year of the war, he admires George's poetic figures in *Das Jahr der Seele* and *Der Teppich des Lebens*: 'These are lyrically formed human beings, not just shadowy impressions. They act and suffer within his magically beautiful, magically protected landscapes.'[56] Lukács's study was published in 1953 as an educational text in the post-war GDR and excoriates the German literary traditions of romantic anti-capitalism and 'spätbürgerliche Innerlichkeit' ('late bourgeois interiority'). His summation of both George and Rilke as the representative poets of the Wilhelmine era is condemnatory but in the former case at least, surprisingly ambivalent. Less so in the more polemically formulated critique of German philosophical traditions in *Die Zerstörung der Vernunft* (*The Destruction of Reason*) published in the following year (1954) in which George is dismissed as a compromised precursor of Nazism.[57]

Walter Benjamin (1892–1940) too, looking back in 1934, only shortly after George's death, focuses on the separation between the earlier symbolist and the later reactionary prophet. Benjamin experienced a love-hate relationship, passionately admiring the early works and the translations but rejecting the prophetic tone of the poems after *Der Teppich des Lebens*.[58] For Benjamin George represents an end, not a beginning. As a *Jugendstil* poet emerging from the aesthetic decadence of late *bürgerlich*/bourgeois culture, 'he stands at the end of a spiritual movement which began with Baudelaire'.[59] The war marks his end, and the figure of Maximin is thus a prophet of the end of the old, not the herald of a new age.[60] Benjamin nevertheless salvages those poems that stand apart from the political events of the time as 'markers of what would have been possible were loneliness and neglect not inevitable'.[61]

Theodor Adorno wrote about the collection of prose pieces *Tage und Taten* (*Days and Works*, 1904) as early as 1934;[62] in 1939 he discussed the correspondence between George und Hofmannsthal; in 1957 dedicated sections of the 'Rede über Lyrik und Gesellschaft' to George's poetry; in 1967 made a radio broadcast on George which would be included in the later *Noten zur Literatur*; and in the same year discussed 'Der totgesagte Park — der Fall Stefan George' in a radio dialogue with prominent scholar and critic Hans Mayer. As a composer in the Second Viennese School Adorno also engaged with George's texts and included discussions of the poet in his late aesthetic theory. Adorno remained fascinated by George but recognized a break at the time of the meeting with Maximilian, expressed in the transition from *Der Teppich des Lebens* to *Der siebente Ring*.[63] He speaks of 'the aristocratic nationalism to which George dedicated himself after the caesura of *Der Teppich des Lebens*, and concludes that 'if anything of George survives it will be just that part that he repudiated after the death of Maximin'.[64] For Adorno, the claim to *Gemeinschaft* of the later work was simply a mask for the Nazi *Volksgemeinschaft* ('folk' or national community) based on a shared racial and national consciousness of 'Aryan' Germans.[65] In this reading George suppresses his heterosexual impulses in order to enable the homosexual ethos of reactionary masculinist *Gemeinschaft*. For Adorno, homosexuality and fascism were linked and the poet's homosexuality is instrumentalized for the sake of the political reading; it is not a recognition of George's homosexuality as a defining and determining part of his sexuality.

Reception of George since the Second World War

A stream of works by friends and disciples mostly in exile of one form or another appeared after the poet's death in 1933, but by 1945 George had fallen from grace in the German literary canon. During the post-war era George was viewed primarily as a proto-fascist, a prophet of the conservative revolution, an advocate of Nietzschean amorality and German grandiosity.[66] In 1948 conservative commentator Fritz Usinger noted that George had been consigned to oblivion by his fellow Germans,[67] tainted by what were perceived to be the pre-fascist politics of reactionary anti-modernism and the homosexual, even paedophile, relations with the young men around him.[68] In 1952 French George-scholar Claude David wrote, 'today, it seems, Germans close their eyes to George's signficance'.[69] It was nevertheless David himself who, in the earliest comprehensive post-war study, *Stefan George, son œuvre pöetique* (1952) put into place the model of the 'two Georges' in order to rescue George's poetry from the biography. For David, George's oeuvre swings between abstention and *Weltflucht* on the one hand, and engagement, tenacity and drive on the other.[70]

Commentators since David have been at pains to come to terms with what they saw as the contradiction between George's greatness as a poet and his espousal of a reactionary politics of charismatic leadership. They split along the lines of historical context: between those for whom the poetry is paramount regardless of context, and those for whom the poetry cannot be separated from the doctrine of 'secret Germany'. Those who value George's poetry in spite of his doctrines, place the early works, especially *Das Jahr der Seele*, above the later demagogic-charismatic works. For these commentators, George was first and foremost a symbolist, responsible for introducing French avant-garde aestheticism to Germany. These commentators typically identified a decisive turn from the early aestheticist to the late charismatic prophet, often finding a loss of poetic power in the later works vis-à-vis the freshness and originality of the early work. However, these critical judgements seemed underpinned by the desire to defend the early work from the association with the later reactionary anti-modernist and foreshadower of Nazism.[71] Yet any neat separation cannot be maintained. Even David held the poet responsible for the consequences of his own and his disciples' myth-making, in particular of those who became committed and active National Socialists later on.[72]

Despite David's post-war advocacy, George's literary fortunes dipped even further as issues of *Vergangenheitsbewältigung* or coming to terms with the past, war guilt and political affiliation dominated literary and cultural debate. George, the man and the poetry, came to represent one of the battlefields in the literary-ideological wars of the late 1960s and 1970s. Adorno, who had engaged closely with the poetry since his youth, noted that George had disappeared from view by 1967 in the student revolution that overtook West Germany.[73] And Manfred Durzak opened his 1974 study of the poet's position and influence with the observation that the poems were no longer read and that the level of reception had dropped to zero.[74] In addition to the condemnation of his political attitudes, post-war commentators from left and right alike viewed George's relations with the young men around him disapprovingly until well into the 1970s. Those few early studies that sought to rehabilitate the poetry did so by divorcing it from the man, his politics and sexuality. Unsurprisingly, George's homosexuality was ignored, alluded to obliquely or dismissed as a perversion that underpins and further discredits the poetry during this period of reception.

The left (with the notable early exception of Klaus Mann) continued to condemn this poet, whose homosexuality and aestheticism rendered him a product of bourgeois decadence and a forerunner and fellow-traveller of Nazism. In one of the most important studies, Gert Mattenklott concluded in 1970 that George's romantic anti-capitalist 'aesthetic opposition' to the politics and society of his time proved to be no protection against fascism, despite its radical protest. Mattenklott linked the 'will to dominate' ('Totalitätsanspruch') of George's aestheticism to the development of German fascism, despite his recognition of the tensions and contradictions in the poetry itself.[75] Klaus Landfried analysed the contradictions between George's aestheticism and his political ambition to establish 'an aesthetically founded state within the state' in 1975.[76] Manfred Durzak, Eckhard Heftrich and others continued to distinguish the poet from his biography and reactionary political views, but against growing opposition.[77]

In the post-Reunification intellectual environment of the 1990s, as the student generation aged, attitudes softened towards the loaded issues of aestheticism and artistic responsibility, leadership, masculinity and homoeroticism in George's life and work. Mattenklott's critical analysis of George's 'aesthetic opposition' to modernity opened the way for Stefan Breuer and others to focus attention on George's adaptation of symbolism and aestheticism from the French to the German literary environment, bringing a sociological perspective to bear on the literary anti-modernism of the late nineteenth and early twentieth centuries. Landfried introduced sociological methodology into the study of the Bund and discussed the nature and effects of the poet's charismatic leadership on those around him.[78] Sociologist Wolf Lepenies identifies *Der siebente Ring* as the turning point for George's Bund from a loose grouping of intellectually and creatively engaged young men to a narrower conception of a 'state within the state' with platonic overtones from around 1907 onwards.[79] As Lepenies, notes, George's aesthetic doctrine of poetics over politics as the means of realizing 'secret Germany' culminated in Stauffenberg's political act against Hitler. Yet Lepenies, like many of the commentators on George's ethos of aesthetic elitism, pays little attention to the poems, focusing rather on the pronouncements made primarily through the journal *Blätter für die Kunst* and by the disciples. Now that the era of its political influence has passed, Lepenies questions the value of the poetry.

It was not until the 1990s that George's star rose again, thanks mainly to Breuer's study of his 'aesthetic fundamentalism'. Breuer's thesis is that George instrumentalized aestheticist poetic techniques in the service of a manipulative narcissism and will to dominate.[80] Literature, for George in this reading, takes over the function of religion that has been weakened by modernity, potentially embodying meaning and the sense of totality lost to the atomized individuals of modern industrial society and containing the seeds of hope for a reawakened *Gemeinschaft*. Breuer introduces his study with reference to Botho Strauß's conservative manifesto of 1993, *Anschwellender Bocksgesang*, to the revival of German anti-modernism in the context of the end of the post-war era, and to the emerging new ways of thinking about German identity.[81] However, as various commentators noted, Breuer largely ignored the poetry in order to focus on the historical sociology of George's environment and influence and the psychopathology of his personality.

Writing in 2010, Osterkamp identified Breuer's *Ästhetischer Fundamentalismus* of 1995 as having initiated a George-renaissance by bringing 'the perspective of cultural sociology to bear on George and his circle as exemplifications of the willingness to believe in the power of charisma and the religious transformation of art'.[82] This was followed by Carola Groppe's *Die Macht der Bildung*, which traced the influence of the George Circle on German thought and behaviour in universities, the arts and education of middle-class youth until 1933, and Rainer Kolk's intellectual history, *Literarische Gruppenbildung* in the following year, which followed the poet's influence until 1945. What is remarkable for Osterkamp is the resistance of these approaches to the poetry: 'They are not interested in the poet's work. They historicize his figure; the poetic work is therefore, inasmuch as they take any notice of it at all, primarily a historical source.'[83] Similarly, Thomas Karlauf's 2007 biography of George, which marks the high point of this wave of interest, reduces the poetry to biographical source material and focuses on the sociological aspect of charisma, conceived by Max Weber as embodied in George.

The renaissance continued, leading to significant reassessments of the issue of continuity in George's work and of the quality of the late poems. Where earlier commentators such as Durzak valued the early symbolist poems to the exclusion of the late politically loaded works, the tendency in more recent reception has been to reject the artificial separation between early and late and to view the body of works as a whole. This has not, however, necessarily resulted in positive re-evaluation. For Braungart, Oelmann and Böschenstein (2001) George's early aestheticism transmutes over time into a conscious political programme, the apocalyptic and admonitory tone of which helped prepare the ground for later social and political developments in Germany. The origins of George's anti-modernism are to be found already, that is, in the earliest aestheticist-symbolist works. For them the interpretative strategy of separation of early and late periods neither deals with the poet's own advocacy of his work as a unity, nor engages with the analytical question of how such a change from the aesthetic to the socio-political sphere came about.[84] For Braungart, George's aestheticist politics represents a reactionary provocation to the progressive aesthetic of modernism.[85] In the same volume Böschenstein interprets George's late work as a radical rejection of the declining *Bürgertum* of the end of the century, finding in it powerful echoes of earlier visionary responses to socio-political conditions in, for example, Hölderlin. Böschenstein links the reactionary modernism of the period from 1907 (*Der siebente Ring*) to the earlier views propagated in the *Blätter für die Kunst*. For Böschenstein, echoing Mattenklott, the late work demonstrates how the modernist poet was able to instrumentalize language as a means to power and hence represents continuity in the oeuvre as a whole.[86]

In 2010 Ernst Osterkamp made a further major contribution to the unitary reading of George's oeuvre, also positing a continuity between the early and late poems, in *Poesie der leeren Mitte*. Reactionary political content in the late work is revealed to be the outcome of earlier tendencies, with individual narcissism mutating into a national syndrome.[87] While Osterkamp does not consider George an advance-guard Nazi, he shows the extent to which George's oeuvre as a whole dictates a nationalist-biological reading of German history as a response to a corrupted present-day modernity, using the criteria of German humanism to create a set of prophetic moments.[88] Osterkamp returns the focus to the poetry but he is not interested in rescuing it from charges of ideological corruption. On the contrary, he aims to show the extent to which the poetry *carries* the toxic ideology of 'secret Germany' as a pre-fascist phenomenon. It is not just George's occasional commentaries or the memoirs of his disciples which are to blame. Where the post-war 69-generation rejected George for his aestheticism, particularly in the early work, and the studies since the late 1890s tended to overlook the poetry for the person and environment, Osterkamp focuses on the alleged instrumentalization of politics, mythology, theology and sexuality 'in a metapolitics of renewal of the world' expressed primarily in the poetry.[89] Those commentators, he writes, who exclude the poetry from their analyses of George's influence, will not be able to understand his historical role since the poetry is its main medium.[90] Osterkamp thus maintains the critique of George as a forerunner of Nazism, begun in the late 1960s by the intellectuals of the student movement (of which he himself was a participant).

George has experienced the extremes of reception as poet, aesthete, charismatic leader and homosexual. Lauded by some, execrated by others, he remains a divisive and controversial figure even a century later. Since Robert E. Norton's *Secret Germany: Stefan George and his Circle* of 2002, three new biographies and two documentary films about George have appeared along with further detailed studies, a comprehensive bibliography, and two handbooks and commentaries.[91] The myth of George the person, of his circle of disciples and the adoration of the figure of Maximin, has been closely scrutinized in four major biographies in English and German over the past two decades (Norton, Karlauf, Kauffmann and Egyptien). Commentators such as Pieger and Schefold, Braungart, Groppe and Kolk have focused on the socio-literary aspects of George's influence, in particular in the late work, in terms of the idea of 'secret Germany', and on the gifted young men, such as Friedrich Gundolf, Ernst Kantorowicz, Max Kommerell and Ernst Morwitz, who became his disciples and maintained the legend. George is generally accepted as interpreter of French aestheticism and symbolism for Germany and as the main representative of lyric modernism alongside Rilke.

Relatively little of this commentary has been dedicated to George's influence on the emergence of male homosexual identity through his poetry during his lifetime. Norton engages with George's homosexuality in biographical and historical terms but not from the point of view of the thematic development of a male homosexual identity in literature. Yet George was the most important influence on homosexual writers and young homosexual men from the First World War era onward. Marita Keilson-Lauritz has identified homosexual strategies of communication through key words and masking and signalling techniques in George's poetry, and in a detailed analysis of George's notion of 'suprasexual love' gives a unique reading of the poet as homosexual.[92] In *Stefan George: Gedichte für Dich* (2011) Christophe Fricker reads the oeuvre sympathetically and compellingly with a view to rehabilitating George's reputation as a poet. In the attempt to deal with the charges of pederasty and paedophilia Fricker tends to apologize for George's role as an advocate for homosexual relations, even to the point of denying the specificity of the appeal to male–male sexuality on the basis of the openness of address to an unnamed and sex-neutral 'du'. Fricker draws attention to the sexualization of the vocabulary of friendship and love as used by George and to the extent to which readings of George have been influenced by hearsay and innuendo rather than detailed analysis. Fricker's advocacy nevertheless is for a body of poetry that is by and large indeterminate in terms of its sexual reference.[93]

With the exception of relatively recent works by Daub and Bisno, the thematization of George's sexuality has remained muted, despite the importance of autobiographical material to the analysis and interpretation of this work. In the final chapter on research perspectives that makes up his review of secondary literature on George from 1955 to 2005, Jürgen Egyptien, for example, identifies important issues such as George's religion, his relationship to the ancient world, or the role of *Jugendstil* for potential further analysis. The themes of homosexuality, homosexual identity and homosexual love are strikingly absent. Keilson-Lauritz's 1987 book, *Von der Liebe die Freundschaft heißt: Zur Homoerotik im Werk Stefan Georges* (*On the Love that means Friendship: Homoeroticism in the Work of Stefan George*) is identified by title only as one of only five specialist studies to appear between 1980 and 1995 before being passed over without further comment.[94] While Egyptien recognizes both the aesthetic unity of George's work across the collections and the modernist self-reflexivity of the language, George's poetic self-recognition as a homosexual and its influence on a generation of German men is ignored.[95] The implication is that sexuality belongs to biography, not literature.

Much analysis continues to view George in terms of obsolete models of pathological narcissism which are incompatible with current views of human sexuality, sexual orientation, or indeed, with contemporary usages of narcissism as a category of personality structure. George's homosexuality is seen as an extreme of narcissism in the classical Freudian sense as late as 1995 by both Peter von Matt and Stefan Breuer.[96] The latter's concept of 'aesthetic fundamentalism' invoked a version of homosexuality as arrested sexual development and narcissistic compensation which takes little account of theoretical advances since Freud first developed the putative link between homosexuality and narcissism in 1914.

Homosexuality in George's Poems

'There is no doubt', writes Marita Keilson-Lauritz, 'that the concept of love in the texts of Stefan George is a homoerotic one'.[97] By developing a set of linguistic masks and signals, George, according to Keilson-Lauritz, was able to evade the prohibitions on the expression of same-sex desire between males. In this strategy, homoerotic content must be masked, but at the same time associated with signals alerting the careful reader to the writer's disguised intent. George's main strategies include the use of the gender-neutral second person ('Du-Gedicht'), role-plays and the use of specific historical contexts, intertextual references, and the use of

certain metaphors and symbols.[98] Keilson-Lauritz traced the homoerotic content
of the poems in detail, using a data-based approach to key words in George's
poetic vocabulary, in particular the word 'Liebe' and its cognates. Keilson-Lauritz
distinguishes between the usage of 'love' and 'friendship' throughout George's
work, and finds that 'love' from *Der Teppich des Lebens* onward is exclusively 'a
matter of men and boys'.[99] Love, moreover means for George the 'search for a
dream-love', which ended with the discovery of Maximin. In contrast to the
platonic homoeroticism of the time, George's love was imagined as corporeal, both
positively as physical contact and negatively as pain. Love is unequal, taking forms
of submission and service ('Dienst') as well as dominance ('Herrschaft') in this
reading, and involves self-exposure and danger, but it is also a dynamic, formative
force, both in the individual and the community sense, and is associated with
abstinence, renunciation and sublimation.[100] While the early poems published in
Die Fibel often expose an autobiographical voice, the poems that George published
in the early to mid 1890s make increased use of roles: 'it is noticeable the extent
to which [...] the self tends more and more to step behind a role'.[101] By the time of
Der Stern des Bundes and after the Maximin-experience, however, the *Rollengedicht*
disappears, leaving the voice of the poet uncontextualized. The use of metonyms
which require feminine agreement in German camouflages the sex of the person
addressed as 'Kind', 'Liebe', or 'Seele'.[102] Erotic motives such as the black flower
in *Algabal*, or the topos of picking or smelling flowers in *Das Buch der hängenden
Gärten* and elsewhere, suggest physical intimacy without sexual specificity, and the
homosocial environments of the monastery, of religious orders, guilds, companies
at arms, groups and leagues more or less subtly orient reader-expectations towards
male exclusivity.[103] Signals of masculinity include male dedications, and male
attributes and environments used symbolically or metaphorically, along with
intertextual references to the classic eras for same-sex love, namely ancient Greece
and the late Roman Empire, or to significant historical and literary figures such as
Plato, Socrates, the lovers of the Theban Band, the Homeric figures Achilles and
Patroclus, or the biblical Saul and David. Through repetition, certain adjectives
come to be associated with same-sex affection — for example 'süss', 'schön', 'neu',
'wahr' — which of themselves have none of these associations.[104]

   The effect of these strategies, as Keilson-Lauritz shows, is to create a powerful
sense of masculinity without necessarily evoking explicit or concrete images of
male attraction, friendship or love. The overall effect is to establish a voice behind
the voices of the various volumes from the *Hymnen* onwards, a lyric persona whose
masculine presence pervades the worlds of these poems, even as it changes and
develops from the 'Rollengedichte' of the *Pilgerfahrten and Bücher der Hirten und
Preisgedichte* through to the prophetic voice of the late works. Keilson-Lauritz
concludes that homoeroticism represents a pervasive background to George's
work as a whole.[105] Nevertheless, George, for Keilson-Lauritz, does not identify
a homosexual constitution in Hirschfeld's sense, and maintained a distance also
from the widely differing individuals who identified broadly in terms of the
'masculine culture' of Adolf Brand's *Gemeinschaft der Eigenen*. In this reading

George's lyric homoeroticism thus remains passive rather than actively present. My aim is to demonstrate how George's lyric voice offered possibilities beyond this to its readership of homosexual men. George charted the recognition of his homosexuality as the defining and determining force of his life and in doing so offered a model of self-revelation to adolescent boys and young men. For the first time in literature he offered them a narrative *life*.

George's Lyric *Vita*

> They are the songs of a wanderer [...] stopping points on a never-ending path which has a definite end point and yet perhaps leads nowhere. Taken together, they form a great cycle, a great novel, completing each other, explaining, reinforcing, muting, underscoring and refining each other.[106]

As early as 1908 Georg Lukács identified Stefan George's works up to *Der siebente Ring* of the previous year as an autobiographical novel in all but form. For Lukács, these works expressed existential loneliness above all. The poet's creation is a lonely man released from all social bonds, who can never belong anywhere.[107] George's titles suggest a romantic-literary confession tracing the steps of the persona's literary-personal development from the retrospectively published *Fibel* (published in 1901 but containing work dating back to the poet's late adolescent years) through the the final volume, *Das Neue Reich* in 1928.[108]

Many literary historians since Lukács have read the poems in terms of George's life, some in a derivative or reductionist manner, others noting the sophistication with which George transformed life events into verse. One of the problems arising from this has been the tendency to identify the poetic voice and persona with the historical figure of George himself without paying due attention to the aesthetic transformation that takes place in the process of writing. Ockenden has noted the extent to which George's poetic oeuvre is routinely reduced to its biographical elements in even the most recent critical studies.[109] Issues of aesthetic autonomy are neglected as the analysis moves seamlessly from the poet's self-stylization amid his circle of adoring disciples to the poems that appear to exemplify this life in the abstracted language of lyric.[110] George himself encouraged this merging of the life and the poetry, as he cultivated his public persona among his disciples, in carefully managed photographic images, in his journal, *Blätter für die Kunst*, and in subscriber volumes magnificently crafted by book-illustrator, Melchior Lechter and only subsequently released for the broader public.[111]

Even during the post-war period in which text-immanent criticism dominated, figures such as Claude David and Ulrich Goldsmith found themselves unable to disregard the life. David's early post-war study of the life and work (1952) was the first extensive biographical reading, and Ulrich Goldsmith similarly notes the closeness of the autobiographical and the poetic from *Algabal* onwards.[112] At a more sophisticated level, Norton reads the late work, particularly *Der siebente Ring*, as a form of secular-masculinist revelation around the figure of Maximin, who will redeem mankind from impure sexuality.[113] Wolfgang Braungart identifies the particularity of George's verse as a performative aesthetics in the lines from the epigrammatic introduction to the final section of *Das Neue Reich*, 'Whatever word and thought I still can frame, What I still love — the features are the same' ('Was ich noch sinne und was ich noch füge | Was ich noch liebe trägt die gleichen züge', IX, 98). Here for Braungart the poet supersedes the separation of aesthetics and ethics which was constitutive of aesthetic modernity. 'George's work achieves the ethical-aesthetic fulfilment of a life' ('Georges Werk ist ethisch-ästhetischer Lebensvollzug').[114] Aurnhammer summarizes this aspect of George's lyric particularity as the 'aesthetic formation of life', 'ästhetische Lebensgestaltung'.[115]

George's lyric *vita* certainly draws on the poet's life, but it also contains material of broader significance as the poet consciously and deliberately traced out his lyric autobiography from the 1890s, creating a record of a homosexual's life in terms of the possibilities and the difficulties of the last decades of the German Second Empire. This was a period of accelerated economic modernization and social upheaval especially for young people of the educated middle class or *Bildungsbürgertum* and for the intelligentsia in general.[116] Already in 1907 Lukács identified the unique existential aspect of George's poetic *vita*. The works up until *Der Teppich des Lebens* radically represent the modernist sense of homelessness in the world, of 'Heimatlosigkeit' and the loss of shared existential values. 'The human being of George's lyrics is lonely, released from all social bonds.'[117] And yet the act of writing represents a reaching out of the isolated self to the other in spite of the impossibility of fulfilment. It is, for Lukács, an existential act independent of the possibility of understanding. 'The content of each of his songs and that of their totality is something that one must understand, yet never can: that two human beings can never become one.'[118]

For Lukács George's poetry expresses the sense of existential loneliness that had come to define the European soul at the beginning of the century. Over the following decade George would document the attempt to come to terms with and overcome this state of being through the creation of the Bund or league with its intense personal relationships and group consciousness. That strategy allied him with other members of 'reactionary modernism', the neo-romantic belief in the possibility of supersession of existential loneliness through various forms of revalidated community. In terms of its homosexual component, George's loneliness, so perspicaciously identified by the young Lukács, represented another form of the Platonic idea of the 'desire and pursuit of the whole' — the fundamental and generic human need to find and connect with others. For the guest Aristophanes in Plato's *Symposium* it takes the form of a parable of the attempts of humankind to overcome the traumatic memory of separation from the other which constituted a part of the original self. For George and the neo-romantic anti-modernists, the memory of oneness or togetherness is explored in other forms, given the no longer traditional social contexts of modernity. The Platonic parable was important because it gave an equal place to homosexual loneliness and pursuit of the whole — namely, of love. For those homosexual men reading George, the radical modernist and the homosexual poet are one: in giving expression to existential homelessness he put the homosexual state into words. The further trajectory of the poems from *Der siebente Ring* onwards in which George attempts to overcome existential loneliness through the evocation of Maximin, the creation of the Bund, and the building of a new wider community, may have represented a wrong turning and a failure as an end point, but can also be read as a detour, one of the learning curves in mankind's 'eight ages' of psychosocial development which did ultimately bring the poet to self-knowledge and object love in the final pages of *Das Neue Reich*.[119]

While Hans Blüher and others were responsible for incorporating homoeroticism into the ideological framework of the youth movement and the *Männerbund*, it was in the poetry of Stefan George that the human aspects of homosexual consciousness were represented as an aspect of subjective and objective identity.[120] George's lyric persona entered and decisively influenced the emerging social imaginary of male homosexuals in Germany, moving through and taking its readers through stages towards a broader and more inclusive sense of self. Through this lyric persona, George recorded an affective biography for a generation of young homosexual men at a critical point in the development of new models of sexual identity in Germany. He mediated individual and group experience in an entirely new way, providing a rich and satisfying range of self-ascribed identification possibilities for the homosexual male. George stepped beyond the tired clichés of earlier isolated figures, mirrored in the daydreams of Aschenbach in *Death in Venice*, and evoked a vibrant and vitalist future, at least until the high point of the Maximin cult in *Der Stern des Bundes*. He refused to countenance the oppressive models generated in psychopathological, criminological and medical fields.[121] He thereby offered an identity to the young men of the following generations who flowed into the youth movements that formed towards the end of the century. George's homosexual identity is present in coded, masked, and signalled form in the early works, but emerges more openly in the ethos of 'suprasexual love' in the Bund and around the figure of Maximin in the early years of the new century.[122]

These adolescents and young men from throughout Germany were predominantly from middle-class educated (*bildungsbürgerlich*) backgrounds. Those among them who responded to the homoeroticism of the groups did not in general identify in terms of the dominant models of Hirschfeld's indeterminate 'third sex', or as the psychologically damaged 'deviants' of Krafft-Ebing's case studies. Nor did they understand themselves in terms of the platonic-pederastic imagery of the older generations, such as writer John Henry Mackay (1864–1933), the members of the *Gemeinschaft der Eigenen*, or the fictive Aschenbach who also belongs roughly to the 1860 generation. 'Friendship' was a powerful expression, but one still not strong enough for the affections they were feeling for others around them, and they needed, and found in George's poetry, a vocabulary with which to express their feelings. Moreover, unlike earlier evocations of Greek or other homosexual environments, George's was founded on the idea of companionship, fellowship and the development of a sense of self in the group. This is what is most striking about the voice throughout his poems. We read and see how the *I*, the *you* and the *we* are formed in words and images over time and undergo a process of self-understanding and ongoing development and change, to the point where the final *I* can face the *you* of the loved other. Of course George's poetry did not just speak to homosexuals; it tapped into many aspects of German male existence at the time, speaking to issues of youth, friendship, and national identity. Indeed one of its great strengths is that it rendered the homosexual experience part of something broader, of a set of experiences of self, society and nation that enabled homosexuals to relate to, and find mirroring in, their wider environment. For this reason Elias' terminology of *wir-Gefühl* and theoretical model of sociogenesis are helpful in describing the recognition of the self in the group and investment in the group identity that constitutes a core value of George's poetry.

George brought together the physical aspects of homoerotic friendship with the spiritual aspects of love and affection in his poetry. The body was not proscribed in George's poetry. While the expression of overt sexual attraction was muted, the body of the young man was recognized in its beauty and adored in its physicality. This represented a major liberation from platonic models of earlier writers and from the pederastic-paternalistic models of the era. George's ideal of love does not eschew the physical. It transforms the body into an ideal, but does not spiritualize it.

George's lyric persona offered several points of identity-formation for young homosexual men. He documented the vicissitudes, trials and tribulations of an individual homosexual existence in the context of his time; in valorizing the figure of Maximin as alter ego and ego-ideal, he created the possibility of an idealized self for isolated individuals who found little self-confirmation from their social surroundings. Through the reading experience of young men throughout Germany this lyric persona contributed to the creation of a sense of group consciousness and group identity that was forward-looking and potentially would deliver them from loneliness and self-hatred.

Notes to Chapter 1

1. The elite corps of the ancient Theban army, known as the Theban or Sacred Band (Ἱερός Λόχος), consisted of pairs of male lovers fighting alongside each other. It was a significant force in ending Spartan domination in the early fourth century BC but was destroyed by Philip II of Macedon in the Battle of Chaeronea in 338 BC. Greek historians Xenophon, Plutarch and Herodotus mention the Band, the latter describing its warriors as 'the first and the finest' ('πρῶτοι καὶ ἄριστοι') among Thebans. Through the mouthpiece of Phaedrus in the *Symposium* Plato refers to an unnamed 'army of lovers' that is assumed to be the Sacred Band. See Leitao, 'The Legend of the Sacred Band', pp. 143–69; and Crompton, '"An Army of Lovers"', pp. 23–29.

2. Sociological and historical research since the late 1960s has comprehensively documented the social pressures and prohibitory forces that determined the emergence of male homosexuality as a modern phenomenon in Europe. On the emergence of modern homosexual identities in Germany, see: Beachy, *Gay Berlin*, Beachy, 'German Invention of Homosexuality'; Greenberg, *The Construction of Homosexuality*; Kennedy, *Ulrichs*; Leck, *Vita sexualis*; Müller, *'Aber in meinem Herzen sprach eine Stimme'*; Oosterhuis, 'Sexual Modernity in the Works of Richard von Krafft-Ebing and Albert Moll'; Oosterhuis, 'Homosexual Emancipation in Germany before 1933'; Oosterhuis, *Stepchildren of Nature*; Tamagne, *History of Homosexuality in Europe*; Tobin, *Peripheral Desires*; Whisnant, *Queer Identities and Politics in Germany*.

3. The revolutionary French National Assembly passed over sodomy in the new penal code of 1791 and hence effectively decriminalized male homosexual relations. This situation passed over

into the Napoleonic Code of 1804 and then into the French Penal Code of 1810. According to Michael Sibalis and Robert Beachy, the decriminalization of sodomy in the German states was not, as is often thought, a consequence of these French developments. See Sibalis, 'The Regulation of Male Homosexuality in Revolutionary and Napoleonic France, 1789–1815' and Beachy, 'The German Invention of Homosexuality', p. 807.

4. Factual material for this section is drawn primarily from Steakley, *The Homosexual Emancipation Movement in Germany*, and 'Sodomy in Enlightenment Prussia'.

5. See Müller, *Aber in meinem Herzen sprach eine Stimme*.

6. Plessner, *Die verspätete Nation*.

7. Plato, *Dialogues*, 1, ed. by Benjamin Jowett (Oxford: Clarendon Press, 1892), p. 509.

8. Gustav Wyneken (1875–1964) established the Wickersdorfer Freie Schulgemeinde in 1906 in line with progressive educational reform precepts, aimed at the creation of new social forms among the young, away from the corrupted society of Wilhelminian Germany. The encouragement of close friendships and relations between teachers and pupils led to problems both within the school community and with the authorities. In his book, *Eros* (1921) Wyneken defended these relationships through recourse to ancient Greek pederasty.

   Adolf Brand (1874–1945) began publishing the homosexual men's periodical, *Der Eigene* in 1896 and built up a group of like-minded contributors. In 1903 he formed the *Gemeinschaft der Eigenen* with scientist Benedict Friedlaender, Wilhelm Jansen, the painter and illustrator, Fidus and others, advocating homosexual love, in particular of an older man for a youth. This was justified as an aspect of masculinity based on a reading of Spartan warrior values, Ancient Greek pederasty and the contemporary writings of Gustav Wyneken. This group rejected the 'third sex' theory associated with Hirschfeld's *Wissenschaftlich-humanitäres Komitee*.

   Benedict Friedlaender (1866–1908) co-founded with Adolf Brand the *Gemeinschaft der Eigenen* and was associated with Magnus Hirschfeld's *Wissenschaftlich-humanitäres Komitee*. He wrote on homosexuality, the law and biological science. In *Die Renaissance des Eros Uranios: Die physiologische Freundschaft, ein normaler Grundtrieb des Menschen [...]* he advocated the revival of 'Greek love'. See: Dougherty, *Eros, Youth Culture and Geist*; Kohlenbach, 'Walter Benjamin, Gustav Wyneken and the Jugendkulturbewegung'; Maasen, 'Man–Boy Friendships on Trial'; Maasen, *De Pedagogische Eros*; Sandfort and others, 'Man–Boy Relationships'; and Williams, 'Ecstasies of the Young'.

9. Werner Jaeger's *Paideia: Die Formung des griechischen Menschen* appeared in three volumes between 1933 and 1947, documenting the German fascination with the idea of Greek-Hellenic education or *Bildung* that had taken various forms in German pedagogy since the late eighteenth century. Jaeger, according to Landfester, found in George's *Teppich* and in later writings by members of the circle of George-admirers, such as Heinrich Friedemann (*Platon: Seine Gestalt*, Berlin: *Blätter für die Kunst*, 1914) important new formulations of platonic Hellenism in the spirit of the new youth movements. Jaeger left Germany for the USA in 1934. See Landfester, 'Werner Jaegers Konzepte von Wissenschaft und Bildung', p. 17; Mattenklott, 'Die Griechen sind zu gut zum schnuppern', pp. 244–48; Oestersandfort, 'Platonisches im *Teppich des Lebens*'; Rebenich, 'Dass ein strahl von Hellas auf uns fiel'.

10. US developmental psychologist Erik Erikson outlined an influential theory of human growth from childhood to old age in eight progressive stages based on Freudian psychoanalysis but focusing on psychosocial rather than psychosexual development. Each of Erikson's eight stages of human growth builds on the preceding stage, ideally to lead the individual through a satisfied, socially integrated and individually productive life. Each stage revolves around a generative conflict, such as trust versus mistrust in infancy, through identity versus role confusion in adolescence, intimacy versus isolation in early adulthood, to integrity versus despair in old age. Each of these nodal points of developmental tension can find resolution, leading to a strengthening of the sense of self; or can fail to find resolution, leading to stagnation and decline. Erikson applied the term 'generativity' for the seventh stage in life in which the individual is concerned in caring for and guiding the following generation. Erikson, *Childhood and Society*, pp. 239–68.

11. 'Jedenfalls ist hier Päderastie annehmbar für den gebildeten Mittelstand gemacht', 'Tagebuch', *Pan* 3/27 (11 April 1913), 640, cited in Shookman, *Thomas Mann's Death in Venice*, p. 16.

12. See DiMassa, 'Stefan George, Thomas Mann, and the Politics of Homoeroticism', pp. 311–33.

13. Renn, *Meine Kindheit und Jugend*, p. 238.

14. See Geuter, *Homosexualität in der deutschen Jugendbewegung*, p. 118–55.

15. See Koebner, *Unbehauste*, pp. 7–10, 14–16; Geuter, *Homosexualität in der deutschen Jugendbewegung*, pp. 148–50; Jungmann, 'Autorität und Sexualmoral in der freien bürgerlichen Jugendbewegung', pp. 679–81.

16. Mosse, *Germans and Jews*, p. 99.

17. Schmalenbach, 'Die soziologischen Kategorien des Bundes', pp. 35–105.

18. For the terms 'horizontal' and 'vertical' identification, see Solomon, *Far from the Tree*, p. 2. As opposed to directly inherited 'vertical' identity (for example, genetic traits, ethnicity, even cultural or religious identifications, language), 'horizontal identity' includes 'independently divergent' characteristics which are not transmitted across generations, but are inherent or acquired. Those individuals who discover such identities in themselves 'must acquire identity from a peer group' or otherwise face a difficult, lonely and potentially conflicted existence. For Solomon, 'while sexuality is not determined by their peers', gay individuals 'learn gay identity by observing and participating in a subculture outside the family'.

19. Hetherington, 'The Contemporary Significance of Schmalenbach's Concept of the Bund', pp. 1–25. See also Aurnhammer, *Stefan George und sein Kreis*, p. 1200.

20. See Weber, *Wirtschaft und Gesellschaft*, p. 669, 678, 679.

21. 'Die Jungen nahmen den strengen Sexualverzicht, den ihnen das Elternhaus nicht hatte aufzwingen können, nunmehr freiwillig auf sich, weil sie dafür durch eine, wenn auch sehr gedämpfte und sublimierte, so doch autoritätslose und also unväterliche Beziehung mit älteren Führern entschädigt wurden.' Jungmann, 'Autorität und Sexualmoral in der freien bürgerlichen Jugendbewegung', p. 678.

22. 'Vereinzelt brach naturgemäss auf dem Weg über die Befreiung der Zärtlichkeit zum alteren Mann auch die sinnliche Komponente gewaltsam durch, aber gewiss nur in einer kleinen Minderzahl der Fälle. Hier fanden sich die verschiedenartigsten Typen nebeneinander: der echte Homosexuelle mit sonst intaktem männlichem Habitus, der ewige Jüngling mit der protrahierten Pubertät, der aus Angst vor dem Weib in der Schulbubenkameradschaft bleiben musste, der fortschrittliche Lehramtsanwärter, der in der Linie der modernen Pädagogik denkend, nach autoritätslosem Kontakt mit der Jugend suchte.' (ibid.) See Geuter, *Homosexualität in der deutschen Jugendbewegung*, p. 27.

23. Bruns, *Politik des Eros*, p. 124.

24. See Doktor, *Die Eulenburg-Affäre*; Domeier, *The Eulenburg Affair*; Domeier, 'The Homosexual Scare and the Masculinization of German Politics before World War I'; Bruns, *Politik des Eros*, p. 119.

25. See Norton, *Secret Germany*, pp. 296–97.

26. Norton, *Secret Germany*, pp. 300–01.

27. Cornwall, *The Devil's Wall*, p. 118; see Bruns, *Politik des Eros*, pp. 53–102.

28. See Bruns, 'The Politics of Masculinity'; Geuter, *Homosexualität in der deutschen Jugendbewegung*, pp. 14–17, 67–109; Blüher, *Die Rolle der Erotik*, passim.

29. Schurtz argued that 'the gendered difference in bonding in historical cultures is a product of adaptive evolution (and therefore innate)'. Harris, 'Love and Death in the *Männerbund*', p. 293.

30. Jungmann, 'Autorität und Sexualmoral in der freien bürgerlichen Jugendbewegung', pp. 697–704.

31. Herf, *Reactionary Modernism*, pp. 1–17; Bruns, 'Politics of Masculinity', p. 319; Brunotte, *Zwischen Eros und Krieg*, pp. 31–87.

32. Blüher, *Werke und Tage*, pp. 353, 355, cited in Karlauf, *Stefan George*, p. 400. A late iteration of this version of pederasty as a non-sexual but homoerotic and homosocial binding and educative force, in relation to George, is to be found in a post-war article by Kurt Hildebrandt, one-time member of the circle, classicist, psychiatrist, and Nazi from 1933. In an article for the *Deutsche Vierteljahrsschrift* of 1950, Hildebrandt reads George's community-building exercise in the Bund as an exercise in pederastic-platonic love, which he equates with *agape* or 'gemeinschaftbildende Liebe' (Hildebrandt, 'Agape und Eros bei George', pp. 84, 93, 101). Hildebrandt's reading is a

late version of Blüher's homoeroticism and Greek pederasty, various forms of which had been popular since the 1860s in discussions of homosexuality, valorizing civic and pedagogical aspects of pederasty. This ideal is cleansed of overt homosexual content and reveals how George's imagery appealed to nationalists of a certain homoerotic type, leading up to Nazism.

33. Wyneken connected with the youth movement in 1912 and participated in the 1913 Erster Freideutscher Jugendtag; Blüher's first studies of the movement were published in 1912, although he had been a member from around the age of fourteen in 1902. See Kröhnke, ' "Wandervogel" und "Homosexuellenbewegung" '.

34. See Karlauf, *Stefan George*, pp. 342–43 for details of the encounter between George and Maximilian Kronberger.

35. Ibid., p. 621.

36. See Robertson, 'George, Nietzsche and Nazism', pp. 197–99. On George's 'cautiously positive' reception of the Nazi government, see ibid., pp. 200–01.

37. Ibid., p. 196, citing Michael André Bernstein, *Foregone Conclusions: Against Apocalyptic History* (Berkeley: University of California Press, 1994), p. 16.

38. Robertson, 'George, Nietzsche and Nazism', p. 196.

39. The classical image of the eternal youth or *puer aeternus* underpinned the youth movement and would feature among the archetypal figures identified by Carl Gustav Jung as essential to the collective unconscious. Jung's thinking may well have been influenced by George's figure of Maximin. The figure of Tadzio in Mann's Death in *Venice* also reflects this imagery *vis-à-vis* the 'senex' or old man, Gustav von Aschenbach. See Dahke, *Jünglinge der Moderne*, p. 131; Franz, *Puer aeternus*, passim.

40. Breuer, *Ästhetischer Fundamentalismus*, p. 60; Dörr, *Muttermythos und Herrschaftsmythos*, pp. 291–92.

41. Breuer, *Ästhetischer Fundamentalismus* 68–72.

42. In fact the term was originally coined by Karl Wolfskehl in 1910 with reference to George's evocation of a Germany other than the Second Empire. Norton, *Secret Germany*, pp. 434–36.

43. See Osterkamp, 'Poesie des Interregnums', pp. 1–26, 'In George, as in most sexually impaired or enfeebled characters a sickly undivested component of infantilism remained, a part of his soul which demanded adoration as the king and ruler', Borchardt, *Aufzeichnung Stefan George betreffend*, p. 29; Kauffmann, *Stefan George*, pp. 116–17.

44. Blüher, *Werke und Tage*, pp. 353, 355, cited in Karlauf, *Stefan George*, p. 400.

45. Norton, *Secret Germany*, pp. 122–23 and 505–11 respectively.

46. See Kauffmann, *Stefan George*, p. 120.

47. Cited in Norton, *Secret Germany*, p. 301.

48. See Keilson-Lauritz, 'Übergeschlechtliche Liebe als Passion', pp. 142–55; Keilson-Lauritz, *Von der Liebe die Freundschaft heisst*, passim.

49. J. A. Symonds, 'Song of Love and Death' is cited in Woods, *Articulate Flesh*, p. 62:

> Stirred from their graves to greet your Sacred Host
> The Theban lovers, rising very wan,
> By death made holy, wave dim palms, and cry:
> 'Hail, Brothers! who achieve what we began!'

50. See Geuter, *Homosexualität in der deutschen Jugendbewegung*, pp. 148–55; Jungmann, 'Autorität und Sexualmoral in der freien bürgerlichen Jugendbewegung', pp. 679–80.

51. Thomas Mann, for example, enthusiastically supported Friedrich Gundolf's article in praise of the war effort in February 1915, whereas George rejected his disciples' arguments out of hand. See Zeller, *Stefan George*, p. 262.

52. Braune, *Erich Fromm's Revolutionary Hope*, pp. 95.

53. Braungart, 'Kult, Ritual und Religion bei Stefan George', p. 260.

54. See Mattenklott, *Bilderdienst*, p. 181.

55. Schirrmacher, 'Dies ist der Pfeil des Meisters'.

56. 'Es sind lyrisch gestalteten Menschen, nicht bloß Eindrucksschatten die innerhalb seiner zauberisch schönen, zauberisch gehüteten Landschaften handeln und leiden' (Lukács, *Kurze Skizze einer Geschichte der neueren deutschen Literatur*, p. 173).

57. Lukács, *Die Zerstörung der Vernunft*, p. 34.

58. See Mattenklott, 'Walter Benjamin und Theodor W. Adorno über George', p. 281.

59. Benjamin, 'Rückblick auf Stefan George', p. 399.

60. Ibid., p. 398.

61. Benjamin, 'Über Stefan George', p. 624.

62. George's title *Tage und Taten* refers explicitly to Hesiod's *Works and Days* (editorial note, George, *SW*, XVII, 94). Hence Morwitz translates the title as 'Days and Works'. However, the more literal translation into English would be 'Days and Deeds'.

63. See Berger, 'Theodor W. Adornos Stefan-George-Rezeption' , p. 213.

64. Adorno, *Noten zur Literatur*, p. 528. It must be noted here, though, that 'Im windes-weben' which Adorno considered so highly, is from the later work, *Der siebente Ring*.

65. Adorno, *Noten zur Literatur*, p. 528.

66. See David, *Stefan George: Sein Dichterisches Werk*, pp. 378–89; Siblewski, ' "Diesmal winkt sicher das Friedensreich" ', pp. 22–23; Egyptien, 'Entwicklung und Stand der George-Forschung', p. 105.

67. Usinger, *Stefan George*, p. 45. Usinger repeated his observation more forcefully a decade later, ibid., p. 46.

68. Of George's friends and associates, the following might be mentioned: Friedrich Wolters 'Stefan George und die Blatter fur die Kunst; Deutsche Geistesgeschichte seit 1890' (1930); Sabine Lepsius, *Stefan George: Geschichte einer Freundschaft* (1935); Albert Verwey, *Mein Verhältnis zu Stefan George'* (1936); Edgar Salin, *Um Stefan George* (1948); Robert Boehringer, *Mein Bild von Stefan George* (1951); Ludwig Thormaehlen, *Erinnerungen an Stefan George* (1962); Edith Landmann, *Gespräche mit Stefan George* (1963), Kurt Hildebrandt, *Erinnerungen an Stefan George und seinen Kreis* (1965), Berthold Vallentin, *Gespräche mit Stefan George* (1967), Ernst Glockner, *Begegnung mit Stefan George* (1972). Ernst Morwitz's *Die Dichtung Stefan Georges* (1934) and *Kommentar zu dem Werk Stefan Georges* (1960) bring together personal memories of interactions and discussions with translations and literary analysis.

69. David, *Stefan George: Sein Dichterisches Werk*, p. 12.

70. Ibid., p. 194.

71. Ibid., pp. 13–14.

72. Ibid., pp. 11, 13–14.

73. Fleming, 'Secret Adorno', p. 99.

74. Durzak, *Zwischen Symbolismus und Expressionismus*, p. 7.

75. Mattenklott, *Bilderdienst*, pp. 177–78.

76. Landfried, *Stefan George*, cited in Egyptien, 'Entwicklung und Stand der George-Forschung 1955–2005', p. 114.

77. Major literary studies include French philologist, Claude David's early post-war *Stefan George: Son Œuvre poétique* 1952 (German trans., *Stefan George: Sein dichterisches Werk*, 1967); Kurt Hildebrandt's *Das Werk Stefan Georges* (1960); Georg Peter Landmann's *Vorträge über Stefan George* (1974); Hansjürgen Linke's *Das Kultische in der Dichtung Stefan Georges und seiner Schule* (1960); Eckhard Heftrich's *Stefan George* (1968); Gert Mattenklott's *Bilderdienst* (1970); Manfred Durzak's *Zwischen Symbolismus und Expressionismus* (1974); Klaus Landfried's *Stefan George* (1975); Marita Keilson-Lauritz's *Von der Liebe die Freundschaft heißt: Zur Homoerotik im Werk Stefan Georges* (1987); and Stefan Breuer's *Asthetischer Fundamentalismus* (1995). See Egyptien, 'Entwicklung und Stand der George-Forschung 1955–2005', pp. 113–16.

78. Petersdorf, 'Als der Kampf gegen die Moderne verloren war', pp. 326–27.

79. Lepenies, *Die drei Kulturen*, p. 320–21.

80. Breuer, *Ästhetischer Fundamentalismus*, p. 239.

81. Ibid., p. 1–4; see also Petersdorf, 'Als der Kampf gegen die Moderne verloren war', pp. 326–27.

82. Osterkamp, *Poesie der leeren Mitte*, p. 14.

83. Ibid.

84. Braungart and others, *Stefan George*, 'Vorwort', p. x.

85. Braungart, 'Kult, Ritual und Religion', p. 257.

86. Böschenstein, 'Stefan George's Spätwerk als Antwort auf eine untergehende Welt', p. 16.

87. Osterkamp, *Poesie der leeren Mitte*, pp. 15–26.
88. Ibid., pp. 115–36. See also Zanucchi, 'Ernst Osterkamp, *Poesie der leeren Mitte*', p. 109: 'The result is a nationalistic-biological distortion of the universalistic educational program of the Weimar Classicism'.
89. Ibid., p. 17.
90. Ibid., p. 15.
91. Norton, *Secret Germany* (2002); Karlauf, *Stefan George* (2007); Kauffmann, *Stefan George* (2014); Egyptien, *Stefan George: Dichter und Prophet* (2018); Aurnhammer and others, eds, *Stefan George und sein Kreis* (2012); Egyptien, *Stefan George: Werkkommentar* (2017); Kolk, *Literarische Gruppenbildung* (1998, repr. 2012); Braungart and others, eds, *Stefan George: Werk und Wirkung seit dem 'Siebenten Ring'* (2001); Groppe, *Die Macht der Bildung* (2001); Böschenstein and others, *Wissenschaftler im George-Kreis* (2005); Raulff, *Kreis ohne Meister* (2009); Osterkamp, *Poesie der leeren Mitte* (2010); Pieger and Schefold, *Stefan George: Dichtung — Führung — Staat* (2010); Frank and Ribbeck, *Stefan-George-Bibliographie* (2000); Rättig, *Stefan George: Das geheime Deutschland, Dokumentarfilm* (2018); Wasner, *Der merkwürdige fall des Stefan George, Dokumentarfilm* (2018).
92. Keilson-Lauritz, *Von der Liebe die Freundschaft heißt*, passim.
93. Fricker, *Stefan George*, pp. 275–79.
94. Egyptien, 'Entwicklung und Stand der George-Forschung, 1955–2005', p. 116.
95. On the recent reception of George, see Ockenden, 'Kingdom of the Spirit', pp. 91–93.
96. Von Matt, 'Der geliebte Doppelgänger'; Breuer, *Ästhetischer Fundamentalismus*, pp. 29–31 and passim.
97. Keilson-Lauritz, 'Stefan George's Concept of Love', p. 207.
98. Ibid., pp. 64–65.
99. Keilson-Lauritz, *Von der Liebe die Freundschaft heißt*, p. 61.
100. Keilson-Lauritz, *Von der Liebe die Freundschaft heißt*, pp. 60–61.
101. Ibid., p. 67.
102. Ibid., p. 75.
103. Ibid., pp. 83–97.
104. Ibid., pp. 98–99.
105. Ibid., p. 13.
106. Lukács, 'Die neue Einsamkeit', p. 121.
107. Ibid., p. 129.
108. *Die Fibel* (*Primer*, including poems drafted between 1886 and 1889, publ. 1901); *Hymnen* (*Hymns*, 1890, reflecting the influence of French symbolist poet, Mallarmé); *Pilgerfahrten* (*Pilgrimages* 1891); *Algabal* (1892); *Die Bücher der Hirten- und Preisgedichte, der Sagen und Sänge und der hängenden Gärten* (*The Books of Eclogues and Eulogies, of Legends and Lays and of the Hanging Gardens*, poems written mostly between 1892 and 1894 and published in 1895); *Das Jahr der Seele* (*The Year of the Soul*, poems written for the most part between 1892 and 1895 and published in 1897); *Der Teppich des Lebens* (*The Tapestry of Life*, poems written between 1897 and 1899 and published in 1899); *Tage und Taten* (*Days and Works*, prose pieces, including the 'Vorrede zu Maximin' in 1904); *Der siebente Ring* (*The Seventh Ring*, including 'Zeitgedichte', poems written between 1897 and 1904, 'Gestalten' 1901–1904, 'Gezeiten', 1899, 'Maximin', 1903–1906, 'Traumdunkel', 1902–1905, 'Lieder', 1892–1905, 'Tafeln', 1898–1905, published in 1907); *Der Stern des Bundes* (*The Star of the Covenant*, poems mainly written between 1908 and 1911 and published in 1914); 'Der Krieg' ('The War', published in 1917); and *Das Neue Reich* (*The New Empire*, trans. By Morwitz as *The Kingdom Come*, including 'Goethes lezte Nacht in Italien', written in 1908, otherwise written between 1909 and 1919, including 'Der Krieg', and published in 1928). While some early poems were published in the *Blätter für die Kunst* and elsewhere, the publication in 1900 of a one-volume edition including the *Hymnen, Pilgerfahrten,* and *Algabal* brought George's work to a broader audience.
109. Ockenden, 'Kingdom of the Spirit', p. 93.
110. Ibid., pp. 90–92.
111. Edward Norton shows the extent to which George's fear of persecution as a homosexual determined his cult of privacy. George's response to the young Hugo von Hofmannsthal's

rejection by letter of his homosexual advances was also underpinned by fear of social, and perhaps even legal, consequences of the matter becoming public. Norton, *Secret Germany*, pp. 122–23.

112. Goldsmith, *Stefan George*, pp. 16–17.
113. Norton, *Secret Germany*, pp. 367–68.
114. Braungart, '"Was ich noch sinne, p. 7.
115. Aurnhammer and others, *Stefan George und sein Kreis*, p. 526.
116. See Petersdorff, *Fliehkräfte der Moderne*, esp. pp 75–140, for an excellent summation of the social environment of change in Germany.
117. 'Der Mensch der George-Lieder [...] ist ein einsamer, aus allen sozialen Banden gelöster Mensch' (Lukács, 'Die neue Einsamkeit', p. 129).
118. 'Was man begreifen muß und was man nie begreifen kann: daß zwei Menschen nie wirklich zu Einem werden können, das ist der Inhalt jedes seiner Lieder und der Inhalt ihrer Gesamtheit'. (Lukács. 'Die neue Einsamkeit', p. 129) Translation from George Lukács, *Soul and Form*, trans. by Anna Bostock (London: Merlin Press, 1974), p. 88.
119. See Erikson, *Childhood and Society*, pp. 239–68.
120. The realm of 'subjective' identity (= 'the sense of self based on individual, personal memory and experience, influenced by collective shared beliefs and cultural narratives') versus 'objective' identity (= the sense of self as 'constituted by the regard of others. At first the way they see your face and understand your name, then through the experience they make with you. In a traditional world the two fit together. You see yourself, roughly, if not entirely, as others see you'.) Heller, 'Cosmopolitanism as Philosophy', pp. 50–51.
121. Examples include the psychopathological (the deviant), the criminal (street-boy, prostitute, sexual predator), the biological (Hirschfeld's 'third sex'), the sentimental elegiac-pastoral (the Greek *paideia*, Gustav von Aschenbach's fantasies.
122. Keilson-Lauritz, 'Übergeschlechtliche Liebe als Passion', pp. 62–135.

CHAPTER 2

Discovering the
Homosexual Imaginary

Finding a Beginning

George's earliest poems date from adolescence and early adulthood (from around 1886 until the early 1890s) and were published retrospectively in the collection *Die Fibel* in 1901, after the sixth major collection, *Der Teppich des Lebens*, when the poet was already in his early thirties. *Die Fibel* thus occupies a place as the opening volume in the poetic autobiography, rendering the poet's poetic beginnings reflexive and historical through the retrospective inclusion of his youthful works. Jürgen Egyptien writes of the poet's self-conscious retrospective identification of this collection in terms of his own coming to awareness of himself as a poet, and hence of the work's forward-looking aspect.[1] The dominant theme is the awakening to life from moribund loneliness and dejection. The tropes of loneliness derive from earlier romantic poetry, but also suggest growing dissatisfaction with the capacity of this poetic language to convey the poet's reality. The lyric voice of a homosexual persona is already perceptible, even if the broader homoerotic themes emerge only gradually and later in *Das Jahr der Seele* and *Der Teppich des Lebens*. The opening 'Geleitverse', written at the time of publication around 1900, stress the conflict between the developing voice and an unresponsive world:

> Das ist des kindes lallen
> Das seine flöte prüft im rohr
> Dem dumpf engegenschallen
> Gebüsch und strom und wind im chor. (I, 9)

> [The murmuring of the child
> That tests his flute with a reed
> The chorus of bush and flood and wind
> That dully drowns him out.][2]

Since his childhood George had been fascinated by languages and in particular by the idea of a secret personal language as a means of withdrawal into an inner realm in which he would have absolute control. Language as a form of mask, and a private language as a form of communication untouched by the German around him, functioned as a source of fantasy and retreat into subjective autonomy and safety. During his adolescence he learned several Romance languages and continued to develop his own secret language.[3] Kaspar senses in George's switching between languages and his fascination with his own self-devised language during the 1890s the signs of insecurity and impending crisis. The secret code in particular expresses his need for self-expression at the same time as fear of exposure and desire for safety (in a potentially threatening legal environment).[4] The 'dark desire' ('dunkler sehnsucht') of the fourth stanza of 'Geleitverse' (I, 9) suggests a less abstract source of the young homosexual man's sense of crisis than existential confusion. In the opening poem (I, 13) fleeting early love leads only to disappointment and pain ('täuschung [...] und schmerz').

The supersession of reality by an undefined erotic ideal takes us to the core of the homosexual experience in a world of prohibition. The line of association in 'Abendbetrachtung' ('Evening Contemplation', I, 16) passes from erotic arousal through aimless wandering while thinking of the (female) loved one ('die Geliebte)' to a cemetery. The economy of the verses is telling: the female loved one is a superficial and fleeting commonplace in a trajectory defined by aimlessness, death and decay. The poetic voice finds little promise of fulfilment even in imagined idealized love. The dominant imagery in 'Herzensnacht' ('Night of the Heart', I, 22) and 'Du standest in der wolken wehen' ('You stood in the blowing clouds', I, 27) is of darkness and exclusion; silence dominates in 'Warum schweigst du ...' ('Why do you remain silent...', I, 23), and winter returns to extinguish the promise of summer in 'Schon künden heissere sonnenstrahlen an' ('Summer beams already announce', I, 26). Life is poisoned in 'Die Sirene' ('The Siren', I, 28), and anger and bitterness dominate in 'Sei stolzer als die prunkenden Pfauen' ('Be prouder than the strutting peacocks', I, 29). In the poems 'Gräber' ('Graves', I, 34) and 'November-Rose' (I, 57) a new note is heard, the beginning of the aesthetics of morbidity that would come to the fore in the later collection, *Algabal*.

The young poet's evocation of unfulfilled expectation suggests conflict between sexual desire and social environment.

> Ich wandelte auf öden düstren bahnen,
> Und planlos floss dahin mein leben.
> In meinem herzen war kein hohes streben
> Es schien mich nicht an schönheit zu gemahnen. (I, 13)

> [I wandered along desolate gloomy paths,
> My life flowing away without a plan
> In my heart was no great striving
> It did not seem to honour beauty]

The feminine associations of beauty ('schönheit') seem to hold little charm for him. And yet he is struck by an image that might yet redeem him.

> Da plötzlich sah ich — o wer sollte es ahnen —
> Ein himmelsbild an mir vorüberschweben ..
> In meinem inner fühlte ich ein beben
> Und Liebe pflanzte ihre siegesfahnen. (I, 13)

> [Then suddenly I saw — oh who might have thought —
> An image of heaven float by me
> In my innermost self I felt a quaking
> And love planted her flag of victory.]

But this image of abstract beauty ('ein himmelsbild') passes by and over him. It arouses a sensation of 'Love' (untypically capitalized in George's original) but has no characteristics and leaves nothing behind. But for the sense of love itself, his feelings are empty and the sonnet ends with a trite formulation of gratitude. And yet the fate that he is thanking has driven him to an act ('tat') of ambiguous significance. It is not the image of love, abstract and characterless, but rather the act that takes him to heaven.

> Ist mir auch täuschung nur und schmerz geblieben
> Und kann ich Dich von glorienschein umwoben
> Anbetend und begeistert still nur lieben:
> So muss ich doch das gütige schicksal loben
> Das mich durch Deine hand zur tat getrieben
> Und zu den sternen mich emporgehoben. (I, 13)

> [Only deceit and pain remain
> And if I can still only love you
> shining in glory, worshipping and passionate
> then I must indeed praise well-meaning fate
> That drove me to action through your hand
> And raised me to the stars.

The sexual implication is clear, as is the ambiguity of the fantasy that drives it, even at this early stage in the poet's life. Karlauf sees the sexual confusion of puberty in these poems; however there is an unmistakable sense of the impossibility and inadmissability of fulfilment of his 'dunkle sehnsucht' that suggests something more than the adolescent frustrations of unfolding sexuality.[5] These early poems describe the confusion of youth, but there is more to the manipulation of the clichés of love poetry than the epigonalism of a young poet. A quiet resolve manifests itself throughout. The poet will not yield to aestheticist negativity in order to resolve life's difficulties. The late adolescent melancholy is shot through with moments of resolution and even restrained vitalism that complicate the *fin-de-siècle* negativity and will find more open expression as George's poetic life passes through the stages of development to maturity. In 'Die Schmiede' ('The Smithy', I, 58) the poet feels himself confined by force into a 'straitjacket of the soul' ('Zwangskleid der Seele') that he retrospectively learns to appreciate in a sinister and perverse twist of self-abasement: 'Er schmiedet zum heil zur befreiung' ('He hammers for salvation for liberation', I, 58). But there is change and growth at the same time:

> Ich fühle in allen tiefen ein gähren
> Mein todesschlaf kann nicht länger währen. (Keim-Monat, I, 66).

> [I feel a moving and stirring in the depths
> My sleep of death can linger no longer.]

In the poem 'Gräber' the garden turns out to be a cemetery:

> Ich wandelt in einem lieblichen garten [...]
> Und meine halboffenen augen starrten
> In seine prunkende herrlichkeit.
> [...]
> Da fuhr ich auf und vor einer gruft

Hielt ich eine steinerne leiche am herzen
Und ward ich geküsst von verwesender luft. (I, 34)

[I wandered in a lovely garden [...]
And my half-opened eyes stared
At its splendid grandeur
[...]
Then suddenly I stopped with a shock
Standing before a tomb holding to my heart
A stone corpse kissing me with putrefying breath.]

Conventional love is repeatedly associated with the garden of death (I, 36). The twinned topoi of sexual arousal and fear of death in the natural environment are derivative of the Catholic late Romantic poet, Joseph Freiherr von Eichendorff (1788–1857).[6] But hints of redemption emerge in the image of the sun which bursts forth, moving beyond sexual guilt and fear. In 'Gift der Nacht' ('Poison of the Night', I, 75) the ageing, solitary poet looks back on a life of Catholicism, lonely masturbation, and guilt, wishing himself again the boy who has not yet experienced sexual desire and regretting the lonely old age that is the penalty for his untamed lusts ('die strafe [...] | Für wilde gelüste' (the punishment [...] for fierce desires). However, George moves beyond guilt to seek participation in life regardless of its later costs ('[Ich] Wollte mit offenen armen | In mein unheil rennen' (I wanted to run towards my doom with open arms) ('Gift der Nacht', I, 75). The poet seeks participation in an indeterminate role as playmate and dancer with nymphs who are imagined as both innocent and seductive. The final line of 'Gräber' suggests sexual disgust when the proffered kiss dissolves into a putrid stench. The desire for participation in the group and the disgust at the women's advances are the poem's two key experiences, and death is the outcome of the dance. Yet the *memento mori* which breaks the illusion comes about through the recognition that he is unable to participate, not that he feels guilty in doing so.

'Wechsel' ('Change', I, 77) plays with the earlier poetic conceit of listing out the physical attributes of the beloved that the poet finds attractive. However, unlike Petrarch and the playful Shakespeare of Sonnet 130, George ends on a note of negative approbation devoid of any sense of attraction, let alone passion:

Heute ist nichts mehr an ihr
Was mir nicht sehr gefiele
Was ich nicht glühend anbetete. (I, 77)

[Now there is nothing about her any more
That does not please me
That I do not ardently worship.]

The qualifier 'sehr', and the trite adverb 'glühend' weaken rather than strengthen the plausibility of the poet's statement of attraction, as does the use of the subjunctive. But most of all, the process of coming to such conviction reveals the strength of the inner opposition that must be overcome for him to worship this woman in the terms of conventional love poetry. The lyric persona finds himself still in the late adolescent phase of trying to convince himself of heterosexual attraction. Similarly, the poem 'Einer sklavin' ('To a slave', I, 78) reduces the words and the identity of the woman to silence, namely to a state in which the poet can continue to reconstruct her in his imagination without recourse to her female reality. And 'In der galerie' ('In the gallery', I, 79) the art-work and the person become indistinguishable as the poet escapes into the 'world of colours' ('welt der farben') and away 'from the dust of the everyday' ('vom staub des alltags') in order to construct a female 'you' whom he then loses amidst the shapes and colours of the art-gallery. In 'Erster frühlingstag' ('First day of Spring', I, 64) the heat of the early northern spring brings self-recognition to a heart that has striven unsuccessfully for love. Against the warmth, beauty and light of southern sensuality, the northern Spring represents an altogether more powerful, profound and problematic sphere of sexuality still beholden to age's wintry custodianship.

> Gierig trinkt seine wonnen ein herz
> Das starker regungen bar
> Zu kleinen lieben sich zwingt
> Und nach einer grossen vergebens ringt. (I, 64)

> [Thirstily a heart drinks its delight
> A heart that strong impulses bore
> That forced itself to small loves
> And strove in vain for great love.]

In 'Das Bild', the dream-image that terrifies the poet is not identified, merely its effect is described: 'Avenging itself and demanding its right, it came in the fears of the night' ('Rächend sich und sein recht verlangend, Kam es in den ängsten der nacht ...', I, 73).

In these early poems a new emphasis emerges as male figures appear, displacing the nymphs, roses and dying gardens of convention. In 'November-Rose' (I, 57) a late-blooming rose adorns the fresh grave of a youth. George's lyric tone and style change perceptibly as the gaze moves from the female to the male and from convention to freedom. The evocation of the youth in 'Erkenntnis' ('Recognition', I, 83) is already accompanied by the tone of hymnic adoration that the poet had tried so hard to evoke in the female object of desire in 'Wechsel'. And in the broken idyll, 'Erkenntnis', the narcissistic-homoerotic figure of the youth suggests a deeper-lying existential problem than mere jealousy, which leads him to suicide. In 'Seefahrt' ('Sea-journey', I, 60) the traditional world of Rhineland Catholic community — of 'the mothers saying their rosary' ('Die mütter beten den rosenkranz', I, 60) — is challenged by the poet's new sense of connection and freedom in the masculine world of the sailors:

> Die freunde lachen — wir eilen fort.
> [...]
> Doch mich verletzt ihr spottend wort
> Bin ich auch nicht viel besser selber –
> Ich steige sinnend in das boot. (I, 60)

> [The friends laugh ... we hurry off.
> [...]

> Yet their sarcasms hurt me
> Even if I'm no better myself —
> Reflecting, I climb into the boat.]

Similarly in the second of the 'Legenden', 'Frühlingswende' ('Turn of Spring', I, 87) a youth, just entering manhood in an imagined early Germanic warrior society, flees his new-found responsibility and the encroaching involvement with women for solitude in the natural environment. The poem ends in an image of narcissistic *thanatos*, of flight into the self, away from society and the group, from rebarbative adult masculinity and seductive femininity.

> Im wasser inmitten der blassgrünen algen
> Und schwanker zum ufer getriebener blumen
> Erblickt er nur immer sein eigenes bild. (I, 90)

> [In the water among the pale-green algae
> And watery blooms swaying towards the shore
> He saw his own image.]

After experiencing the hot kiss of the sun, Icarus is lost among the waves and the poem ends with an exhortation, 'nun hilf dir Ikarus!' (I, 41, 'now help yourself Icarus'), suggesting not merely that the subject is a self-reflexive metaphor but also that no-one other than he can help himself. In the later poems of the *Der Teppich des Lebens* and *Stern des Bundes* the warm sunlight of the male world of Hellas will supplant the cold light of northern Europe that suffuses these poems.

The three Legends that make up the final section of *Die Fibel* are concerned with the boy's passage from adolescence to maturity in a patriarchal world. In the most revealing and explicit of these legends, 'Der Schüler' ('The Student'), a youth on the verge of adulthood finds himself sexually attracted to a younger boy:

> Dass jenes blonde kind der jüngste schüler
> Das oft mich mit den grossen augen sucht
> So gänzlich meinen sinn erschüttern könne. (I, 92)

> [That that blond child, the youngest pupil
> Who often seeks me out with his wide eyes
> Could so completely shake my senses...]

The youth is the product of a loving and stable world-order in which the individual and the group exist in equilibrium and he is due to pass from youth to socially responsible adulthood. The image of transition is stable and both loving and respectful in terms of the relationship of the son to the father and vice versa:

> Dass ich nun bald den höheren grad erringe
> Versprechen mir die väter die mich lieben
> Ja ehren und zu manchem rate ziehn. (I, 91)

> [That now I am about to reach the higher degree
> The fathers promise me, who love me
> Honour me even, and bring me into their counsel.]

Yet the discovery of strange instruments in the depths of untrodden vaults upsets this harmony. In an ancient mirror he sees his own body reflected as a source of mystery that sets him thinking about himself and others:

> Was bringt nun diese wandlung? Doch nicht einzig
> Mein schweifen in den unbetretenen erkern
> Wo ich bei manchem seltsamen gerät
> Den spiegel glänzenden metalls entdeckt
> Vor dem ich meines eigenen leibs geheimnis
> Und anderer zuerst bedenken lernte. (I, 91)

> [What brings about this change? Surely not just
> My wanderings in the untrodden arches
> Where I discovered among strange devices
> The mirror of shining steel
> In front of which I learned for the first time
> To doubt the secret of my own body and of others.]

Karlauf notes the sense of sexual confusion here, and Kaspar senses an early 'Sprachkrise' in the poet's fears and need for safety in the language of secrecy.[7] While mirrored nakedness express the tension between the physical and the mental, the crisis is not merely of language or undefined existential unease.[8] The theme of emerging homosexual identity is already palpable in the tension between past and present insecurity, the recognition of hitherto undefined feelings of attraction to another boy, and the boy's apprehensions for the future. This is the earliest explicit suggestion of the move beyond the discovery of self to that of others as similarly constituted, which lies at the core of George's discovery of the homosexual other and emerging sense of *wir-Gefühl*. It is not self-reflection alone that brings about this change. The change to his existence reaches deeper into his being than the external, mirrored image can represent. The disturbance caused by the blond boy has its origins deep inside the lyric voice.

A journey — 'welch ein wink der fügung!'('what a stroke of fortune!') — offers the diversions of unknown worlds ('unbekannte welten', I, 92), but on return he searches in vain for the stability of old. Neither fasting nor prayer can dispel the thoughts that disturb him or alter the reality of the boy's constitution. As the conflict between the 'joy of which no knowledge speaks' ('glück von dem kein wissen redet', and the stable world of his teachers ('feste welt der lehrer', I, 92) depletes his vital energies, he flees the company of friends and community. However he seeks isolation in order to find himself and to come to a decision, not to escape. Still unsure of what it is that has rendered him an outcast, he nevertheless resolves to move onward in life, not to force himself back into miserable conformity and loneliness in the group:

> Ich weiss nicht ganz was mich auf einmal so
> Von ihnen und den früheren freunden trennt
> Noch welchem nächsten Ziel ich mich ergebe. (I, 93)

> [I'm not quite sure what suddenly separated me
> From them and from earlier friends
> Nor to which goal I should now devote myself.]

Flight is the only form of escape: 'No word will excuse me ... Among the fathers |
there is surely none who might understand' ('Kein wort wird mich entschulden ...
von den vätern | Ist keiner mir gewiss der es begriffe'). The boy faces an unknown
and uncharted future, but it is a future nevertheless:

> Doch es treibt mich auf
> Der alten toten weisheit zu entraten
> Bis ich die lebende erkennt: der leiber
> Der blumen und der wolken und der wellen. (I, 93)

> [Yes, it spurs me on
> To dispense with the old dead wisdom
> Until I recognize the living: of bodies
> Of flowers and of the winds and the waves.]

It will be a much longer journey, however, from this first sense of union to the
recognition of mature object love in the late poems. Unlike the previous two
'Legende', the final poem of the collection, 'Der Schüler' ends with a valorization
of the world of the body against the 'old dead wisdom' of the fathers, as the youth
turns to uncertain life rather than the certainty of death.

The collections of poems published during the first half of the 1890s (*Hymnen,
Pilgerfahrten, Algabal, Die Bücher der Hirten- und Preisgedichte, der Sagen und Sänge und
der hängenden Gärten*) resume the implied *vita*, prepared retrospectively with the
publication of the earlier, juvenile poems in *Die Fibel*, and providing the lyrical-
autobiographical basis for the later openly homoerotic lyrical–personal voice of *Der
siebente Ring* and beyond. Like his lyric persona in 'Der Schüler' George would leave
home shortly after finishing his Abitur (school leaving examination), travelling in
1888 and 1889 to England, Switzerland, Italy, Paris and Spain.[9] *Hymnen* (1890), his
first published book at the age of twenty-two in 1890, reflects the influences of
travel, of his newly discovered Mallarmé and the French symbolists, and, as his
editors note, marks the passage to a mature lyric voice.[10] *Hymnen, Pilgerfahrten,* and
Algabal followed in quick succession.

Where 'Der Schüler' achieves a level of disclosure of homosexual attraction
through the displacement of voice from the poetic self onto the imagined student,
the poems from *Hymnen* (1890) represent an early stage of the poet's own existential
journey. The primary motif is escape from the earlier deadening states documented
in *Die Fibel* into a new openness and vitality. 'Out into the flood!' 'Hinaus zum
strom!' he commands in the opening poem, 'Dedication' ('Weihe'). With adulthood
and maturity comes heterosexual attraction, but it is curiously ambivalent, phrased
in terms of avoidance:

> Nun bist du reif . nun schwebt die herrin nieder .
> [...]
> Zu dir geneigt die segnung zu vollbringen:
> Indem ihr mund auf deinem antlitz bebte
> Und sie dich rein und so geheilgt sah
> Dass sie im kuss nicht auszuweichen strebte
> Dem finger stützend deiner lippe nah. (II, 10)

[Down the goddess gleams,
[...]
She leans to you and offers you a boon.
Her mouth is trembling closer to your cheeks,
So pure you seem to her, so ripe for bliss,
That now she does not shun your hand which seeks
To turn her lips to yours and to your kiss.] (Morwitz 3)

The language of artifice, obscurity and aestheticism of the French symbolist poet Stéphane Mallarmé has been identified as the primary influence in *Hymnen*.[11] In the veiled forms of address using the gender-undefined second person, Keilson-Lauritz identifies the first intimations of the poet's own homosexual identity and suggests that the language of French symbolism is instrumentalized in this collection as a cover for George's homosexuality, rather than being an aesthetic end in itself.[12] There is certainly a curious obliqueness to these poems, rich with impressionist imagery but always moving away and beyond to something other. The poet looks blindly beyond the pearl- and gemstone-encrusted park, deaf to the sounds surrounding him, wedded to his dreams of elsewhere:

Rubinen perlen schmücken die fontänen
Zu boden streut sie fürstlich jeder strahl ·
[...]
Der dichter dem die vögel angstlos nahen
Träumt einsam in dem weiten schattensaal
[...]
Der dichter auch der töne lockung lauscht.
Doch heut darf ihre weise nicht ihn rühren
Weil er mit seinen geistern rede tauscht:
Er hat den griffel der sich sträubt zu führen. (II, 11)

[The fountains rise as rubies, fall in pearls,
Each burst scattering lavishly to the ground
[...]
The poet, whom the birds approach with no fear,
Dreams alone among the wide and shadowed arches.
He also hears the sound's allurements.
But today their melodies may not move him,
Because his speech with spirits holds him bound:
He has to guide the pen that resists] (Morwitz 4)

Similarly the poet lingering in the idyllic natural setting of 'Ein Hingang' ('Parting') seeks redemption in a transfigured imaginary realm:

Wo schiffe gleiten mit erhobnen schilden ·
Wo andre schlafen wehrlos · froh der bucht
Und weit wo wolken lichte berge bilden
Er seiner wünsche wunderlande sucht .. (II, 19)

[Beyond, where clouds are shaped to shining peaks,
And ships advance with tall and carven prows
Or sleep surrendered to the bay, he seeks
The shores of wonder his desires rouse.] (Morwitz 8)

The associative language of French aestheticism and symbolism becomes the means to extending the poet's vocabulary of experience as Keilson-Lauritz implies, into spheres that are as yet unexplored and still off-limits for the young poet.

The following volume, *Pilgerfahrten* (1891) is written in the spirit of both leaving and seeking home. Here the language of French aestheticism becomes the means to extending the poet's vocabulary of experience into spheres that are as yet unexplored and off-limits for the young poet. In the later collection, *Algabal*, in particular this aspect of symbolism and aestheticism will be explored in full. The epigraph gives the tone of the collection:

> ALSO BRACH ICH AUF
> UND EIN FREMDLING WARD ICH
> UND ICH SUCHTE EINEN
> DER MIT MIR TRAUERTE
> UND KEINER WAR. (II, 30)

> [And so I journeyed forth
> And became a stranger
> And I sought for some one
> Who would mourn with me
> And there was no one.] (*Morwitz 15)

The poet sets out and becomes a stranger searching for one who both mourns his loss and yet belongs, himself, to an unspecified home. The antinomy here lies between the poet's alienation and the need to find someone who misses him. The poet in *Pilgerfahrten*, that is, journeys in order to find a home that he has never had or has lost. The editors note the echo of Psalm 69 in George's epigraph, 'I looked for some to take pity, but there was none; and for comforters, but I found none' (II, 110). At this point the homosexual poet is alone, not only as a homosexual but as a human being. There is no-one for him. The recognition of this double sense of loneliness is ubiquitous in the works of this era. For George's late disciple, Morwitz, the opening poems of 'Siedlergang' express the loneliness of lyric voice and the recognition of disillusionment with sensuality as a path to fulfilment.[13] Again and again we read of the loss of idyllic childhood and family community in the wake of the recognition of homosexual maturity, and of the devastating sense of loneliness, all themes adumbrated in *Die Fibel*. Unlike others, however, George does not capitulate to the loneliness and seeks something beyond self-hatred. This is the key to his attraction for so many homosexual men of the time.

The poet oscillates between enthusiasm and disillusionment with various unidentified women, but the language is artificial and the fervour unconvincing, a product of imagination rather than reality. The poem 'Lass deine tränen | Um ein weib' ('Leave your tears | over a woman', II, 36) suggests disappointment in a heterosexual relation to most commentators; however an alternative reading would be that these are tears of frustration and disappointment at the poet's own lack of sexual interest, given the passivity and negativity of earlier imaginings of heterosexual attractions, at the doubts about his own body in 'Wechsel', and the relentless drive for escape from everything associated with the love-poem, even in its aestheticist form in the poems making up *Hymnen*. Here, however he urges

himself to stop bewailing his state and to accept reality: 'Your brooding is false |
relax and stay'. The use of the word 'falsch' ('false') suggests such an interpretation,
underscoring the fatuousness of his imaginings of heterosexual interest. At the
same time, beneath the melting snow something new is beginning to burst forth.
The poet's journeys outward seek aesthetic fulfilment in landscapes and language
that encourage personal evolution and development despite sexual confusion and
humiliation at home. The imagery at this early stage privileges a late romantic
aestheticism:

> Wie winkten mir schon auf der wandrung so lang diese zinnen
> Und so verheissungsfroh!
> Ich muss aus der stätte wo keinerlei gnaden mir warden
> Durch wüsten weiterfliehn ·
> [...]
> An dieser höhe saum
> Entdeck ich auf ihrem haupt eine grünende insel · (II, 42)

> [How these battlements beckoned to me on my long wanderings
> And so full of promise!
> I must leave the place where no mercy was bestowed on me
> Flee on through deserts.
> [...]
> Here from the height I see
> The mountain-top: an island of verdant green ·] (*Morwitz 21)

But the intention is to overcome rather than escape the oppressive sexual environment:

> Schweige die klage!
> [...]
> Suche und trage
> Und über das leid
> Siege das lied! (II, 44)

> [Silence the lament!
> [...]
> Search and bear
> And with conquering song
> Master distress!] (*Morwitz 22)

For Pirro, George's abandonment to the senses offers convalescence through radical
self-regeneration. Sensual pleasure may be destructive of the integrity of the self,
but at the same time it opens up the possibility of rejuvenation and convalescence,
presumably from homosexual orientation, for this critic.[14] However the hope that
he might discover his missing heterosexuality through abandonment to sensual
pleasure is scarcely foreshadowed in these poems. Remnants of the traditional love
poem and the hopes and promises of conventional sexual attraction linger in these
poems, but the future is elsewhere.

> Wir jagen über weisse steppen ·
> Der trennung weh verschwand im nu

> Die raschen räder die uns schleppen
> Führen ja dem frühling zu. (II, 52)

> [Across a plain of snow we speed,
> And parting swiftly lost its sting,
> The whirling of wheels that carry us on
> Leads us into the Spring.] (*Morwitz 25)

The poem, 'Lauschest du des feuers gesange' ('While you listen to the singing flames', II, 35) addresses itself to an unidentified lover with whom the poet enjoys a relationship that may not go beyond the intimacy of a fireside. The dominant theme of these poems is transition from unviable existence in a conventional heterosexual world to a new world characterized increasingly by male companionship and eros. However we cannot yet speak of a developed homosexual worldview. While *Pilgerfahrten* experiments with different voices, a steady refrain of elegiac disappointment runs through them in the voice of the poet as lonely itinerant. In 'Gesichte' ('Visions', II, 39) the male poet imagines his impossible love through female voices, the first a noble woman humiliated by her love for a wastrel, the second a distant admirer of an unknowing man. In these poems love is powerful but prohibited and hence unfulfilled. Love demands physical intimacy and satisfaction: Platonic admiration has no place in George's world, already at this early stage. For this reason, perhaps, the elegiac tone comes to predominate over the subject: love, not its manifestations, the lover, not the object, is the problem. Despite this pervasive sense of disillusionment and disappointment, *Pilgerfahrten* intimates travel as a metaphor for change in its title.

An early commentator and friend of George, Carl Rouge, noted the dramatic as opposed to lyric nature of this volume, in which George takes on different voices in a passive rather than active mode. For Rouge, the absence of a unifying voice obliges the reader to create one himself; and yet the substratum is missing for us to do this.[15] Pirro also sees the exploration of different modes of subjectivity through masking and transformation as endangering the stability of the self. These commentators view George's subjectivity in the poems as oscillating between self-control and existential experimentation. This tension between restraint and liberation can be re-evaluated in terms of individual desire and social norm.[16] For Robert Vilain, the central figure of *Pilgerfahrten* instrumentalizes the figures of imagined desire ('a companion or a lover') as a means of continuing his poetic journey.[17] George remains fixated on his personal journey forward, in a state of egoistic necessity, into the uncharted territory of a homosexual life, using the characters and events of his real world to populate an imaginary world in which his own progress is paramount.

A Path to the Self: *Algabal*

In the following cycle, *Algabal* (1892), George takes on the mask and the voice of the boy-emperor Heliogabalus (reigned AD 218–22), who became synonymous with decadence, depravity and debauchery, including homosexuality, for historians from Gibbon onwards and was a popular figure for the symbolists and decadents of the end of the nineteenth century.[18] However in these poems George takes his experimentation with masks, historical costume and role-playing further, seeking answers to his search for self, while goading and provoking his readers with tropes of French modernity. In his 1986 study, *Die literarische Décadence um 1900*, Wolfdietrich Rasch noted how provocative was George's rejection of the conventions of German lyric in favour of symbolist and aestheticist motifs borrowed from French poets, Baudelaire and Mallarmé.[19] Rasch sensed in the extremism of *Algabal* a level of protest extending beyond aestheticist rejection of the natural world to suggest a radical and dynamic existential critique.[20] However this critique focuses and instrumentalizes the language of French symbolism and aestheticism in a spirit rather different from that of Mallarmé and his associates. George's language in *Algabal* already seeks breakthrough to something new and different; even the revised inscription to Wagner's eccentric patron, Bavarian king Ludwig II, suggests a new level of connection to his present. For Zanucchi, George was struggling with the collapse of values that represented modernity's dark side.[21] However, George's confrontation with Mallarmé led to an engagement with and problematization of aestheticist nihilism that would find a way forward through contemporary French and German vitalism.[22] Like French novelist, Huysmans in *A Rebours (Against the Grain*, 1884), he will come to reject narcissistic aestheticism as a way of life, and seek redemption, albeit of a quite different kind from the former's rediscovered Catholicism.

Despite its copious use of the motifs of contemporary *décadence*, including the Narcissus myth, the aestheticization of artificiality against nature, and the pervasive imagery of violence and death, *Algabal* represents a form of Nietzschean transvaluation of values, rebuilding a sense of self through the provocation and defiance of existing norms in the poetic realm.[23] In his early analysis of George, Claude David identified a strain of Nietzschean individualism 'beyond good and evil', in the Emperor, 'wo ausser dem seinen kein wille schaltet' ('where no will reigns except his own', II, 60). Similarly Kolk speaks of Algabal's décadent-aestheticist abandonment of morality as a manifesto of Nietzschean 'revaluation of all values'.[24] For Eckhard Heftrich, the image of Algabal leaning over his own childhood like Narcissus over the water, is homoerotic and backward-looking.[25] For Klaus Landfried, too, the figure of Algabal enables George to express an extreme of narcissism. In 'Grosse tage' ('Great Days', II, 78), for example, the emperor looks back nostalgically to his youth.[26]

> O so werde wieder knabe der im haine ruhe sucht
> Inne hält er eben eng vor eigener gedanken wucht.
> [...]
> Trätest du an meine seit mit mir und kein schatten nur! (II, 78)

[Be again the boy who wanders through the woods to be alone,
Stops, afraid of thoughts that face him, of a sudden, as his own,
[...]
Oh, that in the flesh, not only as a shadow you were here!] (Morwitz 35)

Narcissism is still a loaded word in relation to male homosexuals. For Freud, narcissism signified a state of being in love with, and sexually focused on, oneself.[27] It represented an indispensable stage of individual sexual development. Homosexuals in this line of thinking had become fixated at this relatively undeveloped stage of sexuality, unable to move beyond self-love. In their search for sexual partners they sought out only that which they saw in themselves. Unable to engage with others as complete persons, only seeking displaced ego images and vehicles for immediate instinctual gratification, they were thus incapable of object-love, and would remain solitary all their lives. Post-Freudian psychoanalytic doctrine embedded this understanding of male homosexuality as at best a transitional stage of Oedipal development during adolescence and at worst a fixation and deviation from proper sexual development, which must be overcome in order to achieve heterosexuality.[28] However contemporary psychoanalysis recognizes that most adults — not just homosexuals — can be viewed as narcissistic in the sense of passing through and retaining powerful aspects of self-love. Healthy narcissism is a condition for, not an impediment to, object-love, and homosexuals are as capable of moving through a valorizing and self-confirming narcissism as are heterosexuals.[29]

For homosexual men of George's era, the obstacles to this progression were considerable. The social forms of individual validation were by and large closed to those men who accepted their homosexuality, since the socially mirrored images they received of themselves were humiliating, degrading and alienating. The narcissistic focus on self functioned as a strategy to avoid social obliteration. Narcissistic egoism is also a means of exploring and discovering the self, not merely of isolating it. George's progress from isolation through narcissism to self- and finally object-love demonstrates this as an extraordinary trajectory, against which the dominant images of male homosexual figures such as Dorian Gray, Tonio Kröger or Gustav von Aschenbach are indeed damaged and impeded from self-fulfilment. This is not to say that George's homosexual *vita* was an ideal: it can be criticized in retrospect regarding both political attitudes and individual relationships. But that scarcely differentiates it from heterosexual models of the era.

The mask and the role-play of *Algabal* provide a form of release of suppressed and repressed feelings and desires. Homosexual eros appears as just one more form of decadence or perversion alongside all the others in the ideational context of nihilistic aestheticism; indeed it pales in comparison to Algabal's cool dismissal of his brother's 'dear' blood, the death of the Lydian slave or the smothering of the banqueting guests under a rain of flowers. George uses the themes and motives of European *décadence*, including homosexuality, to distance himself and to explore his divergent responses to the world around him.[30]

Like the pond of Ovid's myth, the underworld of *Algabal* reveals the poetic voice in his isolation protecting him from the world beyond by creating a self-enclosed frame. In the opening poem, 'Ihr hallen prahlend in reichem gewande'

('O halls that boast of such fabulous treasure', II, 60), George builds an antithesis between the surface world of objective nature and human normality and the lower world of subjective passion.[31] And while the lower world is defined by morbidity and decadence, Algabal's aestheticism suggests something more than Salomé's regressive necrophilia. His cultivation of the black flower, for example, represents an act of desired generativity, regardless of the powerful association with death and prohibition:

> Wie zeug ich dich aber im heiligtume [...]
> Dunkle grosse schwarze blume? (II, 63)
>
> [How can I evoke you in sacred bounds,
> Strange, and large, and sombre bloom?] (Morwitz 30)

Algabal functions as a foil for George. The historical reputation of the emperor, the imagery of decadent sexuality (in, for example, the black flower), and the suggestion of aversion to the female body imply some of the defining characteristics of the homosexual of the time:

> Ich riss die priesterin von dem altar [...]
> Sie hatte wie die anderen ein mal (II, 81)
>
> [I tore the priestess from the altar [...]
> She had, like the others, a stain] (*Morwitz 37)

This text reveals the mixture of resentment and misogyny arising from repression of sexuality, the sense of living in an inverted world (where life is death), the narcissistic turn inward towards identifications and projections, the fantasy of omnipotence and the grandiose ego-ideal, and the contempt for normality.

The evocation of the narcissistic aesthete imagined in a position from which he could project his hatred, resentment and exclusion provocatively rejects the norms of Wilhelminian Germany, and implies that there is a life beyond, even if that life is imagined in a sphere of death. In Erich Ebermayer's later story, *Dr. Angelo* (1924), the protagonist commits suicide and dies as a metaphoric guest of the decadent emperor, suffocated by the perfume of the flowers with which he has filled his room at the point where social censure is about to put an end to his love of the young men around him. Ebermayer's story reflects the power of George's social imaginary for those lonely homosexual men decades later, whose dreams, partially fulfilled, turn out to be still beyond reach.[32]

With *Algabal* George frees himself from the *mauvaise foi* of his contemporaries, in particular those associated with anarchist Adolf Brand's homosexual advocacy group *Die Gemeinschaft der Eigenen* when dealing with their erotic longings. For all its sensuous imagery, George's poetry lacks the cloying, dishonest sentimentalism that was to be found in the pages of the *Gemeinschaft* journal, *Der Eigene*. Thomas Mann would later unmask Aschenbach's sentimental and paedophilic day-dreams of Tadzio as a terrifying orgy of sexual violence in the writer's anguished unconscious. George's lyric voice manifests a dynamic sense of truthfulness to itself from its earliest beginnings. This honesty of emotion characterizes that voice in its journey through the following volumes. It will not cease until it discovers the object love of the final poem of the last volume, *Das Neue Reich*, dedicated to Bernhard von Uxkull-Gyllenband decades later, 'Du schlank und rein wie eine flamme' ('You like a flame, unflawed and slender', ix, 111). Over the following decade, in *Das Jahr der Seele* (1897) and *Der Teppich des Lebens* and *Lieder von Traum und Tod* (1900), George's poetic *vita* takes on an affirmative aspect for which the nihilistic aesthete of *Algabal* is of no further use.

In the process of working against oppression and through depression, even as he flirted with the emerging themes of reactionary modernism, George began to create a homosexual imaginary, a redemptive sphere which would bind him and others into a new sense of community and build the promise of new life. George's journey would take him to a point of self-recognition beyond the narcissism and megalomaniac projection of the early and middle years to a statement of mature homosexual identity in the final poems of his collected works. In the highly charged social and political context of early twentieth-century Germany George envisioned an uncompromised homosexual life on his own terms, offering a radically new form of imaginary existence to men like himself reading his work and recognizing themselves.

Valorizing Male Eros in the *Bücher*

In a letter to Viennese writer Hugo von Hofmannsthal, George noted the end point which he had reached with *Algabal*.[33] In the following collections, the *Bücher der Hirten und Preisgedichte, der Sagen und Sänge, und der Hängenden Gärten* (1895), George liberates his lyric compass from the single voice of the boy-emperor in ancient Rome to multiple voices in three stylized cultural-historical spheres: ancient Greece, the Christian Middle Ages and oriental Babylon. These three collections represent a neo-romantic journey through imaginative realms, each of which stipulates and sanctions different areas of experience.

> Sie enthalten die spiegelungen einer seele die vorübergehend in andere zeiten und örtlichkeiten geflohen ist und sich dort gewiegt hat · dabei kamen ihr bereiflicherweise ererbte vorstellungen ebenso zu hilfe als die jeweilige wirkliche umbegung [...] Jede zeit und jeder geist rücken in dem sie fremde und vergangenheit nach eigner art gestalten ins reich des persönlichen und heutigen und von unsren drei grossen bildungswelten ist hier nicht mehr enthalten als in einigen von uns noch eben lebt. (Foreword to III, 7)

> [They mirror a soul which has temporarily taken refuge and found shelter in other eras and regions. Here conceptually inherited imaginings came to my aid, just as did the tangible environment of the moment [...] In every age, a spirit which shapes and integrates what is alien and past transfers it to the realm of the personal and the present. And nothing of what has been presented here of our three great worlds of education is other than what still lives on in some of us.] (★Morwitz 346)

The final sentence gives the key to George's vision: the personal and subjective reading of these imagined spaces corresponds to the imaginative-experiential needs of the emerging male homosexual symbolic imaginary, one in which only that is retained from 'our three great worlds of education' which still 'lives on in some of us'. The formulation is deliberately ambiguous, the address to a first-person community, an in-group or *wir-Gruppe* appealing in different ways to different readers, to be sure. As Schneider writes, these poems represent a natural order in which the individual is part of an emotional world which goes beyond that of the ancients.[34] For the first time, the homosexual can begin to read himself into an imaginative environment in which self and world are in equilibrium, and in which positively valorized male eros and male attachments become increasingly dominant.

George was still a young man in his twenties during the first half of the 1890s, and like many homosexual men was torn between sexuality and society. Ida Coblenz has figured large in biographies of George, with some commentators still clinging to the belief that she was the love of his life.[35] She was the daughter of a local Bingen merchant, introduced to George by his brother, Friedrich (Fritz), who was in a state of despair at what to do with Stefan and his peculiar penchant for versifying. Unhappy in her home environment, Ida was attractive, lively and creative. She responded readily to the invitation to get to know this eccentric poet who had already fled his hometown. He, for his part, as the poems of this period demonstrate, was still seeking personal stability. She offered friendship, empathy and social and intellectual companionship; he offered intellectual intimacy and an escape from the toxic relations at home. Each found in the other what they thought they wanted and needed; both ignored in each other that which did not suit their needs. She sensed his lack of sexual interest, and ignored the absence of physical attraction (she found him physically repulsive); he utilized her charm in order to maintain the pretence that he could find a place for himself in that world, even as he wrote poems articulating its impossibility and attesting to a different love. That each used the other during these early years is hardly new or surprising in the annals of friendship, love and sexual development.[36]

George traces the emergence of homosexual eros in the young man still coming to terms with the absence of heterosexual passion as he responds to the homoerotic world that emerges in these poems of exploration and discovery of his personal imaginary. The tendencies that will increasingly populate this imaginary world and influence those around him become clearer in these poems, the fascination with ideals of leadership, following, renunciation and abstinence, and loyalty unto death, the unity of body and soul. In 'Der Tag des Hirten' ('Shepherd's Day', III, 14) the melancholy narcissism of the 'Legenden' is transformed as a shepherd leaves his flocks in a Zarathustra-like ascent to self-recognition and self-validation in the open sun of the mountain-peaks. 'Der Ringer' ('The Wrestler', III, 22), the first of the 'Lieblinge des Volkes' ('Favourites of the People', III, 22) uses the Greek tradition of eulogy to express homoerotic admiration of the wrestler's body). In the following poem, 'Der Saitenspieler' ('The Lyre-Player') an effeminate singer re-creates himself through his song as the hero of his listeners' dreams:

Verschwiegen duldend schwärmen alle knaben
Vom helden ihrer wachen sternennächte. (III, 23)

[And every boy in secret anguish, worships
The hero of his sleepless, starlit hours.] (Morwitz 47)

In 'Erinna' a female persona expresses longing for her male lover:

> So war Eurialus beim rossetummeln
> So kam Eurialus geschmückt vom mahle — (III, 24)

> This is Eurialus astride a stallion.
> Like this I saw him coming from the banquet. (Morwitz 47)

The *Preisgedichte* take as their models Roman poets such as Propertius and Catullus, linking the worlds of past and present and intimating the dynamics of love, jealousy, affection and animosity among close-knit circles that these ancient poets so strikingly evoked in settings long since gone. The classical address only partially disguises the contemporary reference to friends from the early 1890s such as Albert Saint-Paul ('Damon') and Waclaw Rolicz-Lieder ('Kallimachus'), suggesting both transparency and opacity in the lyric persona's engagement with his present. The fraught relationships behind these poetic addresses are transformed into poetic moments of truth:

> Stets im verkehre mit himmlischen Dingen umfloss uns
> Etwas wie himmlischer glanz (III, 29)

> [Always communing with heavenly matters, a something
> Sheathed us like heavenly gleam.] (Morwitz 49)

It was the moment of recognition in the relationship with Ida Coblenz ('Menippa') that the dream was over ('Kein wunderding erscheint mir mehr die narbe deines kinns'; 'The scar | Upon your chin no longer seems a miracle', III, 30); he sympathises and shares with Sidonia (based on an unknown person) the pangs of unreciprocated love for the young Demotas; discovers friendship through poetry with the young Paul Gérardy ('Phaon'); explores 'radiant youth that burns for action' ('strahlende[] jugend/die ganz in taten die sie wirken will/lebt', III, 36) with the young Ludwig Klages ('Isokrates'); experiences unfulfilled love for the young poet, Edmond Rassenfosse ('Antinous').[37]

In fantasies of chivalric loyalty, self-sacrifice and renunciation, the poet relives and rehearses the medievalism that had sustained the late nineteenth-century homosexual imagination. Here the dominant value is loyalty ('Treue') and the lonely knight's vigil becomes symbolic of homoerotic worship from afar. Loyalty or faithfulness here focuses on the ideal of faithfulness (to a man), rather than the individual lover (regardless of sex). These poems recapitulate the processes of abstraction and transformation of feelings and desires imagined in the chivalric *Männerbund*. 'Treue' will become the motto of the Bund, a synonym for the bonding of homosexual men in the recognition of their commonality, their exclusion from normative society. 'Treue' and 'Liebe' become interchangeable, since physical love is forbidden. Both find ideal expression in the admiration of the lonely knight who finds succour in his sacred mission and in the imagined bonds of brotherhood with his fellow knights. In this emotional environment of idealized chivalry, the nominal object of worship, the lady, becomes an empty distant image as passion is displaced onto the 'brother-in-arms', love becomes loyalty and war becomes the symbolic framework of justification of the new value-system of homoerotic loyalty:

Sie bluten willig im gefechte
An meeresküsten kahl und grau
Und geben freudig ihre rechte
Für eine blasse stolze frau.
Sie retten in den grossen nöten
Wenn engel mit dem giftespfeil
Zur strafe unerbittlich töten —
Sie dulden zu der andren heil. (III, 50)

[They head for bouts of strength and leave
Their blood on coasts of ashen shale,
Their dexter hand they gladly give
To shield a woman, proud and pale.
In times of bitter need they save,
When angels with their poisoned arrows
Kill without pity for punishment,
They suffer for the other's good.] (*Morwitz 58)

In 'Der Waffengefährte' ('The Comrade in Arms') George rehearses the ideal of chivalric-homoerotic friendship between two knights:

Nun ist mein bruder eingeschlafen
— Die schwerten klangen heute scharf —
Und ich bin froh dass ich den braven
Dieweil er ruht behüten darf.
Er stützte sich mit seinem schilde
Ich nahm sein haupt in meinen schooss
Aur seiner wange zuckt es milde
Um seinen bart erbarmungslos. (III, 52)

[And now my brother is asleep
— Today the clash of swords was keen
And I am proud that I may keep
The rest of such a heart serene.
He leaned against his shield, I took
His head upon my knees, his cheek
Had something of a tender look,
His bearded lip was stern and bleak.] (Morwitz 59)

Love mingles with war, intimacy with heroism. He takes his friend's sleeping head in his lap just as he accepts his saving grasp in a moment of rescue. In the second section of the poem, the death of the warrior-lover leads from the individual to the group, from the lonely knight through his friend to the Bund, the group that validates the indistinguishable core values of 'Liebe' and 'Treue':

So unterlag er doch der feinde tücke . .
Er focht mit wenig treuen wider scharen
Er fiel [...]
Und fürsten kamen gar zum trauersaale
Es hoben sich gemurmelte gebete
Der männer lob D (III, 53)

> [Yet he was trapped by crafty foes, with few
> And faithful men against a horde he vied,
> He fell [...]
> And to his burial even princes came,
> Muffled prayers were heard,
> The praise of men.] (*Morwitz 60)

The ties binding the 'band of brothers' (the *comitatus*, the Theban Band, the chivalric knights, the 'brothers in arms' in their different socio-historical iterations) are not merely horizontal, for each other. They are also vertical, focussing on a higher ideal of themselves as members of a Bund, for whom honourable death is a form of apotheosis. This idea will become a dominant theme in the poetry of George's middle period. The prohibition of physical love underpins this displaced erotic fantasy in its medieval form in 'Der Waffengefährte':

> Wohin ich mich nach seinem tode kehre?
> Wer wehrt von mir des rauhen lebens stösse?
> Ich werde fallen ohne seine grösse —
> O sei es nicht zu fern vom pfad der ehre. (III, 53)

> [Now he is dead, where shall I turn? What hand
> Will keep the hounds of ruthless life at bay?
> Without his greatness I shall fall. May
> It not be too far from the path of honour!] (*Morwitz 60)

There is a hint of suicidal self-doubt in these lines of the younger man abandoned in life through the death of his lover. However, heroic death is implicit in the warrior ethos of feudal-chivalric Europe and ancient Greece. A structure of commonality has evolved in the band of brothers or Bund, to deal with this loss, providing a supra-individual ideal into which individual death transmutes itself. Here we find an early stage of the Bund mentality that George would turn into a modern cult for his disciples based on the idealization of the heroic warrior-youth Maximin in *Der siebente Ring*. The abandoned knight-lover's intimation of his own death, with its suggestion of suicidal self-doubt, is redeemed through the sense of the lover and the community of knights as a supra-individual entity in which the individual is transfigured into the group through death in the service of the ideal (of 'ehre', 'honour'). Homosexual loneliness is assuaged through transfiguring images of abstinence, self-discipline, self-sacrifice, asceticism or death which prepare for states of union with an idealized leader/brother. The imaginative representation of the ambivalent brothers/lovers-in-arms imagery of the first part of the poem prepares for the fuller development of the Bund, which would become dominant in George's late work. This is one of the main functions of these collections of poems in George's oeuvre. Transfiguring individual loneliness into homosexual fantasies of collectivity, or *Gemeinschaft*, they create a correspondence between his own life and an ideal-typical stage in the life of the homosexual individual.

'Treue' is the dominant theme of the *Buch der Sagen und Sänge*. This idealized knightly-chivalric world depends on the bonds of loyalty and love between men. The validation of homoerotic relations is displaced and projected, to be sure, in this poetic setting, but it is a means of validating male love and companionship in a deeper sense as something more than just homoerotic attraction. Love between men is here validated as something deep and lasting, bound by an oath of loyalty just as powerful as that of marriage.

The fantasy of the Bund or *comitatus* in its historical guises fulfilled two functions in the male homosexual imaginary. It provided both the lover and a group identity for homosexual men who lacked both. In histories of gay literature, the emphasis has been laid primarily on the individual-sexual and psychogenetic aspects of the emergence of a homosexual identity in Western societies and literatures. German, more than British or French, literature of this period focuses on the needs of the homosexual individual for a group identity and experience. The recognition of the need for such an identity, and the poetic-imaginary fulfilment of the individual's sense of *wir-Gefühl* comes to the fore in George's work, whereas figures such as Mackay, Ebermayer and Thomas Mann focus on the individual love relationship, more often than not fantasized rather than real, in a more or less alienated group environment determined primarily by the heterosexual bonds of family and society.

Of course, George's message appealed to a wider group than to homosexual men alone. This is indicative of the power of his reformulation of idealized masculine roles in an era of significant disruption of traditional gender roles. However it remains strikingly obvious that the two groups of young men who were most strongly drawn to George were homosexuals and Jews, both seeking inclusion alongside reinforcement and validation of their sense of masculinity in the case of young homosexual men, and confirmation of national identity as Germans in the case of young Jewish men. (George himself was thought by many contemporaries to be both Jewish and homosexual, where both identities involved feminization and absence of masculine identity in the popular imagination.[38])

The last of the 'Sagen und Sänge', 'Das Bild' ('The Image', III, 56), finishes with the speaker's exhaustion before the adored image. The idealized lover's healing gifts come too late:

> Ich glaube mein arm ist bald zum umfangen zu matt
> Auf meinen lippen erlosch die brennende liebe

> I doubt
> My arm would have power to clasp, for the hour is sped,
> The fiery love on my lips has burned itself out.
>
> (Morwitz 61)

The period of waiting and dreaming is over and the persona of the chivalric knight is transformed into the freer, disillusioned voice of the travelling minstrel ('der fahrende Spielmann') in the final section of this book: 'Was ich gestern nicht erriet | Heute bin ich es gewahr' ('Yesterday I did not know | What today is my despair', III, 58; Morwitz 62).

Die Bücher der hängenden Gärten take the imagined experience further afield into an oriental-exotic realm in which the values of the chivalric community are erased from memory:

> Vergiss mit uns im bund
> Die würde so dir anvertraut

Und küsse froh den grund
Wo gold- und rosenschein
Der weichen wünsche frevel sühnt · (III, 73)

[Forget together with us
The office conferred on you.
Rejoice and kiss the ground
Where rains of rose and gold
Atone for langour, lust, and sin] (*Morwitz 67)

The 'gram der mich abermals leise bestahl' ('the grief which once more has imperilled my days', III, 74, Morwitz 68) is dissolved in the imaginative evocation of a natural-sensual sphere. The aesthetic realm takes precedence over the reality of being and world:

Zierat des spitzigen turms der die büsche erhellt
Verschlungnes gefüge
Geschnörkelte züge
Verbieten die lüge
Von wesen und welt. (III, 77)

[Glint of the pointed pagoda
In shrubbery furled,
With extricate fusion
And lacy inclusion,
Dispels the illusion
Of being and world.] (Morwitz 69)

In this realm of words and imagination, nothing is pre-ordained. Where the Greek utopia focuses on individual florescence and expiration and the feudal-chivalric world idealizes the loyalty and belonging in the Bund community, the oriental fantasy of the *Hanging Gardens* explores a world of power, violence and the senses. Like Algabal's dark unnatural empire of stone and precious metals, this bright natural world of sensual experience, escape and abandonment is inherently amoral:

Da schloss ein breites licht aus wolkenreichen
Es wanderte versöhnend auf den leichen
Verklärte die betrübte trümmerstadt
Und haftete verdoppelt an der stelle
Wo der Bezwinger durch die menge stob
Der kühn dann über eines tempels schwelle
Die klinge rauchend zu dem gotte hob. (III, 75)

[An ample light from dark horizons sped,
It dwelt consolingly upon the dead
And touched the sad and ruined town to wonder.
It clung with double splendours where the crowd
Scattered before the victor, as he rode
Into a temple, unappalled and proud,
And swung his dripping blade against the god.] (Morwitz 68)

From within this world of oriental splendour a sequence of love poems emerges. The love is prohibited and compelling but at the same time innocent. The tone is quite different to the provocative licence of *Algabal*:

> Wenn ich heut deinen Leib nicht berühre
> Wird der faden meiner seele reissen
> Wie zu sehr gespannte sehne. (III, 86)

> [If I do not touch your body now,
> Then the fibre of my soul will snap
> Like an over-stretched bow-string.] (*Morwitz 73)

> Als wir hinter dem beblümten tore
> Endlich nur das eigene hauchen spürten
> Warden uns erdachte seligkeiten?
> Ich erinnere dass wie schwache rohre
> Beide stumm zu beben wir begannen
> Wenn wir leis nur an uns rührten
> Und dass unsre augen rannen —
> So verbliebest du mir lang zu seiten. (III, 88)

> [When behind the flowered gate our own
> Breath at longed-for last, was all that stirred,
> Did we feel that fancied ecstasy?
> I remember how when softly one
> Touched the other, we began to sway
> Like the fragile reeds — without a word.
> Tears rose in our eyes and had their way.
> Very long like this you stayed with me.] (Morwitz 74)

The symbolist suggestiveness enables the mixing of the sensuous detail of the flowers with the physical sensuousness of the lovers' proximity to each other. But the lyric voice remains an innocent in a world of actions and emotions. Danger comes into this world from outside:

> So denke nicht der ungestalten schatten
> Die an der wand sich auf und unter wiegen
> Der wächter nicht die rasch uns scheiden dürfen
> Und nicht dass vor der stadt der weisse sand
> Bereit ist unser warmes blut zu schlürfen. (III, 88)

> [Then do not fear the formless shadows pressed
> Against the wall in high and nether swerve,
> The guards who can divide us at a nod,
> The sand that traps the town in glaring rims
> And is athirst to suck our tepid blood.] (Morwitz 74)

> Mürber blätter zischendes gewühl
> Draussen um des edens fahle wände
> Jagen ruckweis unsichtbare hände
> Die nacht ist überwölkt und schwül. (III, 90)

> [Brittle foliage sibilant and massed,
> Loosed by unseen hands to flight and fall,
> Drives against our Eden's ghostly wall.
> The night is close and overcast.] (Morwitz 75)

Voices of the water spirits in the final poem of the collection ('Stimmen im Strom', 'Voices in the River', III, 99) promise release from the poet's life of reflection and creativity in an oceanic movement which signifies both watery death and erotic liberation:

> Müdet euch aber das sinnen das singen ·
> Fliessender freuden bedächtiger lauf
> Trifft euch ein kuss: und ihr löst euch in ringen
> Gleitet als wogen hinab und hinauf. (III, 99)

> [But if reflection and singing tire you
> — Flowing joys in thoughtful motion —
> A kiss will release you from struggling
> You will glide as a wave up and beyond.] (*Morwitz 78)

In this final book George moves towards self-understanding by exploring the *lieux de mémoire* of the homosexual imagination of the past. These three past worlds of male homosexuality provide the basis for the move outward and beyond anything that has gone before as George begins to imagine for himself and his readers a new group consciousness, a sense of the 'we' that exists in a bright, sunlit natural world, quite different from the depressive and melancholic evocations of lonely sexuality of earlier writers. In this world, released from the obligations of hererosexual socialization, the poet will begin to explore the male body and to discover the forces of attraction that go beyond mere libido. Influenced by the youth movement of the 1890s and beyond, George would begin to evoke the bonds of male homosexual community and group identity under the rubrics of loyalty and love. Important here is the level to which individual loneliness is transfigured and a sense of group is evoked. Other, less salutary aspects of this spiritual movement will become clearer in the following decade.

George's Inclusive Imaginary

At this point in his creative oeuvre George has begun to move towards the proactive imaginative stance in relation to his own wishes and desires that would make him such an important figure in the context of the time. For early commentator, Hans Dietrich, George's work is 'incandescent with the poet's intention to redeem his brothers. But before he can do this, he must be released himself.'[39] It is the encounter with the other that is crucial, and George's early poems thus become in Lukács's term, songs of a wayfarer on a spiritual pilgrimage to discover love.[40] Dietrich identifies in George's disciples Friedrich Gundolf and Friedrich Wolters the early spokesmen for and intermediaries of George's message. In their 'Introduction' to the third issue of the short-lived magazine, *Jahrbuch für die geistige Bewegung*, Gundolf and Wolters put into the form of a manifesto their sense of frustration and desire for change at the end of the first decade of the new century. As acolytes and associates of George, they put into words what he had created for them, namely the belief in a totality of which they were a part.

> Die pessimisten sind nicht wir, die an ein vollkommenes und unverlierbares glauben, sondern die, welche alles gewesene bloss als eine vorstufe für ein imaginäres kommendes ansehen.[41]

[It is not we who are the pessimists. For we believe in a perfect and imperishable totality. Rather the pessimists are those who view everything that has existed as nothing more than the preliminary stage for an imaginary coming order.]

The term 'Freundschaft' had held homoerotic associations in certain contexts since the German Enlightenment and Romantic periods. Under the heading 'Freundschaftskult', Gundolf and Wolters redefine homosexual love as part of something broader and greater than the scientific, legal, forensic and medical categorizations that had emerged over the previous decades.

> Man hat sich auch nicht gescheut in offener wie versteckter weise auf die ausschreitungen hinzuweisen die ein solches kultivieren der freundschaft früher hervorgebracht haben soll und jetzt hervorbringen könne. Wir fragen nicht danach ob des Schillerschen Don Carlos hingabe an Posa, des Goetheschen Ferdinand an Egmont, der leidenschaftliche enthusiasmus des Jean Paulischen Emanuel für Viktor, Roquairols für Albano irgend etwas zu tun hat mit einem hexenhammerischen gesetzesabschnitt oder einer läppischen medizinischen einreihung: vielmehr haben wir immer geglaubt in diesen beziehungen ein wesentlich bildendes der ganzen deutschen kultur zu finden. (ibid.)

> [Earlier writers did not hesitate to draw our attention openly or covertly to the extremes to which the cultivation of friendship is believed to have led and can still lead. Let us consider the devotion of Schiller's Don Carlos to the Marquis de Posa, or of Goethe's Ferdinand for Egmont, or Emanuel's passionate infatuation with Viktor or Roquairol's with Albano [in Jean Paul's *Hesperus* and *Titan* respectively *PM*]. We do not question these loves or view them in terms of a legal witchhunt or a foolish medical classification. On the contrary we have always understood these relations to represent an essential formative element for German culture as a whole.]

'Freundschaft' is not merely sexual eros: it is a dynamic force, a formative demiurge that extends through the individual to the group as a pedagogical and state-building principle. As an expression for what was in fact homosexual love it had functioned as a means of differentiating between physical and emotional attraction without recourse to the more abstruse terminology of platonic love. However, it was highly charged in contexts such as those identified above, in which the physical and the emotional began to merge. Even in the language of the *Gemeinschaft der Eigenen* in the first decade of the century, such *Freundschaft* remained an indirect but powerfully suggestive concept.[42]

Gundolf and Wolters make clear their criticisms of the very groups that were agitating for changes to the law regarding homosexuality, members of Hirschfeld's *Komitee* and Brand's *Gemeinschaft*, as antithetical to the spirit of the new community of men embodied in the earlier youth movements and in heightened form in George's circle.

> Dass wir nichts zu tun haben mit jenen keineswegs erfreulichen leuten die um die aufhebung gewisser strafbestimmungen wimmern, geht schon daraus hervor dass gerade aus solchen kreisen die widerlichsten angriffe gegen uns erfolgt sind.[43]

[We have nothing to do with those far from agreeable people who whine about the lifting of certain criminal sanctions. Indeed these people are responsible for the most obnoxious attacks on us.]

For the homosexual individual of the time, the ideas of homosexual eros and social nurturing promised something entirely new: the sense of belonging to a like-minded community.

Ohne diesen Eros halten wir jede erziehung für blosses geschäft oder geschwätz und damit jeden weg zu höherer kultur für versperrt. [...] Es ist auch nicht ein moralisches vorurteil was heute noch die menschen gegen diese freundschaft empört, ihnen ist gleich unverständlich, im tiefsten grund widerlich die liebe des Dante zu Beatrice wie des Shakespeare zu seinem freund: es ist die abneigung des amerikanischen, pathoslos gewordenen menschen gegen jede form der heroisierten liebe.[44]

[We consider any form of upbringing that does not include this *eros* to be nothing more than business or chatter and hence closed to all higher culture. [...] People's outrage today against this *eros* is not of the nature of a moral judgement. To them, the love of Dante for Beatrice or of Shakespeare for his unnamed friend is equally incomprehensible and equally abhorrent. It is the reluctance of the modern human being, having become Americanized and incapable of passion, to accept any form of heroicized love.]

That they were exaggerating the level of inclusiveness of even the youth movement is unimportant here; the main issue lies in their pointing to a shared world in which homosexuals could experience a sense of *wir-Gefühl* — and everything that it proposed in terms of interpersonal relations. For the first time homosexual men were included in this worldview as something other than objects of medical, legal or religious proscription. This type of thinking was far from unique at the time: calls for change, 'breakthrough' or fundamental alteration of current social relations formed the core of the youth movement. It was to be expected that such ideas would influence the new social movements of the early century, in particular the youth movement. Hans Blüher's works on the *Wandervögel* provided the theoretical underpinning for the homosocial aspects of the youth movement, and the ideas recur in the ever-more polarized form in the context of the post-war men's movements. Nevertheless, George's poetry offered both the recognition of the pathway, and the destination itself, a detailed imaginary universe of the male homosexual, through poetry of extraordinary beauty at this time. His fascination with, and exploitation of, the aesthetics of the underworld in the work of Baudelaire and Mallarmé led him to the creation of a new, positive imaginary for homosexual men. George's volumes came to include homosexual men in the here and now of a lived world. The hopes, promises, and fantasies of the lonely homosexual imagination enter the realm of a literature of life and community with George and are fundamentally changed. Contemporary fictional characters Fenny Skaller (John Henry Mackay) and Gustav von Aschenbach (Thomas Mann) are backward-looking in comparison with George's poetic voice as the realization of a living homosexual imaginary.

Homosexual Love in *Das Jahr der Seele*

The 23-year-old George met and fell in love with the seventeen-year-old Hugo von Hofmannsthal in 1891. Hofmannsthal (1874–1929) belonged to a respected, well-established upper middle-class Viennese family. At seventeen he was still a school student, handsome (to judge from the photographs) and a published poet, intellectually precocious with a reputation beyond his years. George was an impressive, if eccentric figure, and after a brief first meeting sometime around early December 1891, the younger man put his feelings into the verses of the poem, 'Herrn Stefan George | einem, der vorübergeht' ('To Mr Stefan George | one who passes by') [45] The poem is homoerotically suggestive, albeit more of Hofmannsthal's own hidden desires than of sexual attraction towards the older man:

> Du hast mich an dinge gemahnet
> Die heimlich in mir sind (Wien, im dezember 1891)

> [You reminded me of things
> That are secret inside me] (Vienna, in December 1891; trans. PM)

Hofmannsthal's later poem from the same year, 'Der Prophet' ('The Prophet'), is indicative of George's ability to both attract and intimidate those who recognized in him a reflection of their own deeper natures. George recognized the emergent poet of genius but was also smitten by the handsome young man. A meeting took place and in letters over the next weeks George gave expression to his desire for a soul-mate and more:

> Lassen Sie sich durch die geheimtuende aussenseite nicht erschrecken! [...] Schon lange im leben sehnte ich mich nach jenem wesen von einer verachtenden durchdringenden und überfeinen verstandeskraft die alles verzeiht begreift würdigt und die mit mir über die dinge und die erscheinungen hinflöge [...][46]

> [Don't let the secretive exterior scare you off! [...] For a long time now I have longed to have in my life a person of that disdainful, penetrating and highly refined power of understanding that appreciates everything, forgives, and can soar above the things and appearances of the world with me [...]]

Hofmannsthal's answer also suggests something more than an encounter of the intellect in this 'halbverschleiertes Bekenntnis' ('partly-veiled confession'[47]):

> Ich kann nur mich selbst geben ... ich kann nicht anders, mein Wesen gießt den Wein seines jungen Lebens aus ... wer nehmen kann, nimmt. [...] ich möchte Sie gerne halten können, Ihnen zu danken, daß Sie mir Tiefen gezeigt haben aber Sie stehen gerne, wo Ihnen schwindelt, und lieben stolz den Abgrund den wenige sehen können. [...] *Ich* kann auch das lieben was mich ängstet.[48]

> [I can only give myself ... I can do nothing else, my being pours out the wine of its young life ... whoever can take, takes. [...] I would like to be able to hold you, to thank you for showing me depths. For you like to stand on the dizzying heights and proudly love the abyss that few can stand to see. *I* too can love what scares me.]

But the younger man was unable to match the older in confronting his sexual and existential crisis, and the affair spun out of control. George appears to have approached

Hofmannsthal with sexual advances or propositions that the latter was unable to entertain. Hofmannsthal retreated into the pose of the ambushed schoolboy, called in his parents and put an end to George's hopes, leaving him bewildered, incensed, hurt and offended. He faced scandal, ostracism and even legal repercussions, given the legal situation and the possibility of exposure as a homosexual preying on an adolescent school-student. His position was jeopardized and he responded by threatening Hofmannsthal indirectly with a duel.[49] Nevertheless, a rapprochement took place within the year, in which each of the men maintained a reserve based on deeper understanding of the other, with George still perhaps maintaining hope of something more in his letter containing the poem, 'Maiwind fuhr übers brache feld' ('Winds of May blew across the fallow field').[50] George's behaviour in pursuing Hofmannsthal set a pattern for his later behaviour which he replicated with Gundolf and others, before he met Maximin Kronberger, whose death obviated the possibility of the disappoinment that George had experienced with Hofmannsthal, and who would be transformed into the poetic figure of Maximin.[51]

Hofmannsthal similarly retained his distance but continued to correspond with George, while becoming a figure of Viennese respectability and never coming out as a homosexual. Both admired each other's poetic gifts and George enlisted Hofmannsthal into the circle of contributors to *Blätter für die Kunst*. Hofmannsthal recognized that George represented a radical new departure in German lyric at the end of the century despite his outsider status, and that he must remain at least externally on good terms. He remained cautious, seeking publication, connections and literary networks elsewhere, all the while maintaining cordial relations where possible with George.

George was at pains to encourage the younger poet's active collaboration and the 'Ballade des äußeren Lebens' of 1894, which made Hofmannsthal's name, appeared in *Blätter für die Kunst* in 1896.[52] Some time around December 1895 George dedicated the second edition of *Pilgerfahrten* to the young Hofmannsthal for publication in November 1898.[53] In May 1897, Hofmannsthal wrote warmly to George in anticipation at receiving a copy of the still unpublished *Jahr der Seele*. George responded with a powerful expression of hope of reigniting their relationship and of understanding of their differences and of the different paths they had taken over the previous years, including the poem 'Heut lass uns frieden schliessen' ('Today let us make peace').[54] In 1902 the two reached a level of intimacy again in letters in which George intimated their similarities as well as differences:

> Ich glaube dass kaum eines der drückenden gespenster worunter Sie dulden mich verschont hat. In meiner jugend war ich stark genug um auch das widrigste zu besiegen und ohne hilfe — später aber wär ich gewiss zusammengebrochen hätt ich mich nicht durch den Ring gebunden gefühlt. das ist eine meiner lezten weisheiten — das ist eins der geheimnisse! woran Sie am schmerzlichsten leiden ist eine gewisse wurzellosigkeit [...][55]

> [I think that I too have been little spared those oppressive ghosts that you have suffered. In my youth I was strong enough to overcome even the most adverse of turns without help. Later, however, I would have collapsed under their weight had I not felt myself bound by the Ring. This is one of my last

wisdoms — this is one of their secrets! What you suffer from most painfully is
a certain rootlessness [...]]

In his response, Hofmannsthal reprises his earlier refusal to face aspects of himself
that he finds reflected in George. The passive-aggressive denial of transparency in
this discussion seems calculated to provoke the older poet.

> Auf das Tiefe und Geheimnisvolle, das Ihr Brief enthält, will ich lieber mit
> Nachdenken als, für jetzt, mit Worten mich einlassen. Das furchtbare Wort
> 'Wurzellosigkeit' hab ich selbst in fahlen Stunden in mir gefunden; das
> Geheimnis des Ringes, das Sie andeuten, vermochte ich vielleicht dann und
> wann zu ahnen. Wie glücklich werde ich sein, vieles Wahrheit für mich werden
> zu lassen, was in Ihren Werken mir noch Gleichnis ist, freilich tief bewegendes
> Gleichnis.[56]

> [For now I would rather forgo the words in order to reflect on the depth
> and mystery that your letter contains. I have discovered that terrible word
> 'rootlessness' in myself even in pale hours; the secret of the Ring that you hint
> at, I might have guessed from time to time. How happy I will be to let that
> become truth for me which is still parable in your work, admittedly deeply
> moving parable.]

The relationship limped along for a few more years, moving uneasily back and forth
between intimacy, self-revelation and business-like pragmatism until it petered out
altogether in early 1906.[57] While Hofmannsthal seems to have been unable to face
his homosexuality, George seemed unable to relinquish the narcissistic demand for
capitulation of the other. Having made an advance, George then required complete
submission, a pattern of affect that would persist and determine his adult object
relations. But by this time, George was occupied with an altogether more ambitious
project of homosexual love, namely the 'secret of the Ring', and the idealization of
Maximin as narcissistic ego-ideal.

Das Jahr der Seele appeared six years after the traumatic meeting with Hofmannsthal, by which time the relationship had survived considerable strains. The
influence of the younger poet continues to be felt in this and following collections.
Hofmannsthal himself was powerfully moved by the opening poem, 'Komm in den
totgesagten Park' ('Come to the park they say is dead', IV, 12), and the later poem
in the collection, 'Soll nun der mund der von des eises bruch' ('Shall lips which
anguish sealed', IV, 70) was written with Hofmannsthal in mind. The former poem
was completed at the end of 1891 when the two had just met and reveals George's
mixture of intensity and distance.[58] The relationship would continue to influence
George's work until the end of the century. George had originally intended to
dedicate *Das Jahr der Seele*, his fifth volume, to Ida Coblenz. However he had
broken off contact with her as a result of her admiration for the work of, and later
intimacy with and marriage to, the poet Richard Dehmel. George appears to have
been envious of Dehmel's success as poet and translator. He claimed to loathe
Dehmel's poetry and considered the poet himself beneath contempt.[59] He viewed
Ida's initial enthusiasm and later intimacy as treachery and cut off all contact. The
volume was dedicated in 1897 to his sister, Anna Maria Ottilie.

In *Das Jahr der Seele* George embarks on the journey of self-discovery as a homosexual man for the first time. In fact many of the poems in this volume were written over the same period as the *Bücher der Hirten- und Preisgedichte*, from the poem 'Soll nun der mund der von des eises bruch ...' originally given to Hofmannsthal in December 1891 through to the poems that were collated in summer 1895 as a handwritten manuscript. However George's sorting and selection of the poems into a path of development is evident. Some later poems, including the dedicatory poem to Ludwig Klages of late 1897, were added. With this volume, the narrative and structuring aspects of George's work became evident.[60]

Das Jahr der Seele expresses a new-found sense of self, of openness to the world, and even of intimacy with others. The excursus into the artistic interior in *Algabal* and the *Bücher* had taught George that it is a lonely world, and that the lyric *I* is alone unless he can find love. What that love might be took George decades to discover. In the collections of the next decades, he would travel through narcissistic projection and displacement to object love. The lonely knights of the *Bücher der Sagen und Sänge*, who find solace in loyalty, discover the other as self. It will be a long journey for these allegories of homosexual men to discover the other as other, no longer a narcissistic displacement of existential aloneness.

A sense of attachment is expressed, new to the poet after the inward-turned nihilism of *Algabal* and the fantasy of the *Bücher*. But attachment to what? *Das Jahr der Seele* begins the process of reconciling the *ich* and the *du* in what is in effect the documentation of a first homosexual love affair in the first section, 'Sieg des Sommers' ('Triumph of Summer').[61] The extension of the self alone through poetic imagination that provided so little personal consolation in the previous volumes gives way to a new sense of the self in *Das Jahr der Seele*, as something both addressing and addressed in these poems. As George wrote in his preface, 'Selten sind sosehr wie in diesem buch *ich* und *du* die selbe seele' ('Seldom are the *I* and the *you* so much the same soul as in this book', IV, 7).

The poet opens himself up to places, feelings, and above all, to people, his immediate associates and friends. *Das Jahr der Seele* represents a step forward in the poet's *vita*, in which he recognizes for the first time, the attraction of attraction, the desire to be with others, whom he experiences through himself, through his poetic voice, reconstructing their feelings, imagining them and empathizing with them. *Das Jahr der Seele* was one of George's most popular works. Lacking the aestheticist language of earlier works and exploring the soul of the young man, it is among his most accessible works.[62] In these poems, we sense the homosexual poet for the first time in a state of acceptance of his sexual orientation and even of a level of inner contentment. Here the homosexual creative consciousness begins building its world, recognizing its community, wondering at its coherence and beauty.

The opening poem, 'Komm in den totgesagten Park', with its origins in and perhaps reference to the affair with Hofmannsthal, expresses both aestheticist weariness in its autumnal images and a vital forcefulness in the repeated verbal imperatives of the lyric voice, urging an unnamed other to come and discover something 'they say' is dead.

Komm in den totgesagten park und schau:
Der schimmer ferner lächelnder gestade ·
Der reinen wolken unverhofftes blau
Erhellt die weiher und die bunten pfade.
Dort nimm das tiefe gelb · das weiche grau
Von birken und von buchs · der wind ist lau
Die späten rosen welkten noch nicht ganz ·
Erlese küsse sie und flicht den kranz ·
Vergiss auch diese lezten astern nicht ·
Den purpur um die ranken wilder reben
Und auch was übrig blieb von grünem leben
Verwinde leicht im herbstlichen gesicht. (IV, 12)

[Come to the park they say is dead, and you
Will see the glint of smiling shores beyond,
Pure clouds with rifts of unexpected blue
Brighten the ponds and the colourful paths.
Take the grey tinge of boxwood and the charm
Of burning-yellow birch. The wind is warm.
Late roses still have traces of their hue,
So kiss, and gather them, and wreathe them too.
Do not forget these last asters either,
Nor the scarlet on the twists of vine,
And what is left of living green, combine
To shape a weightless image of the autumn.] (*Morwitz 81)

In fact this 'dead' park reveals itself to be beautiful beyond earlier imagining, warm, even, and imbued with a powerful sense of life that lives and dies. Beauty is to be found despite the associations of death and social censure in the opening line. The image of the shimmering, beckoning opposite shore will become a topos of the homosexual imaginary in later poems. The dark ponds ('Weiher') here do not suggest the winter of suicide, as in so many of the stories of German provincial naturalism. They are bright and colourful. The remnants of life, still powerfully present in their final moments, engender recognition, love and, potentially, rebirth on both the literal and symbolic levels. Love can be discovered in this sheltered autumnal park. The verbs progress from coming to take a look, to kissing, *not* forgetting or consigning to oblivion, and finally to weaving a wreath — of love, not death. The poem moves from passivity to active engagement with life, ignoring social prejudice exhorting the other to discover the beauty of the muted colours and to embrace the life of roses, asters and vines, images of love, death and physical enjoyment respectively, even at this late point to weave a wreath to life, not death.

This park represents a seminal and significant moment in George's homosexual imaginary, as a place in which the individual, personal homosexual self communicates to an other (Hofmannsthal) the discovery of the possibility of an alternative existence to that of convention. It is the forcefulness in spite of the dying environment which is striking in this poem and which suggests the later critique of Hofmannsthal in 'Der Verworfene' ('The Outcast', v, 49) in *Der Teppich des Lebens* and contrasts with the precocious world-weariness of the latter's 'Ballade des äußeren Lebens'. Hofmannsthal thought that he could maintain the distinction between the inner and the outer lives; George was committed to overcoming it. Each of the men would remain preoccupied with the other for years to come.

In his 'Gespräch über Gedichte' (published February 1904 in *Der Neue Rundschau*, Berlin) Hofmannsthal has one of his interlocutors, Gabriel, expand on Keats's idea of 'negative capability' in his description of the poetry of *Das Jahr der Seele*, finding in it 'all of the deepest and most secret conditions of our inner selves most curiously interwoven in a landscape' ('alle die geheimsten und tiefsten Zustände unseres Inneren in der seltsamsten Weise mit einer Landschaft verflochten').[63] For Hofmannsthal, George's greatness lies in the poetic externalization of the inner world, which simultaneously expresses the interiorization of the outer world. Hofmannsthal's interlocutor reflects further on the dynamic of inner and outer worlds in the process of poetic perception:

> Wollen wir uns finden, so dürfen wir nicht in unser Inneres hinabsteigen: draußen sind wir zu finden, draußen. Wie der wesenlose Regenbogen spannt sich unsere Seele über den unaufhaltsamen Sturz des Daseins. Wir besitzen unser Selbst nicht: von außen weht es uns an, es flieht uns für lange und kehrt uns in einem Hauch zurück.

> [If we want to find ourselves, then we should not descend into our inner selves: it is outside that we are to be found, outside. Like the rainbow that has no substance, our soul stretches itself above the inexorable abyss of being. We do not possess our self: it blows on us from without, it flies from us for a long time and then returns in the puff of a breath.]

The act of writing poetry is for Gabriel a symbolic act symbolizing the momentary loss of self in the act of penetration of another's existence, a poetic quality that Hofmannsthal recognized and admired in George's poetic voice, but was incapable of himself.[64]

George's synthetic mode, bringing together the inner and outer worlds, is driven by the libidinal self, which for the homosexual is problematic at this stage of historical and individual consciousness. At the point where the libido expresses sexual energy outward to the world, that world, far from receiving, refuses or at best allows only indirect access. The situation of the 1890s is indicative of this situation for both men, namely at this time of consolidation of the idea of a homosexual identity and of a potential life (i.e. a *vita* or trajectory passing through stages of personality development through interaction with the external world, as opposed to a series of disconnected anonymous sexual acts). Both were still young, albeit past the normal age of narcissistic self-preoccupation. Yet George's alternating grandiosity and vulnerability particularly in the early letters to Hofmannsthal suggest an unresolved narcissistic conflict between self-identity and world.

It is hardly surprising that such a conflict would characterize the psychological experience of a homosexual man of this time. It was a historical point at which the idea of a homosexual identity had begun to unfold as an internalized life possibility on the one hand, but a point at which the rebuttal of such an identity in subject–

object relations was still the norm on the other. The homosexual experience was one of frustration between inner and outer world, of the individual's interactive experiences with reality. At that point at which the individual could seek to engage as an adult homosexual male with a social environment that did not offer a reciprocal understanding, the discrepancy between self and world became clear, leading to a renewed flight to self, to narcissistic self-idealization on the one hand and fear of, and even flight from, the world on the other. In such a case, where a 'stable but dynamic view of the self [...] is a normal component of identity, pathological narcissism is defined by unstable and/or maladaptive regulation of self-image'.[65] The choice is between renewed inwardness, leading to a surcharge of narcissistic self-absorption, or acceptance of the social order and willing deflection of these libidinal energies onto socially acknowledged points of access, resulting in de-validation of self. George and Hofmannsthal represent these two trajectories respectively.

The female gendered addressee continues to be present in this volume even as the poet is coming to terms with his homosexual desires. The latter are recognized but they remain in the inner realm, subjective and without representation. The only object can be the woman, but the poet's discomfort is communicated in the stilted expression, the use of small capitals in the typeface ('IHR', 'SIE'), the playing with reader expectations. In the second poem the social imperative of heterosexual address is recognized:

> Ihr rufe junger jahre die befahlen
> Nach IHR zu suchen [...] (IV, 13)

> [O urges from the years of youth which sweep
> Me on in quest of her [...]] (Morwitz 81)

But the implications are masked:

> Ich muss vor euch die stirn verneinend neigen
> Denn meine liebe schläft im land der strahlen. (IV, 13)

> [Before you I must bend denying brows,
> In lands of light my love is chained in sleep.] (Morwitz 81)

George appears to be on the verge of announcing his homosexual object orientation in this poem. The voices that ordered him to seek a woman are rejected, for he has found his love asleep in the land of shining light ('ein reich der sonne' — 'a kingdom of the sun' — is one of the tropes of utopian homosexual subjectivity in George's work). But the lyric voice does not manage to either express its real interest or to embrace 'her' in the second stanza:

> Doch schickt ihr SIE mir wieder [...]
> Ich will sie diesmal freudig anerkennen. (IV, 13)

> [But if you should send her back, [...]
> I shall acknowledge her this time with glad acclaim.] (Morwitz 81)

The poet's words remain in the modality of will, the realm of a hypothetical desire that fails to realize itself because it does not exist. There is no engagement with the

reality of the woman as desired object in this poem. 'She' remains nebulous and
unreal. It is all about the absence in George's life. Similarly in 'Ja heil und dank dir
die den segen brachte!' ('Oh, hail and thanks to you who eased my stress', IV, 14)
the idealized woman remains several removes from reality:

> Ich werde sanfte worte für dich lernen
> Und ganz als glichest du der Einen Fernen
> Dich loben auf den sonnen-wanderungen. (IV, 14)

> [I shall devise a gentle word for you,
> And praise you on our sunny paths as though
> You were the very one for whom I long.] (Morwitz 82)

Many have commented on the obliqueness of this poem, asking what the real
feelings are and to whom they are directed.[66] Friendship, love, companionship,
understanding, and sexual attraction are not so neatly separated and defined for the
young poet. The settings of *Das Jahr der Seele* are urban natural spaces, gardens and
parks, in which the liaison with the unnamed woman is imagined as a public event
in performative terms. The personal satisfactions of socially approved intimacy and
companionship act as a powerful counterweight to homoerotic desire which even
when awakened must remain anonymous, covert and detached. Social identity and
individual identity are closely related in these early poems of *Das Jahr der Seele*,
evoking the last enamelled images of a late summer *belle époque:*

> Die wespen mit den goldengrünen schuppen
> Sind von verschlossnen kelchen fortgeflogen S (IV, 19)

> [The wasps with scales of golden-green are gone
> From blooms that close their chalices.] (Morwitz 83)

It is a 'remembrance of things past' even as winter descends ('eh [das Land] im
nahen sturm vereise', 'before the land is frozen in the coming storm', IV, 19):

> Ich schrieb es auf: nicht länger sei verhehlt
> Was als gedanken ich nicht mehr verbanne ·
> Was ich nicht sage · du nicht fühlst: uns fehlt
> Bis an das glück noch eine weite spanne. (IV, 21)

> [I wrote it down: No more can I conceal
> What, as a thought, no longer I can shun,
> What I restrain, what you do not feel:
> For us, joy remains a long way off.] (*Morwitz 84)

This social, performative relationship will not last: the poet recognizes at the end of
the first section ('Nach der lese', 'After the harvest') that it will finish, leaving the
remains of love under a blanket of snow:

> Ich lasse meine grosse traurigkeit
> Dich falsch erraten um dich zu verschonen
> Ich fühle hat die zeit uns kaum entzweit
> So wirst du meinen traum nicht mehr bewohnen
> Doch wenn erst unterm schnee der park entschlief
> So glaub ich dass noch leiser trost entquille

Aus manchen schönen resten strauss und brief
In tiefer kalter winterlicher stille. (IV, 22)

[I leave you to guess at my great sadness
In order to protect you
Time will scarcely have parted us
Before you will be absent from my dreams.
But when the snow has made the park a tomb,
Faint comfort, I believe, may still be told
By lovely residues: a note, a bloom,
In winter stillness, bottomless and cold.] (*Morwitz 84)

The identity of the other in these poems is unclear, both in terms of George's biography and in the literary terms of the narrative of *Das Jahr der Seele*. What does emerge, is that regardless of this person's identity, and for all the friendship and mutual concern of past years, the poetic voice is moving on to something new and different. Whether the person is male or female is uncertain, but also in some ways unimportant: whether based on the experiences with Ida Coblenz or with one of the George's male friends of the time. The importance lies in the ambiguity itself and in the sense of liberation from past closed forms of existence, symbolized in winter ice and snow into new, warmer human relationships, the dynamism of which is driven by homosexual libido.

In the final poem of 'Nach der lese' the remnants of the relationship, flowers and letters, like mementoes of the novel of adultery, remind us of the relativities in George's homosexual autobiography, of the similarities between the forbidden loves of women in socially approved marriages and of homosexual men living out socially approved roles, both leading double lives in their emotions. Where the novel of adultery in the second half of the nineteenth century confronted the difficulties of representing female desire, the emerging literature of homosexual identity sought ways of rendering desire socially inoffensive without losing sight of it altogether. George traces a path from suppression to recognition of the power of desire in *Das Jahr der Seele*.

Over the course of the second section, 'Waller im Schnee' ('Pilgrims in the Snow') the relationship of the friends and would-be lovers disintegrates under the pressure of the lyric persona's self-questioning and with the sense of promise of something new and better in the coming spring:

Zu raschem abschied musst du dich bequemen
Denn auf dem weiher barst die starre rinde ·
Mir däucht es dass ich morgen knospen finde ·
Ins frühjahr darf ich dich nicht mit mir nehmen. (IV, 32)

[To rapid parting you must needs agree,
For riven is the water's frozen rind,
Perhaps a bud will be tomorrow's find!
I cannot take you into spring with me.] (Morwitz 88)

The third section, 'Sieg des Sommers' brings new life and adventures, ending on a seafaring note of journeys yet to begin. While the nature of the love affairs and attractions in this section is not clarified, a new freedom and openness is palpable. In the final poem the lyric persona's joy at the prospect of travel is undeterred even by the prospect of the other's pain at the prospect of his leaving and doubtful return:

> Ich aber horche in die nahe nacht
> Ob dort ein letzter vogelruf vermelde
> Den schlaf aus dem sie froh und schön erwacht —
> Der liebe sachten schlaf im blumenfelde. (IV, 45)

> [But I shall listen through the dusk, if there
> The last call of a bird will tell me of
> The sleep which yields a wakening fresh and fair
> In flowered field-the satin sleep of love.] (Morwitz 92)

This final stanza expresses the poet's feelings for the person he has left, listening in the night for the bird-call that announces the awakening from sleep. The ambivalence of this ending is clear: on the one hand the call of life, and on the other the care for the woman who was dear to him, perhaps loved him, but could not keep him from that inchoate but emerging sense of a life still undiscovered:

> Lieder wie ich gern sie sänge
> Darf ich freunde! noch nicht singen · (IV, 49)

> [Songs as I'd like to sing,
> friends! I cannot yet.] (*Morwitz 93)

In the 'Überschriften und Widmungen' ('Superscriptions and Dedications') George preserves those experiences from his youth that are of importance to him:

> Was ich [...]
> aus reicher jugend eben
> In das leben über-rette. (IV, 49)

> [What I [...]
> from youth's riches
> Salvage over into life.] (*Morwitz 93)

He ends the section with a sense of hiatus and threshold of the traveller-pilgrim just approaching the middle of life, before looking back over his past in 'Erinnerungen an einige Abende innerer Gesellikeit' ('Recollections of Evenings of Inner Companionship'):

> Bei seiner reise mittag bald zurück
> Bald vor sich zum gewölke bängen fragens
> Hat lange sich der rastende gedreht ..
> Durchwallt ist ganzer erden berg und tal
> Soviel an glück und tränen hinter ihm.
> Was kann noch sein? Soll er das haupt hier betten
> Als an des weges marken oder soll er
> In hellern höhen lauter noch frohlocken ·
> In wildern schluchten tiefer noch erstöhnen ..
> So war dies alles erst der morgengang? (IV, 56)

> [The traveller pauses midway on his road,

And after looking back on what he traversed,
Probes forward into clouds with timid doubt.
The hills and valleys he has crossed are worlds!
Behind him so much joy and stress! Can there
Be more to come? Shall he lie down to slumber
As if this were the journey's end, or venture
To brighter peaks, to jubilate more loudly,
Or moan more hopelessly in wilder chasms?
Was all this nothing but a morning's walk?] (Morwitz 96)

The journey and the return mark a threshold, over which the poet steps into a new sense of self-understanding and of identity. The motif of the pilgrim returning to his hometown as a site of significance suggests a new attitude to his life: to his past as having a significance of religious dimensions, as the force that created him, and as the beginning of life that now has a trajectory and a meaning. He is now mature and actively searching where earlier he was passive and receptive. Nevertheless he is still involved in the struggle to come to terms with the inner and the social self. In the poems of 'Nachtwachen' ('Nightwatches', IV, 63) he revisits a past in which he failed to take adequate account of the other in his preoccupation with himself:

Nicht nahm ich acht auf dich in meiner bahn
In zeiten feucht und falb worin der wahn
Des suchens fragens sich verlor. (IV, 64)

[I did not heed you and I went my road
In months of mist and greyness, when the goad
To ask, the urge to quest abate.] (Morwitz 99)

The relationship with the woman lacked passion and engagement from the beginning, but since the return of the traveller, it has been problematic, undermined by other amatory relationships of unclear status and nature:

Verschweigen wir was uns verwehrt ist
Geloben wir glücklich zu sein
Wenn auch nicht mehr uns beschert ist
Als noch ein rundgang zu zwein. (IV, 89)

[Then let us conceal what is denied us
And vow to be happy
Even if the one thing which is not denied us
Is walking together once more.] (*Morwitz 106)

The poems of the long final section, 'Traurige Tänze', represent the poet returned from his summer journey to his familiar world, resuming a life in which lack of fulfillment vies with the memory of past love:

Wo sieche seelen reden
Da lindern schmeichelhafte töne ·
Da ist die stimme tief und edel
Doch nicht zum sang so schön. (IV, 90)

[Where sick souls speak

> There sweet sounds sooth
> There the voice is deep and noble,
> Any yet cannot sing so beautifully.] (*Morwitz 106)

The temptation to acquiesce to convention vies with the recognition that the past cannot be returned and that the present is no longer satisfactory:

> Der hügel wo wir wandeln liegt im schatten ·
> Indes der drüben noch im lichte webt (IV, 107)

> [The hill where we are roaming lies in shadow,
> While that beyond is all enmeshed in light] (Morwitz 112)

A sense of a possible future is adumbrated as a hope, but it lacks outline, depth and even self-belief against the safety of home. Voltaire's ending of *Candide* is referenced obliquely in the final lines of 'R. P'. in the spirit of acceptance of the familiar and safe:

> Was frommt die weisheit dem bezirk des wahnes nahe
> Die uns mit grellem blenden schreckt und überwältigt
> Des einen unkund wo sie bürde wird und frevel?
> Wie friedenlos . du allerbleichster unsrer brüder ·
> Durchirrst du deine traurigen und weiten lande!
> Wann wirst du müde neue felder zu erobern
> Und lernest einmal pflanzen pflegen und dich freuen
> An dem was blüht und grünt und reift in dreien gärten? (IV, 80)

> [Of what use is wisdom on the verge of madness,
> That frightens and overwhelms us with its glare and glitter,
> But does not know when it becomes a weight and trespass?
> How restlessly, you palest of our brothers,
> You wander aimlessly through the sad extent and breadth of your lands!
> When will you weary of the conquest of new regions
> And learn at last to plant and tend with care and pleasure
> What grows, and blooms, and ripens in a threefold garden?]
> (*Morwitz 104)

The tenor of 'Traurige Tänze' is renunciation alongside indeterminate hope:

> So hältst du immer wach die müde stirn
> Und gleitest nicht herab von steiler bösche
> Ob auch das matt erhellte ziel verlösche
> Und über dir das einzige gestirn. (IV, 110)

> [Thus you hold your tired head up
> And you don't slip on the steep cliff face
> Even if the distant goal loses its light
> And the one star above you flickers out.] (*Morwitz 114)

Companionship consists in the sharing of disappointment:

> Da brachet der abendhauch
> Ihr die erlösende kunde:
> Meine trübste stunde

Nun kennest du sie auch. (iv, 117)

[The airs of evening blew
Her signs of saving grace:
The saddest hour I face,
You know it now — you too!] (Morwitz 116)

In 'Überschriften und Widmungen' George wrote the following poem to A.H., identified as August Husmann, an unknown reader of his poetry somewhere in Germany, who had written to George in March 1897, thanking him for his 'sympathetic verses':[67]

Du sanfter seher der du hilflos starrest
In trauer über ewig welke träume
Gib eine hand! Wir zeigen dir gefilde
Um saaten der erlösung hinzustreun.
Wir wollen gerne sie — verborgene wunder —
Mit unsrem blut und unsren tränen pflegen
Und heiter lächelnd wirst du uns umarmen
Wenn sie vor den erstaunten blicken blühn. (iv, 78)

[You, gentle seer, who muse so helplessly
And sadly over dreams which never flowered,
Give us your hand, and we shall show you fields
Where harvests of redemption can be sown.
With offerings of our blood and tears we gladly
Would tend them, miracles which still are hidden.
And you will clasp us, smiling and elated,
When they unfold before your startled eyes.] (*Morwitz 103)

While the imagery of 'Komm in den totgesagten park' speaks to many, not merely to homosexual men, the theme of belatedness and marginality as the points of entry into a new life, spoke particularly to those who had always had to watch from the sidelines of society. The collection as a whole reflects an honesty to a self that is still partial:

Zu sternen schau ich führerlos hinan
Sie lassen mich mit grauser nacht allein, (iv, 24)

[Without a guide, I look to the stars,
They leave me alone in the gloomy night.] (*Morwitz 85)

But it nevertheless seeks the promise of a life as yet unlived. The way forward remains unclear. However there are signs of things to come. Earlier in the collection, at the end of the winter, when the 'victory of summer' is imagined, the lyric persona looks up and across the river where:

Drüben an dem strand ein bruder
Winkt das frohe banner schwenkend. (iv, 33)

[Over there on the shore a brother
Beckons with his joyful banner.] (*Morwitz 80)

The sense is strong of something more than emancipation from the private stresses

of self-denial. The image of the brother under the joyful banner, beckoning from
the other shore, promises something new and different, a sense of group identity, of
a march forward, united under the flag of happiness. In this image the band begins
to emerge from its background, intimating the path that George would follow over
the next decade.[68] If the community of homosexual men throughout Germany was
a quiet one, of isolated souls finding a sense of themselves through the recognition
of a shared identity of peripherality and exclusion, George is intimating here
something more and greater, not merely a community, but a band of brothers. Not
the lonely imagination, nor even the two lovers against the world, but a movement,
a social grouping of a different nature. In subsequent volumes this mission will be
taken to extremes, characterized by narcissistic projection and idealization in the
works dedicated to Maximin and the Bund, defined as the group of those who are
chosen and who belong. However at this point in *Das Jahr der Seele* the contribution
to the homosexual imaginary takes the form of the communication of the new
idea of the joyful brother, and of the possibility of belonging to each other and
experiencing happiness and fulfilment together. The twelve poems in the third
section, dedicated to various men from George's inner circle of friends, suggest the
type and the constitution of the group that the poet would collect around him from
this time onward:

> Wie ein erwachen war zu andrem werden
> Als wir vergangenheit in uns gebändigt
> Und als das leben lächelnd uns gehändigt
> Was lang uns einzig ziel erschien auf erden.
> Auf einmal alle stunden so nur galten:
> Ein mühevolles werben um die hohe
> Die uns vereinte . die in ihrer lohe
> Gestalten um uns tilgte und gewalten. (IV, 42)

> [Like an awakening to different becoming
> When we had broken off the dream of old,
> And smiling life permitted us to hold
> The only thing we wanted in this world.
> And all at once the meaning of our days
> Was to tirelessly seek that ideal
> That unites us and in its heat
> Obliterates the shapes and forces around us.] (*Morwitz 91)

This is what makes George's poems unique: the generation of a sense of
community, and the appeal to a state of mind that was ubiquitous among the
members of the youth generation, those experiencing adolescence after the turn of
the century, namely of the end of possibilities and the need to create a future. The
homoeroticism of these poems sends out a strong message to George's homosexual
readers that here, for the first time, was a poet for them.

However George still had a long road to travel. It led to narcissistic projection
and charismatic leadership in the search for connection to the group. The Bund
that begins to unfold in George's imagination in *Der Teppich des Lebens* and comes
to coalesce around the image of Maximin in *Der siebente Ring* projects the self into

an ideal relationship with the other as an undifferentiated male community. The coming together in the ideal group symbolized in Maximin as leader and follower, and the casting off of the traumatized, individuated self, that would prove so attractive to the youth of his day, however, represents a narcissistic stage, not an end point in the development of George's lyric self. George charted the path through the false promises of masculinism in the nascent homosexual imaginary, providing a powerful repository of images, and a vision of a future community, both of which turned out to be illusory.[69] This aspect of his work culminated in disappointment and disillusionment in the wake of the war, but not in cynicism: indeed it will be argued that the experiences of the war led George beyond his unclearly formulated mission of reactionary anti-modernism and towards simple object love, and engagement with the other, beyond the infatuation with the narcissistic projection of self in the group in the final poems of *Das Neue Reich*.

Das Jahr der Seele is central to George's persona, since it marks the threshold point in the dynamic process of self-formation of the homosexual poet, throughout which the conflict rages between the social and the individual self — a battle that the poet will end through the creation of an idealized alter ego and ego-ideal who is at once lover and god. Around this ideal figure he will assemble the friends of past and present, among whom those who share his homoerotic feelings will be privileged members. This grouping or Bund will come to represent the social self, the *wir-Gefühl* that does not yet exist for the homosexual in Germany of this time:

> Nicht ist weise bis zur letzten frist
> Zu geniessen wo vergängnis ist. (IV, 100)

> [It is not wise to enjoy until the very end
> That which must pass away.] (*Morwitz 110)

This book of poems is about finding self-fulfilment through love, as he repeatedly exhorts his partner(s) to do, and as he himself seeks to do. Finally his advice is to leave behind the dead ashes of past relations:

> Ihr tauchtet in die aschen
> Die bleichen finger ein
> Mit suchen tasten haschen —
> Wird es noch einmal schein!
> Seht was mit trostgebärde
> Der mond euch rät
> Tretet weg vom herde
> Es ist worden spät. (IV, 114)

> [You dip your pale fingers
> into the ashes,
> Searching, feeling, groping through them
> Will light return again?
> Accept the counsel of the moon
> Its gesture of consolation:
> Step away from the hearth
> It has gotten late.] (*Morwitz 115)

And yet the memory of the experience is ultimately what remains important:

> Doch alle dinge die wir blumen nannten
> Versammeln sich am toten quell. (IV, 118)

> [But all the things we thought were flowers
> Gather together at the dead well.] (*Morwitz 116)

At the end of *Das Jahr der Seele* the poet has bidden his love farewell, but has not yet discovered his own course. The tone is bleak, particularly the final image of past hopes and desires gathered 'at the dead well'. The interchangeability of 'ich und du' at various points in the work is nowhere more evident than in these exhortations to the lover, realizing the poet's preface: 'selten sind sosehr wie in diesem buch ich und du die selbe seele' ('in this book, to an almost unprecedented extent, the I and the you represent the same soul'). They are at the same time exhortations to himself to overcome the limitations of his present life.

Where in the *Bücher* the lyric voice experiments with the romantic imagery of antiquity and the Middle Ages as a means of extension and liberation of the inhibited self, in *Das Jahr der Seele* the poet seeks — but does not yet find — engagement. He draws powerfully on the rhythms and themes of folk poetry, in particular of the natural world. Like Goethe and Heine, George evokes the simplicity and directness of folk-poetry without cliché. However there is an important difference: George's language is accessible to the homosexual reader in a way that earlier lyric is not. Not merely is the sex of the second person undisclosed and the forms of address cleared of the traditional vocabulary and associations of heterosexual attraction and love; the imagery itself is new and different, and constitutes the formation of an imaginary world, a new homosexual imaginary in German literature. These poems may express unfulfilled longing and the failure to connect, but the intention is unmistakeable, namely to begin speaking to other men in the language of physical and emotional attraction, not of the etherealized platonic love of so many of George's contemporaries. These poems thereby evoke a joint sense of selves, a 'wir' as a community of souls who share a sense of loneliness and longing on the one hand, but also intimations, as if for the first time, of fulfilment, even happiness, on the other.

George's homosexuality emerges alongside and in the context of feelings of loneliness, friendship, intimacy, loss, grief, excitement, and wonder. But his consciousness is mapped as a totality, not merely in its sexual aspect. In this sense the full sequence of George's works as the lyric autobiography of a homosexual man of his era and generation is mapped into the poetry as the unfolding of a personality, not as a static statement of sexuality nor as a set of homosexual fantasies of idealized Greek or other love. Those men reading these poems and able to intuit the unspoken processes of self-formation of the homosexual, re-living the threshold experiences of loneliness, love, self-recognition, fear, hiding behind camouflages, aliases and masks, yet recognizing signals of likeness from others, were able to reach a new level of self-understanding, self-acceptance, and, most importantly for this study, recognition of an imaginary world that was theirs to share for once. These mid-period poems begin to see a way forward beyond the Romantic solipsism of the earlier *Bücher:* they begin to see the possibility of a 'we' that is more than just the awareness of the existence of others. It is an unspoken but emergent sense of homosexual desire that fuels the need for closeness in these poems. The body, not the soul, initiates intimacy. Patterns of heterosexual expectation are found wanting and the lyric persona pushes back against them, even though he cannot yet enunciate his desires. These strategies are not conscious or deliberate: they map the emerging homosexual individual; they do not recreate in retrospect.

The pressure to express love and desire in terms of a female addressee comes from within as well as from outside in the homosexual poet of the 1890s. It is not merely the homosexual's response to social censure and legal menace; it reflects the true state of ambivalence in the emerging homosexual who is between the subject and the group, and cannot liberate himself into the homosexual love poem which does not yet exist for him:

> Im offnen leben wo ihr all euch gleichet ·
> Wo ihr fast niemals wie ihr fühlet saget (IV, 73, an Paul Gérardy)

> [In daily life, where one is like the other,
> And hardly ever says what stirs within him.] (Morwitz 102)

In the early poems — up until *Das Jahr der Seele* — the ambiguity of address (in terms of the sex of the addressee) expresses the impossibility — yet — of address to a man. The *wir-Gefühl* that is essential even to the lyric mode retains its traces in the imperative to address love to a woman even as the poem announces its homoeroticism. George is not addressing a female recipient; it is the social form of the lyric that expects and demands a type of address. George's early poetry expresses the contradictions between lyric and homosexuality. The male lover is not yet a lyric — or even literary — entity. In the final poem of *Das Neue Reich*, George will achieve this in one of German literature's superlative love poems.

Theodor Adorno suggested in 'Lyrik und Gesellschaft' ('Lyric Poetry and Society') that the lyric mode includes a social moment even in its most personal and subjective states. Adorno finds the traces of social determination in the rhythmic and semantic interstices between feeling and word. George, more than any other, withstands the social determination of the word by rescuing the origins of pure language from its social forms.[70] For Adorno, George's poetry suppresses the heterosexual drive, and with it, the drive towards 'otherness' itself.[71] Homosexuality is here simply a cipher in the poetic theory of pure language: he pays no attention to George's psychology. While recognizing the narcissism of George's stand, he misrecognizes the homosexuality in the poetic voice as merely the expression of an enforced narcissism, a turning inward to sameness. This assumption perpetuates attitudes toward homosexuality that George's poetry undermines. Yet George's greatness as a poet lies in his breaking through to the recognition of the homosexual other. While the idealization of Maximin and the Bund during the first decade of the century represented narcissistic grandiosity, George moved towards object love as the men he loved died or were mutilated in the war.

George's volumes from *Das Jahr der Seele* onward created a sense of the 'we'. This was not an unproblematic process. As Germany lurched towards modernity the sense of social and cultural crisis proved ambiguous: on the one hand opening up unheard-of possibilities for change and at the same time enabling radical socio-political experimentation. George's volumes from the beginning of the new century cannot be separated from his 'aesthetic fundamentalism' (Breuer) or 'reactionary modernism' (Herf). George's increasing infatuation with the idea of the corporate body of men, sharing a unified set of emotional, sexual and ideational interests, in which he would play the role of master and prophet, led to malaise, disillusionment and disappointment, as beloved figures were damaged and departed, and George himself came to see its shortcomings in the wake of war and fragmentation of the group around him.[72]

A New Sense of Self: *Der Teppich des Lebens*

In a letter to Ida Coblenz of early September 1895 George already — at the age of twenty-seven — reviews his life as a series of stages expressed in the successive volumes of his poetry:

> Ich stehe wieder an einem wendepunkt und blicke auf ein ganzes leben zurück das wie ich fühle von einem ganz anderen abgelöst wird. Ich möchte es mit der herausgabe meiner bücher schliessen. Ich möchte Hymnen Pilgerfahrten und Algabal im ersten, Hirtengedichten Sagen und Sänge und Hängende Gärten im zweiten und die letzten gedichte als Annum animae oder Jahr der Seele im dritten vereinigen.[73]

> [I'm at a turning point again and look back on a whole life that I feel is being replaced by a completely different one. I would like to close it with the publication of my books. I would like to combine *Hymns*, *Pilgrimages* and *Algabal* in the first, *Eclogues and Eulogies*, *Sagas and Songs* and the *Hanging Gardens* in the second, and the last poems as *annum animae* or *Year of the Soul* in the third.]

Der Teppich des Lebens (limited edition, 1899/1900; first public edition, 1901) occupies a central position in George's oeuvre.[74] The decision to publish *Die Fibel*, the collection of poems from the late 1880s largely predating *Hymnen* at this point suggests that George was now consciously formulating this life in verse as a literary mission.

The interchanges between an angel and the lyric persona dominate the *Vorspiel* (*Prelude*) to *Der Teppich des Lebens*. For George's disciples, the angel of the *Vorspiel* was a visionary figure and manifestation of the path forward, for others a less transcendental figure, but no less powerful in its gift of liberation and guidance.[75] The living voice of the poet and the imagined voice of an angel are separated, the one lurching towards depression and despair, the other holding the keel even, enabling its precious cargo to maintain a sense of equilibrium through the evocation of arrival at better shores. The angel is both an idealization and a mirror image of the lyric persona ('Und seine stimme fast der meinen glich', 'And his voice was almost like my own', v, 10), the voice of revelation to the lyric persona of the inner conflicts that disturb him:

> Und ER: Was jetzt mein ohr so stürmisch trifft
> Sind wünsche die sich unentwirrbar streiten. (v, 11)

[And he: What now buffets my ears so stormily
Is the strife of wishes inextricable from each other.]

The source of the poet's distress is the gloomy life of service under the master's yoke ('des herren joch [...] Zu düster und zu einsam war sein dienst', v, 13, 'the master's yoke [...] too gloomy and lonely was his service'). But the angel's role is not to settle the persona's conflicts by granting permission; rather he stands by to help:

In meinem leben rannen schlimme tage
Und manche töne hallten rauh und schrill.
Nun hält ein guter geist die rechte wage
Nun tu ich alles was der engel will. (v, 12)

[Dark days ran through my life
And many voices sounded harsh and shrill,
Now a good soul holds the scales in balance
Now I do all that the angel wills.] (*Morwitz 119)

The angel appears naked to the poet, enveloped in springtime blossoms. He is a herald of happiness, but there is also a threatening, even sinister undertone to the poet's immersion in the perfume of fresh roses:

Ich badete beglückt
Mein ganzes antlitz in den frischen rosen. (v, 10)

[In delight I bathed my brow,
And cheeks, and mouth in newly-opened roses.] (Morwitz 118)

In *Algabal* the rain of heavily scented flowers brings the death of the revellers, and later, in Ebermayer's *Dr. Angelo*, the protagonist commits suicide by closing himself up in a flower-filled room, in reference to George's earlier image of the dying revellers. This is a love-death, a suicide brought on by the prohibition of homosexual love. The implication here is also that George's suffering is the result of prohibition of that which he desires, and the gloomy service which renders his life miserable is the pretence of heterosexuality.

The naked angel saves the poet from the suicidal despair and desperation of his loneliness, splitting and projecting the imaginative capacity, and is thus able to hold the scales of life and imagination in balance, guiding the bark of life 'Zur stillen insel zum gelobten port' ('To the silent island, the promised port', v, 12).

Ich mag nicht atmen als in deinem duft.
Verschliess mich ganz in deinem heiligtume!
[...]
So fleh ich heut aus meiner dunklen kluft. (v, 11)

[I cannot breathe save in your sweet presence,
Enclose me wholly in your sanctuary!
[...]
Thus now I plead from my dark chasm.] (*Morwitz 118)

This image of the angel guiding the vessel of life into safety is a comforting one which, at this point, enables the poet to imagine a future other than despair:

Ich forschte bleichen eifers nach dem horte
Nach strofen drinnen tiefste kümmerniss
[...]
Da trat ein nackter engel durch die pforte. (v, 10)

[When pale with zeal, I searched for a refuge,
After writing lines full of grief and apprehension,
[...]
A naked angel stepped through my doorway.] (*Morwitz 118)

The angel will be transformed throughout the course of the volume, reflecting
the changes in George's self-perception, and becoming a narcissistic self-image, a
mirroring of self in an externalized self-object, which represents a greater wholeness
or totality. George's sense of moving from depressive isolation to euphoric union
with the angel traces his recognition of the narcissistic self-object in his verse as a
stage of regeneration, not of balance or equilibrium in itself.

By the seventh poem of the 'Vorspiel', a hierarchy of communication and influence has been established, consisting of the angel, the persona of the poet, and the
disciples, the 'Jünger' or 'kleine schar' of young men who have raised the pennant
of 'Hellas ewig unsre liebe' ('Hellas eternally our love', v, 16), in which the lyric
persona is validated through his (messianic) role as transmitter of the angel's truths:

Ich bin freund und führer dir und ferge.
Nicht mehr mitzustreiten ziemt dir nun
Auch nicht mit den Weisen · hoch vom berge
Sollst du schaun wie sie im tale tun.
[...]
Drüben schwärme folgen ernst im qualme
Einem bleichen mann auf weissem pferde
Mit verhaltnen gluten in dem psalme:
Kreuz du bleibst noch lang das licht der erde.

Eine kleine schar zieht stille bahnen
Stolz entfernt vom wirkenden getriebe
Und als losung steht auf ihren fahnen:
Hellas ewig unsre liebe. (v, 16)

[Now I am your friend, and guard, and guide,
So you may no longer share the feuds
Even of the wise. My peaks provide
Views of valleys and their multitudes.
[...]
There, in swirls of incense, solemn throngs
Follow an ascetic on a white
Horse, and passion smoulders through their songs:
'Long the world shall have the cross for light!'

Only few have chosen silent ways,
Proudly distant from the active drove,
And the words their banners flaunt are these:
'Hellas, our eternal love!'] (Morwitz 121)

The final line with its four stresses, is unique in the 'Vorspiel'.[76] The hellenic love that these men share is not merely homoerotic; it is also free of guilt:

> Du sprichst mir nie von sünde oder sitte.
> [...]
> So lieb ich dich: [...]
> [...]   weges-sicher
> Nicht weisst von scham von reue oder fluch'. (v, 17)

> [You never speak of sin or morals
> [...]
> So I love you when [...]
> [...] Secure in your intent,
> You know nothing of shame or repentence or curse.] (*Morwitz 121)

And it is a group phenomenon anticipating breakthrough to a new state of communal being:

> So komm zur stätte wo wir uns verbünden! (v, 19)

> [Then come to the place where we are united] (Morwitz 122, modified PM)

> Ein bräutliches beginnliches entschleiern ..
> Nun spricht der Ewige: ich will! Ihr sollt! (v, 20)

> [A first and bridal lifting of the veil,
> Now the Eternal says: I will! You must!] (*Morwitz 123)

The role which emerges for the poetic voice as a result of this experience is that of the prophet, the role which predominates in biographical and other representations of the real George. The angel corresponds to the idealized self that will later be manifested in the figure of Maximin. The poet as prophet will become the conduit of a new way of being for the homosexual men around him, moving from the depression of the opening poems to the euphoria of 'Hellas ewig unsre liebe'.

George himself provided a gloss on this poem, suggesting that German youth release itself from the superficial education and underlying old-soldier brutality of the Wilhelminian era for a new, broad conception of their Germanness.[77]

> Dass ein strahl von Hellas auf uns fiel: das unsre jugend jetzt das leben nicht mehr niedrig sondern glühend anzusehen beginnt: dass sie im leiblichen und geistigen nach schönen maassen sucht: dass sie von der schwärmerei für seichte allgemeine bildung und beglückung sich ebenso gelöst hat als von verjährter lanzknechtischer barbarei: dass sie die steife gradheit sowie das geduckte lastentragende der umlebenden als hässlich vermeidet und freien hauptes schön durch das leben schreiten will: dass sie schliesslich auch ihr volkstum gross und nicht im beschränkten sinne eines stammes auffasst: darin finde man den umschwung des deutschen wesens bei der jahrhunderwende.[78]

> [That a ray of Hellas fell on us: that our youth no longer views life as low but begins to see it glow: that it seeks beautiful proportions in body and soul; that it has released itself from enthusiasms for shallow general education and superficial happiness, and spurned the brutalities of old soldiers; that it rejects as ugly the rigid uprightness as well as the bowed yoke-bearing of those around

them, wanting instead to stride through life with beauty with heads held upright and free; finally that it also sees its identity as a people as broad, not in a limited tribal sense: this is the direction in which the German character has turned as the century changes.]

However George's commentary indicates something more than 'general and rather abstract Philhellenism' in the context of a manifesto for the rebirth of Germany that later commentators such as influential scholar of Hellenic pedagogy or *paideia* Werner Jaeger found in it.[79] This redeeming angel comes, like the brother in *Das Jahr der Seele* (IV, 33), swinging the banner of freedom on the opposite shore:[80]

> Da trat ER mir entgegen fahnenschwinger
> Im herbstes-golde und er hob den finger
> Und lenkte mich zurück in seinen bann (v, 13)

> [Then he, the banner-bearer, crossed the glow
> Of autumn and with lifted finger drew
> Me back into his spell] (Morwitz 119)

The lyric persona looks back with disbelief to the ascetic lifeworld of his earlier self, intoxicated now with the promise of the future:

> Dein geist zurück in jenes jahr geschwenkt
> Begreift es heut nicht welche sternenmeilen
> Vom ort dich trennten wo die menschen weilen (v, 24)

> [Back to the vanished years your spirit leant
> And failed to grasp what starry fathoms ran
> Between you and the worlds of other men.] (Morwitz 125)

The linkage of Hellenistic, homoerotically tinged imagery with the sense of breakthrough into a new life represents the dawning consciousness of the homosexual man of the possibility of community as well as of self, borrowing from, while rejecting, the spiritual asceticism of the Christian myth of the leader and the creation of a new community of believers. These early evocations of the stirrings of homosexual group identity in the Bund of young men, glow golden in the reflection of Hellenic innocence and are dedicated to the body as well as the soul:

> Dir ruft die erde zu der ihr entstammt (v, 24)

> [The earth from which you hail is calling you] (Morwitz 125)

> Der nackten glieder gleiten in den wellen, (v, 25)

> [And in the stream the glide of naked limb.] (Morwitz 125)

With this volume a controversial aspect of George's poetic persona begins to manifest itself. The poet's self-stylization as master and prophet has come to define George in his biography and his aesthetics. It is problematic but deeply intertwined with the poet's coming to a sense of self and homosexual community. Far from remaining static, this role also follows a trajectory during his adulthood. It becomes pronounced over the following decade only to be quietly withdrawn in *Das Neue Reich*, in which the final stage of George's poetic life is registered. In the reading which follows, George's involvement with the circle or Bund of disciples and followers represents a particular convergence of individual psychological, group psycho-social, and national historico-political factors which define his original homosexual imaginary in Germany at this time.

For Adorno, the appearance of the angel marks the beginning of George's decline into nationalism.[81]

> Perhaps one may be permitted to speculate that George's succumbing to a frenzied nationalist positivity derived from the fact that he suppressed his instinctual attraction to the other sex, and with it to the Other as such, and restricted himself endogamously to what resembled him the way the voice of the wretched angel from the prologue to these poems does.[82]

He uses the curious term 'endogamous' ('endogamisch[]') here to express the fixation on sameness and the self rather than difference and the other, indicating the angel's inward-turned, narcissistic and homosexual significance. The metaphor of marriage within the group binds together George's politics with his sexuality. For Fleming, 'Adorno reads George's homosexuality as his primary form of rejecting Otherness as such.'[83] For Adorno, that is, the angel is an indication of the link in George's work between narcissism, homosexuality and fascism. Homosexuality is the libidinal expression of the narcissistic fixations which generate fascist nationalism. Adorno fixes homosexuality to narcissism via Freudian theory, and thence to an image of German nationalist inward-turnedness ('endogam') which, for him, as for Lukács and other left-wing commentators, typified the late George and prefigured Nazism; he does not see the emancipatory moment in the trajectory of George's poetic life. While Adorno's linkage of the psychology of homosexuality with the politics of fascism seems blinkered by today's standards, there is nevertheless a moment of truth in his connection of homoeroticism, narcissism and depressive negativity. Adorno sees the negativity alone, but George's desperation at the gloominess and loneliness of homosexual existence leads him in a direction at once liberating and harmful at this moment in German life.

In the 'Vorspiel' George imagines the creation of a homosexual community in radically different terms for his own and following generations. The angel which guides him forward towards a new positivity is the mouthpiece for hellenic homoeroticism but in an entirely different spirit from that of earlier generations. Here the sun of Hellas is physical, warming and life-affirming where in the fantasies of Aschenbach, for example, Tadzio as Phaedrus becomes the de-corporealized bringer of death. While George's symbolism may have spoken more widely, it certainly spoke specifically to homosexual men. However it also contained the seed of its own destruction:

> Verweilst du in den traurigsten bezirken
> Wo ruhmlos tat der starken wie der bleichen
> Begraben wird so lenkt — wie ohn entweichen
> Zu jeder lust der leib — mein ruf zum wirken.
> [...]
> So komm zur stätte wo wir uns verbünden!
> In meinem hain der weihe hallt es brausend

Sind auch der dinge formen abertausend
Ist dir nur Eine — Meine — sie zu künden. (v, 19)

[If you are prisoned in those hopeless tracts
Where deeds of both the wan and vital pale
Unsung, then — as the body without fail
To all delight — my word exhorts to acts.
[...]
Then come to where we work in unison,
Where through my sacred grove a paean rings:
Though tens of thousands be the forms of things,
You shall give voice to one alone: my own.] (Morwitz 122)

George spoke to a 'nation' of outsiders, of young men, Jews and homosexuals in particular, who would come to call themselves 'secret Germany', transfixed by the lyric transformation of loneliness into connectedness. George expressed the affective lives of these young men in an autobiography divested of individuality but suffused with experience. Adorno's identification of the mixture of narcissistic self-imaging and proto-fascist rallying in the final lines of poem X of the 'Vorspiel' is prescient. However this reactionary-modernist poetic moment does not last, and it never completely obscures liberationist individualism in the move through and beyond the Bund.

In poem XIV of the 'Vorspiel' the addressed persona emerges from (privileged) isolation onto the streets:

Du stiegest ab von deinem hohen hause
Zum wege · manche freunde standen neben
Du suchtest unter ihnen deine klause
Und sahst dich um gleichwie in andrem leben.
Dich werden deine gipfel nicht mehr schützen
Doch wie seither in lauterstem gewande
Wirst du an deines nächsten arm dich stützen
Und bliebst wie vormals gast von fernem strande
Den vielen — die du immer meiden möchtest.
Vergeblich wäre wenn sie dich umschlängen
Und töricht wenn du zwischen ihnen föchtest.
Sie sind zu fremd in deines webens gängen.
Nur manchmal bricht aus ihnen edles feuer
Und offenbart dir dass ihr bund nicht schände.
Dann sprich: in starker schmerzgemeinschaft euer
Erfass ich eure brüderlichen hände. (v, 23)

[You left your house above and took the road
Which wound below, and many a friend was near,
And there you tried to found your own abode
And gazed as though you saw another sphere.
Your summits will no longer be your screen,
But in a robe unsullied as before
Upon your neighbour's arm you now will lean,
And yet you are a guest from alien shore
To all the many whom you wished to shun.
Their clasp could never hold you, and to fight

> Their battles in their ranks were idly done.
> For them your patterns are too recondite.
> But sometimes pure and seldom fires shine
> From them and show their nearness does not stain.
> Then say: 'I take your brother-hands in mine,
> Allied in strong community of pain'.] (Morwitz 124)

At the moment of descent, life is transformed: friends are standing by and '[you] looked around as if in another life'. This moment of transformation is articulated in a way that gay men of an age to remember just how closed life could, and had to, be (myself included) can only recognize as extraordinarily prescient in the era of equal rights and gay marriage. Suddenly the familiar life of family, friends and neighbours appears new and transformed in the moment of openness and acceptance. No longer protected by isolated peaks or his lofty house, the emergent 'you' now finds the supporting arm of the neighbour, but remains a foreign guest to all of those whom he had earlier avoided. And yet even they show nobility of feeling and their community is not a disgraceful one. The 'you' is charged to speak his recognition of their community of suffering and to take their hands as a brother, not a foreigner.

Rieckmann reads in this poem a covert reproach to Hofmannsthal. For Rieckmann, the relationship between George and Hofmannsthal was sealed after their first encounter in 1892 and 'threw its shadow over every aspect of their relations until their final break and beyond'.[84] This relationship was defined by their opposed attitudes to the possibilities available to them as homosexual men on the personal level and in the context of a homophobic civil society:

> Die eine, durch George repräsentiert, die sich also absolute ästhetische Opposition gegen die bürgerlichen und pseudochristlichen Werte der wilhelminischen Gesellschaft verstand; die andere, durch Hofmannsthal vertreten, die den Versuch unternahm, diese opponierende Haltung in die bürgerliche Gesellschaft zu integrieren mit dem Ziel, diese Gesellschaft von innen heraus zu regenerieren.[85]

> [The one, represented by George, saw himself in absolute aesthetic opposition to the bourgeois and pseudo-Christian values of Wilhelmine society; the other, represented by Hofmannsthal, attempted to integrate this opposing attitude into bourgeois society with the aim of regenerating this society from within.]

Hofmannsthal had recently turned from poetry to the 'hohes haus' of theatre.[86] George's point, for Rieckmann, is that Hofmannsthal would never be a man of the people and that his attempts at theatrical relevance would necessarily fail. Still in his aestheticist robes ('in lauterstem gewande') on the supporting arm of a well-meaning member of the public, he would remain a foreigner. Rieckmann's interpretation is persuasive. However, the final lines remain ambiguous in this reading, since they suggest greater, not lesser identification with the group in the end. George's point of biographical reference may well have been Hofmannsthal, but the group with whom he should be associating is that of other men, homosexuals like himself, whom he has eschewed in favour of convention and social standing. Not the distinction between elite theatre and the common man, but rather between the alienated homosexual and the group or Bund of men who can accept, even love, each other. If he accepts himself, George suggests, he may find brotherly affection rather than alienation, and a sense of community, not disgrace, among other homosexual men. George would again express the intimacy that he felt he shared with Hofmannsthal, by confiding many years later in July 1902, his need for the support of the Bund or circle of close friends in order to alleviate overwhelming sensations of rootlessness and loneliness.[87]

This poem also contains a self-reflexive moment, despite the second-person address. The descent into a world of other homosexuals who reveal themselves to be a community of friends suggests the experience of George himself in these early years of discovery of others around him, such as Carl August Klein, George's first disciple of many, on whose friendship the poet would rely, despite his public persona of lofty independence.[88] Here we can already sense a tension between the roles of the sovereign master and the individual still discovering himself through the exploration of others. This tension will continue even through the most hieratic of the volumes, *Der Stern des Bundes*.

In the final poem of the 'Vorspiel', the poet looks back over time and events; he stands alone at the end of life, bereft of friends save one:

> Kein freund war nahe mehr · sie alle gingen
> Nur ER der niemals wankte blieb und wachte.
> [...]
> Mit der betäubung wein aus seinem sprengel
> Die dichten schatten der bedrängnis hindernd
> Des endes schwere scheideblicke lindernd
> So stand am lager fest und hoch: der engel. (v, 33)

> [All had withdrawn and gone was every friend,
> But he who never faltered, watched and stayed.
> [...]
> Delaying anguish in its sullen spate
> With numbing wine shed from his aspergill,
> And easing tortured glances of farewell,
> The angel at the bed stood tall and straight.] (Morwitz 129)

The angel looking over him in his last moment is strong and sure, his only point of meaning. Everything and everyone else is gone. The angel is his poetic self, his life in language, the sole remaining trace of his existence and identity. What follows is a series of images, moments and figures from that life, including those dear and meaningful to him, such as Gundolf, Hofmannsthal and others, transformed into the poetic *vita*, eternalized as the poet's symbolic imaginary (creating and feeding into the *wir-Gefühl* of the emergent group).

Stefan George was the creator of a group consciousness which had become timely. At a crucial point in German history his particular genius gave voice to a homosexual identity as a national symbolic imaginary, spearheading a movement generated by influences as diverse as the aestheticist exploration of states and sensations of the French symbolists, the radical self-questioning of German and European identity by thinkers in an emergent philosophical environment of vitalism (such as Nietzsche and his followers), the psycho-social recognition of homosexuality as a state of being in the fields of psychiatry, criminology and the law, the radical sexual experimentation of the German youth movements, themselves born of new vitalist philosophies, and the existence of a large body of men no longer content with sexual anonymity, loneliness and social exclusion. These men were now seeking something more than recognition as pariahs, requiring a sense of themselves as a 'we-group', an identity defined not by self-hate and exclusion, but by self-acceptance and inclusion. For all the problems of group identity in Germany at this time that George's poetry would come to embody, he gave voice for the first time to a living, hoped-for homosexual social imaginary, making the imaginative transition from self-denial and retrospective fantasy to self-realization. Those who could identify with 'Hellas ewig unsre liebe' proved all too willing to follow George even further in his mission of self-realization.

Germany had generated the conditions for the emergence of a dynamic and constructive male homosexual imaginary, and Stefan George was its primary creator. However he came to understand this role in terms of a charismatic leadership that turned out to have ruinous consequences, if not for him, then for many of his followers:

> In seinen blicken lesen wir erfreut
> Was uns erkannt ist im erhellten traum (v, 32)
>
> [And in his glances joyfully we read
> What in prophetic dreams he knows will come.] (*Morwitz 129)

From this time onward, George is increasingly seduced by the charismatic role as prophet and leader, merging homosexual identity with a vision of warrior-masculinity drawing on Hellenic and Germanic-medieval models and, at least until war broke the dream, sacrificing individual attraction and love to the pursuit of the whole, structured around the relation of leader and group. George merged the roles of poet and charismatic leader over the following decade. However the poetry never became the vehicle for ideology that George's fiercest critics have maintained, and this stage in his life and writing turned out to herald something other than the transformation into the narcissistic-charismatic genius and precursor of fascist modernity of commentators such as Mattenklott and Osterkamp.

George was not alone in his fantasies of charismatic leadership. His dream emerged in the environment of radical change, 'breakthrough' and searching for new paths into the future that characterized parts of German society, particularly the youth movement that provided the crucible for change at this time.[89] Hans Blüher, for example progressed in this environment from historian of the *Wandervogel* movement to spokesman for a fascist doctrine of masculinism based on the validation of suppressed homoerotic libido as a society-building force. The mixture of radical ideas and social unrest in German-speaking Central Europe at this time produced a plethora of more or less charismatic-prophetic leadership figures. George's intention may have been to valorize the homosexual in himself and others through the creation of the Bund, but the outcome was fatally compromised by the nature of his condition of entry — to become a disciple — as the criterion for existential authenticity.

George's later disenchantment with the masculinist model of homosexuality, which he nevertheless continued to embody at least in his presence and public perception, led to steady withdrawal and retirement during the 1920s and until his death in Switzerland, sick, prematurely aged and out of reach of the Nazis who would destroy him if they could not enlist him. In the poetry from the wartime period onwards, however, the dream was over. Disenchantment battled love in a conflict, the roots of which can be found as early as in *Der Teppich des Lebens*. Unlike most of the established homosexual writers by the 1920s, such as Erich Ebermayer, Albert Rausch (*aka* Henry Benrath), Ernst Glaeser and others who quietly acceded, or heterosexual writers such as Gottfried Benn and Gerhart Hauptmann who showed themselves compliant under Nazism, George and his followers kept their distance, refused to comply, or emigrated as Jews or as political dissenters.[90] It is my thesis that George began to realize in the years 1917–18 the extent of his failure and that the poems published as final in his poetic life attempt to make good a trajectory that had traced an arc of tragedy for him as a person and for many of his followers. In this he represents another face of reactionary anti-modernism, like Thomas Mann or any of the others who realized either just in time or too late that theirs had been a false messiah. George's difference was that he was a homosexual who insisted on his identity. In an environment during the 1920s in which homosexual and post-war masculinity were evolving in unforeseen ways, courted by an emergent Nazism seeking the support of disaffected and alienated men in the era of post-war depression, homosexuals were also a successful target, seeking inclusion in the national community as well as validation of their masculinity. George had prepared his disciples for these later developments in his writings and activities up until the early years of the war, but came to the sudden and traumatic recognition of what he had done at the point where the Bund disbanded in order to join the war. Nevertheless, the tension between the two sides of George, the prophet and charismatic leader, and the homosexual man able to love other men, manifests itself much earlier than this.

The themes of leadership, following, choice, election and admittance are to be found in the poems of the 'Vorspiel', in which the grim experience of loneliness is alleviated in the first instance through the recognition of a redeeming other — a figure neither religious nor holy at this stage — who promises release from loneliness. The selves of these poems are young men, some in historical costume, but the voices ring modern and lonely. The promise of community is amplified through the adoption of a single voice, associated with a charismatic-prophetic, but still unidentified figure:

> Verweilst du in den traurigsten bezirken
> [...]
> So komm zur stätte wo wir uns verbünden!
> In meinem hain der weihe hallt es brausend
> Sind auch der dinge formen abertausend
> Ist dir nur Eine — Meine — sie zu künden (v, 19)
>
> [If you are prisoned in those saddest of regions
> [...]
> Then come to the place where we unite!

> Where through my sacred grove a paean rings:
> Though tens of thousands be the forms of things,
> You shall give voice to one alone: my own.] (*Morwitz 122)

A mounting sense of crisis and urgency expresses itself in the latter poems of the 'Vorspiel', of existential loneliness and the need for redemption, transmitted in images of need and answering voice:

> Da — ohne wunsch und zeichen — bricht im kerker
> Ein streif wie schieres silber durch den spalt. (v, 20)

> Then through the chink a glint, a silver band
> Breaks unheralded and undreamed, into the prison!] (*Morwitz 123)

The references to homosexual love are present:

> Dass wir der liebe treuste priester wol
> Sie suchen müssen in verhülltem jammern (v, 21)

> [We, who are love's most faithful priests, must quest
> For it with hidden grief and hollow eyes.] (Morwitz 123)

The 'Eternal' speaking to the prisoner in poem XI promises release in the here-and-now into the group, and it is imagined in passive rather than active sexual terms. His agency extends no further than acceptance in terms of an unveiling:

> Ein bräutliches beginnliches entschleiern ..
> Nun spricht der Ewige: ich will! ihr sollt! (v, 20)

> [A first and bridal lifting of the veil,
> Now the Eternal says: 'I call — you must!'] (Morwitz 123)

In a world of conventional sexuality it is the shared intimacy of male friends that leads to a breakthrough communicated in the word but underpinned by sexual imagery. A new dance takes the place of the traditional round of the sexes, communicated by the secret: 'Und das geheimnis lehrte neuer tänze' (v, 26, 'And teaches the secret of new dances'):

> Doch ist wo du um tiefste schätze freist
> Der freunde nächtiger raum · schon schweigt geplauder
> Da bebt ein ton und eine miene kreist
> Und schütteln mit der offenbarung schauder.
> Da steigt das mächtige wort — ein grosses heil —
> Ein stern der auf verborgenen furchen glimmert
> Das wort von neuer lust und pein: ein pfeil
> Der in die seele bricht und zuckt und flimmert. (v, 25)

> [But in a room with friends, by night you find
> The rarest treasures, soon a silence reigns,
> And then a glance is born, a trembling sound,
> And revelation pulses through your veins.
> The regnant word ascends, the magic seal,
> A star in furrows of which no one knows,
> The word of new delight and new ordeal,
> A shaft that stabs the soul, and throbs, and glows.] (Morwitz 125)

The 'Vorspiel' announces a new order in the language of this-worldly redemption, implying an existential revolution of the isolated male individual onto the unified group, and is spiritual and physical, even sexual. But it remains an unfulfilled promise in the 'Vorspiel' and throughout this volume, a call to subordination and obedience to a vaguely imagined higher power.

The call to arms still has the innocence of boyhood adventure attaching to it. But like the literature of empire, it harbours something dark, threatening, even malign, configuring male libido in terms of structures of power and battle. As many commentators have indicated, the themes of love, loyalty and submission remain complex and unsettling. Even separated from the later history of Nazism, the affirmation of warrior values in the service of an ideology of homosexual — or at least male-to-male — love in various pre-modern contexts is a questionable strategy of sexual enfranchisement, whether in the context of an idealized feudal warrior-hierarchy or a monastic-hieratic setting. In *Der Teppich des Lebens* and through the following two volumes, *Der siebente Ring* and *Der Stern des Bundes*, a tension exists between love as individual affection and love as submission to an idealized group imaginary.

> Was uns entzückt verherrlicht und befreit
> Empfangen wir aus seiner hand zum lehn
> Und winkt er: sind wir stark und stolz bereit
> Für seinen ruhm in nacht und tod zu gehn. (v, 32)

> [He gives in fief from his own hand
> That which delights and frees us, gives us glory
> He beckons, and we are strong and proud, ready
> To serve in his greater glory,
> To go into the darkness and to die.] (*Morwitz 128)

The themes of leadership, authority and subordination, inclusion and exclusion as the homoerotic criteria of membership of the Bund are pursued in a group of poems each conceived on a character type: the disciple, the elect or chosen, and the rejected or abject. 'Der Jünger' ('The Disciple') expands on the theme of redemption through subordination. It is a poem in which identity is achieved through self-abnegation of religious dimensions. The being to whom the disciple pledges absolute allegiance occupies a space between a god and a feudal lord — implicitly as an act of homosexual love. The evocation of the pre-modern relationship of fealty is powerful as a historical reminiscence, perhaps, but as an enactment of a state of modern being, it suggests degradation rather than ennoblement in equating love with submission.

> Ihr sprecht von wonnen die ich nicht begehre
> In mir die liebe schlägt für meinen Herrn. (v, 47)

> [You speak of pleasures that I do not desire
> I pulse with love that binds me to my lord,] (*Morwitz 135)

Against the disciple, the rejected, outcast or abject one ('Der Verworfene') remains stranded on the shores of convention, unable (as opposed to unwilling) to make the commitment of self that is represented as an act of love and loyalty at once. He is too afraid to respond to his inner promptings and hence is destined to a life on the periphery, disqualified from a sense of community by the failure to have developed his inner self:

> Du horchtest ängstlich aus am weg am markte
> Dass keine dir verborgne regung sei ..
> In alle seelen einzuschlüpfen gierig
> Blieb deine eigne unbebaut und öd. (v, 49)

> [You pried too tensely on the road, the market,
> Lest there be shades of moods you might have missed.
> Your soul, which slipped into the soul of others
> So greedily, was itself left unsown and waste.] (*Morwitz 136)

George's analysis of abjection focuses on the dynamic of failure in the relationship between individual and normative community. The outsider's overwhelming need to be a part of the community which rejects him blocks his ability to look inward and find authenticity in himself. And yet without community, authenticity is impossible. The abject character, that is, seeks validation among others where he should seek authenticity among his own.

The poem may well have been written with Hofmannsthal in mind. After the initial love affair, Hofmannsthal kept his distance from George, at once admiring the poetry but rejecting the homosexuality, not merely the homosexual relationship that the slightly older poet was offering. For George Hofmannsthal was denying something in himself that George had at once recognized and reciprocated. Hofmannsthal quickly recognized that his privileged Viennese *bürgerlich* environment was incompatible with George's sexual modernism, and opted for convention. He also recognized and was repelled by George's narcissistic-charismatic personality, not merely the homosexual attraction, and in his later poem 'Der Prophet' the title figure suggests George as a seductive, sinister and lethal presence:

> Sein Auge bannt und fremd ist Stirn und Haar.
> Von seinen Worten, den unscheinbar leisen,
> Geht eine Herrschaft aus und ein Verführen,
> Er macht die leere Luft beengend kreisen
> Und er kann töten, ohne zu berühren.[91]

> [His eye enthralls and his aspect is strange.
> From his words, so seemingly soft,
> Emanates a domination and a seduction,
> He makes the empty air circulate threateningly
> And he can kill without touching.]

George's figure of the chosen or elected one ('Der Erkorene' v, 48) is neither the disciple nor the master, but a figure who idealizes both in one: he is chosen by and anointed to a higher force to which he remains responsible. It is not difficult to see in this figure, anointed at birth and favoured in life, the 'golden boy' of the homosexual imagination: the 'boy next door' who seems to have everything in addition to normality.[92] The chosen one lives the inner and the outer worlds at once, enjoying both as his birthright without conflict or contradiction. This figure allows himself to be chosen and accepts the leadership of the circle. Embodying all the attributes of heterosexual masculininity but at the same time acknowledging the higher power that made him a homosexual, he is the wish-fulfilment image of the socially isolated, self-hating homosexual of his time. In contrast to this figure, the abject character fails to rise to the existential challenge of being both a homosexual and a member of a self-affirming society. Since the first meeting with Hofmannsthal, it seems evident that George was seeking such a character in figures such as Friedrich Gundolf and Maximilian Kronberger, before settling for one who could not disappoint him: the idealized and projected figure of Maximin.

The following poems of *Der Teppich des Lebens* provide a commentary on the ideal of life in the circle of loving members. In 'Das Kloster' ('Monastery') the communal life of men is evoked in which each is linked to the other in love, not lust:

> Umschlungen ohne lechzende begierde
> Gefreundet ohne bangenden verdruss
> So flieht im abend schluchzen wort und kuss ..
> Und solches ist der frommen paare zierde:
> Von ebnem leid von ebner lust verzehrt
> Zur blauen schönheit ihren blick zu richten
> Geweihtes streben göttlichstes verzichten —
> Wie einst ein mönch aus Fiesole gelehrt. (v, 51)

> [They clasp but do not crave. They are united
> As friends who never fret and never fear,
> The evening drains a word, a kiss, a tear,
> And this the faith to which the pairs are plighted:
> To keep delight and grief alike restrained,
> To lift their glances up to azure beauty,
> Divine renouncing, consecrated duty
> As once a monk of Fiesole ordained.] (Morwitz 137)

That sublimated sexual love is in question here, is scarcely veiled by the monastic setting or the reference to early Renaissance painter, Fra Angelico, the Dominican monk of Fiesole, and is suggested by the pairing of figures in the community.[93] More important than physical sex is the companionship that binds in suppressed and shared longing and the release from fear, frustration and cynicism in the wider world. Is this an alternative for the homosexual life — now, in Germany at the end of the nineteenth century, as it had been in the Tuscany of Fra Angelico? The evocative images of peaceful community in this poem provide a balance to the more unsettling imagery of fealty, submission and warrior love-death discussed above.

The opening poems of the final section, *Lieder von Traum und Tod* combine George's profound feeling for German folk poetry in landscape and nature with intimacy in the personal address to figures from the poet's immediate circle of friends (including Sabine and Reinhold Lepsius, Albert and Kitty Verwey, Cyril Meir Scott, Carl August Klein, Richard Perls and others). These poems to individuals have nothing of the imperious charismatic prophet, whether we consider the undertones of love and attraction to Cyril Meir Scott, 'Ein knabe der mir von herbst und abend sang' ('A boy who sang to me of autumn and evening', v, 64–66), despite his avowed revulsion at homosexual relations,[94] or the final farewell to Richard Perls in 'Fahrt-Ende' ('Journey's End', v, 73). Against the rejection of the aesthetics of decadence in 'Den Brüdern' ('To the Brothers', v, 71) in favour of the 'more insistent call' of stronger, vitalistic forces, the poet weighs up the pressure to conform and disappear into the crowd in 'Lachende Herzen' ('Laughing Hearts'):

> Die ihr mich schlinget in euren geselligen reigen
> Nimmer es wisst wie nur meine verkleidung euch ähnelt
> Spielende herzen die ihr als freund mich umfanget:
> Wie seid ihr ferne von meinem pochenden herzen! (v, 77)

> [You who entwine me in turns of gregarious dances,
> Never aware that my mask is what renders me like you,
> Hearts full of frolic, you who in friendship embrace me,
> Oh, how remote from you all is my heart and its pulsing!]
> (Morwitz 150)

Yet the final poems of 'Tag-Gesang' and 'Nacht-Gesang' reveal the love which drives the poet's beating heart:

> Du ergingst dich in strahlen
> Bekränzt und erlaucht
> Hast dein schimmerndes haar
> Dann in blüten getaucht. (v, 79)

> [You were circled with glory,
> And wreathed, and sublime,
> Then you dipped your glossy locks
> Into blossoms of lilac and thyme.] (*Morwitz 151)

George provided a spiritual biography in which homosexual men could recognize both the possibilities of a life of personal and community identity while confronting the difficulties of life at this time. He confronts the melancholy of the lonely, sexually isolated individual, seeking comfort in the appearance of normality and reliving the relapses into sexual insecurity and depression:

> So ring ich bis ans end allein? so weil ich
> Niemals versenkt im arm der treue? sprich!
> 'Du machst dass ich vor mitleid zittre · freilich
> Ist keiner der dir bleibt · nur du und ich' (v, 31)

> [So to the end I must contend alone
> And never rest in faithful arms? Reply!
> 'You stir me to compassion, for no one
> Indeed remains with you — save you and I'.] (Morwitz 128)

The angel of his image of self and ego-ideal remains even when the hope for community fades. It is the poems that have created the *wir* of the collection:

> Uns die durch viele jahre zum triumfe
> Des grossen lebens unsre lieder schufen (v, 33)

[We who through many years composed and spoke
Our odes in praise of magic life, [...]] (Morwitz 129)

This human and intimate appeal remains a powerful antidote to the charismatic-prophetic current which emerges in *Der Teppich des Lebens* and will dominate the following two volumes, *Der siebente Ring* and *Der Stern des Bundes*.

So far we have followed George's lyric-existential trajectory from earliest stirrings of homosexual attraction, through withdrawal into aestheticist *Verinnerlichung* (internalization) in *Algabal* and imaginative self-liberation in the *Bücher*. The opening of the *Bücher* suggested the arrival at a new stage of self-discovery in which the imaginative journey inwards is at the same time an exploration outwards as the homosexual imagination begins to populate its world. *Das Jahr der Seele* began with the combination of scepticism towards, and acceptance of, the received world. The park at the beginning is 'said to be dead' ('totgesagt') but the poet himself finds beauty in the fading year as autumn moves to winter. In this volume the inner world of vicarious sensuality confronts reality and discovers unexpected possibilities, even promises of self-fulfilment, in an increasingly open engagement with homosexuality as a defining characteristic of his life and writing. *Der Teppich des Lebens* weaves the threads of homosexual self-understanding into the fabric of life in all their colours and textures. The poems of this collection overcome the limitations of the lyric self to create a sense of 'we' that is more than just the awareness of the existence of others. The lyric experience of the *wir-Gefühl* in these poems lifts them beyond the romantic solipsism of the *Bücher der hängenden Gärten*, which expressed longing for a sense of closeness to an other but was unable to achieve it. The body not the soul initiates intimacy. In *Der Teppich des Lebens* George discovered his voice as emergent leader of a group of young men in which an inchoate new sense of male–male love was expressing itself as physical attraction, affection, fealty and submission, leadership and domination. In the process he began to play out a narcissistic fantasy as charismatic prophet and at the same time to reveal the ego-weaknesses of a homosexual man of this time working towards self-understanding.

Notes to Chapter 2

1. Kaspar, 'Die Fibel', in Egyptien, *Stefan George — Werkkommentar*, p. 5.
2. Morwitz does not include *Die Fibel* in his translation. Translations from this volume are by the author unless otherwise noted.
3. Norton, *Secret Germany*, p. 64; Karlauf, *Stefan George*, pp. 61–62.
4. See Kaspar, 'Die Fibel', in Egyptien, *Stefan George — Werkkommentar*, p. 13.
5. Karlauf, cited ibid., p. 9.
6. Voß, 'Überschriften und Widmungen', in Egyptien, *Stefan George — Werkkommentar*, p. 217, notes the intertextual references to Eichendorff, Hoffmann, Novalis and the *Nachtwachen des Bonaventura* in the 'Überschriften und Widmungen' section of *Das Jahr der Seele*.
7. Karlauf, cited by Kaspar, 'Die Fibel', in Egyptien, *Stefan George — Werkkommentar*, pp. 9, 13.
8. Ibid., p. 17.
9. Merklin, 'Hymnen', in Egyptien, *Stefan George — Werkkommentar*, p. 23
10. 'George ist nun sicher, das Neue gefunden zu haben, die "umwälzung" ist gelungen und ein neues Selbstbewußtsein spricht aus den Briefen an die alten Freunde' [George is now certain that

he has found something new, the "revolution" has succeeded and a new self-confidence speaks from the letters to the old friends] (Editors' note, *SW*, I, 88).

11. Merklin, 'Hymnen' in Egyptien, *Stefan George — Werkkommentar*, p. 35.

12. Keilson-Lauritz, cited in Merklin, 'Hymnen', in Egyptien, *Stefan George — Werkkommentar*, p. 34, fn. 54.

13. Pirro, 'Pilgerfahrten', in Egyptien, *Stefan George — Werkkommentar*, p. 57.

14. Ibid., p. 51.

15. Pirro, 'Pilgerfahrten', in Egyptien, *Stefan George — Werkkommentar*, p. 48, citing an essay from 1920 by Carl Rouge.

16. Pirro, 'Pilgerfahrten', in Egyptien, *Stefan George — Werkkommentar*, p. 49.

17. 'On one level the central figure seeks deeper understanding of himself and his calling, and to this end sometimes needs a companion or a lover; on another level, the companion-figures, usually women, represent seductive distractions from or corruptions of his poetic mission or spiritual journey'. Pirro, 'Pilgerfahrten', in Egyptien, *Stefan George — Werkkommentar*, p. 51, citing Vilain, 'Stefan George's Early Works', p. 56.

18. See Egyptien, *Stefan George: Dichter und Prophet*, pp. 45, 72; Oswald, 'Oscar Wilde, Stefan George, Heliogabalus'; Oswald, 'The Historical Content of Stefan George's *Algabal*'.

19. Rasch, *Die literarische Décadence*, p. 174.

20. Ibid., pp. 175, 178.

21. Schneider, 'Das Buch der Hirten- und Preisgedichte', in Egyptien, *Stefan George — Werkkommentar*, p. 97.

22. Zanucchi, 'Algabal', in Egyptien, *Stefan George — Werkkommentar*, p. 85.

23. Kolk, *Literarische Gruppenbildung*, pp. 29–30.

24. David, *Stefan George: Sein Dichterisches Werk,* p. 95, cited in Rasch, *Die literarische Décadence*, p. 177; Kolk, *Literarische Gruppenbildung*, p. 30.

25. Heftrich, *Stefan George*, p. 43.

26. Landfried, *Stefan George*, pp. 56–57.

27. Freud developed his theories of narcissism from around the time of the *Drei Abhandlungen zur Sexualtheorie* (1905) onwards. The essay *Zur Einführung des Narzißmus* appeared in 1914. See Laplanche and Pontalis, *Das Vokabular der Psychoanalyse*, pp. 317–24.

28. 'It would take the normalization of self-love under the rubric of healthy narcissism and its ally self-esteem — the transformation of love of self from impediment to love of the other to the very condition of the same — to unsettle this truism' (Lunbeck, 'The Narcissistic Homosexual', p. 63).

29. See ibid.

30. The original reference is to Ælius Lampridus' biography of Heliogabalus in the *Historia Augustus*, see Editors' notes to 'Becher am boden', *SW*, II, 123–24; and Zanucchi, 'Algabal', in Egyptien, *Stefan George — Werkkommentar*, p. 71.

31. Zanucchi, 'Algabal', in Egyptien, *Stefan George — Werkkommentar*, p. 91.

32. The emperor Heliogabalus reputedly staged a banquet at the end of which his guests were suffocated by the overpowering perfume of masses of rose-petals raining down on them. The episode is represented in Lawrence Alma-Tadema's painting of 1888, 'The Roses of Heliogabalus' (Collection Juan Antonio Pérez Simón, Mexico). In 'Becher am boden', the emperor has masses of fragrant petals rain down over his banqueting guests, smothering them with 'Manen-küsse | Euch zu segnen'. See Oswald, 'Historical Content', pp. 204–05. French novelist Emile Zola would use this motif in his 1875 novel, *La Faute de l'abbé Mouret*. Zola, George and later Ebermayer are likely to have been familiar with this story from the 'Life of Elagabalus' in the late Roman collection of biographies, *Historia Augusta*.

33. Letter to Hofmannsthal, 10 January 1892, cited in Schneider, 'Das Buch der Hirten- und Preisgedichte', in Egyptien, *Stefan George — Werkkommentar*, p. 97.

34. Schneider, 'Das Buch der Hirten- und Preisgedichte', in Egyptien, *Stefan George — Werkkommentar*, p. 102.

35. For a most recent example, see Schloon, 'Das Buch der Sagen und Sänge', in Egyptien, *Stefan George — Werkkommentar*, p. 124; Höpker-Herberg, 'Ida Coblenz', in Oelmann and Raulff, *Frauen um Stefan George*, pp. 84–102; Viering, 'Nicht aus Eitelkeit', pp. 203–39.

36. The most detailed and reliable account of this relationship is to be found in Karlauf, *Stefan George*, pp. 124–44.
37. Schneider clarifies the identities of these figures: Antinous is Edmond Rassenfosse, who had hosted George in Tilff and whom George met again in Brussels in March 1894. According to Morwitz, Isokrates was Ludwig Klages, whom George had met in July 1893. George was struck by Klages's youthful energy and passion, but distanced himself from the person, as the final lines of the poem suggest. Schneider, 'Das Buch der Hirten- und Preisgedichte', in Egyptien, *Stefan George — Werkkommentar*, pp. 110–12.
38. Rieckmann, *Hofmannsthal und George*, p. 133.
39. 'Überglüht von dem Willen, seine Brüder zu erlösen. Aber zuvor muß er selbst erlöst werden [...]') Hans Dietrich [Hans Dietrich Hellbach], *Die Freundesliebe in der deutschen Literatur*, p. 150.
40. Hans Dietrich [Hans Dietrich Hellbach], *Die Freundesliebe in der deutschen Literatur*, p. 151. Keilson-Lauritz identifies this social and ethical dimension to George's early work, *Kentaurenliebe*, p. 60.
41. Gundolf and Wolters, *Jahrbuch*, p. 5.
42. Alexander von Gleichen-Rußwurm's study, *Die Freundschaft,* published in 1911 represents a codification of this indirect terminology of sexual interest.
43. Gundolf and Wolters, *Jahrbuch*, p. 7.
44. Ibid., pp. 6–7.
45. Karlauf, *Stefan George*, pp. 81–82.
46. George–Hofmannsthal, *Briefwechsel*, p. 13.
47. Hofmannsthal to George, in George–Hofmannsthal *Briefwechsel*, p. 14.
48. Ibid.
49. George–Hofmannsthal, *Briefwechsel*, pp. 15–16; Dürhammer, *Geheime Botschaften*, p. 126.
50. George–Hofmannsthal, *Briefwechsel*, pp. 38–40.
51. Goldsmith, *Stefan George*, p. 33.
52. George–Hofmannsthal, *Briefwechsel*, pp. 80–81.
53. Editors' note, *SW*, II, 110.
54. George–Hofmannsthal, *Briefwechsel*, pp. 116–18.
55. Ibid., p. 166.
56. Ibid., p. 169.
57. George and Hofmannsthal corresponded sporadically from December 1891 until March 1906. On the relationship, see Karlauf, *Stefan George*, pp. 9–27, 196–205 and passim, and Egyptien, *Stefan George*, pp. 80–89, 105–09, 121–27, 140–45, 232–42 and passim.
58. See Dürhammer, *Geheime Botschaften*, p. 131.
59. See Karlauf, *Stefan George*, pp. 137–38 and Norton, *Secret Germany*, pp. 139–40.
60. Karlauf, *Stefan George*, p. 207.
61. Zanucchi, 'Algabal' in Egyptien, *Stefan George — Werkkommentar*, p. 184.
62. Rieckmann, *Companion to the Works of Stefan George*, p. 10.
63. Keats's term identified the poet's willingness to recognize truths beyond the reach of reason, logic or even hitherto accepted language and vocabulary, as opposed to the philosopher's requirement for linguistic and conceptual clarity.
64. In Hofmannsthal's 'Über Gedichte' two connoisseurs of art, Gabriel und Clemens, discuss poems by Goethe, Hebbel and George. The essay appeared in *Der Neue Rundschau* in February 1904.

> GABRIEL.   Er vollbrachte eine symbolische Handlung. Er starb in dem Tiere, Clemens, weil er sich einen Augenblick lang in dies fremde Dasein aufgelöst hatte, weil einen Augenblick lang wirklich sein Blut aus der Kehle des Tieres gequollen war.

> GABRIEL.   He carried out a symbolic act. He died in the animal, Clemens, because he dissolved himself for a moment into the being of this foreign existence. For a moment it was his blood that was pouring out of the animal's throat.

65. Cf. Kealy and others, 'Pathological Narcissism and Maladaptive Self-Regulatory Behaviours', p. 156; cf. also Pincus and Lukowitsky, 'Pathological Narcissism and Narcissistic Personality Disorder'; Ronningstam, 'Narcissistic Personality Disorder'; Gabbard and Crisp-Han, 'Many Faces of Narcissism'.

66. See for example, Zanucchi, 'Algabal', in Egyptien, *Stefan George — Werkkommentar*, pp. 183–84. Egyptien follows Faletti and earlier commentators in assuming that the addressee of 'Komm in den totgesagten park' is female. However, there is no sexual identification in this text and the assumption is made on the basis of biographical associations with Ida Coblenz. Egyptien, 'Herbst der Liebe', in Egyptien, *Stefan George — Werkkommentar*, p. 24.

67. See Editors' note, *SW*, IV, 141.

68. On the interpretation of this figure, see Goldsmith, *Stefan George*, pp. 117–18.

69. Hans Blüher, historian of the *Wandervogel* movement developed an influential philosophy of masculinism based on homosocial urges.

70. See Fleming, 'The Secret Adorno', p. 98.

71. Adorno, *Noten zur Literatur*, p. 531.

72. George's influence persisted long after his death among specific groups. *Castrum Peregrini*, the foundation created by his followers, Wolfgang Frommel and Gisèle van Waterschoot van der Gracht, had its origins in the war years as a place of refuge and was made a foundation in the fifties. However in 2018, in the wake of years of rumour and formal journalistic investigations, insalubrious aspects of the *Castrum Peregrini* were revealed, and the link with George formally broken.

73. Kauffmann, *Stefan George*, p. 99.

74. See Editors' note, *SW*, v, 94.

75. See Lehnen, 'Vorspiel', in Egyptien, *Stefan George — Werkkommentar*, pp. 257–58; Aurnhammer, *Stefan George und sein Kreis*, p. 758.

76. See Editors' note, *SW*, v, 106.

77. Editors' note, *SW*, v, 106.

78. *Blätter für die Kunst*, Vierte Folge. Erstes und Zweites Heft. 1897, in Stefan-George-Stiftung, ed., *Einleitungen und Merksprüche der Blätter für die Kunst*, p. 23.

79. See Landfester, 'Werner Jaegers Konzepte von Wissenschaft und Bildung', p. 17; Mattenklott, 'Die Griechen sind zu gut zum schnuppern', pp. 244–48; Oestersandfort, 'Platonisches im *Teppich des Lebens*'; Rebenich, 'Dass ein strahl von Hellas auf uns fiel'.

80. The German expression 'vom anderen Ufer' meaning 'homosexual' is identifiable only as far back as 1935 (in Küpper's etymological dictionary). However, it seems possible that it was Hofmannsthal himself who coined the expression in referring obliquely to George's advances to him in a letter to Hermann Bahr in 1892. After the meeting, Hofmannsthal had expressed in a poem his own suppressed homosexual feelings: 'Du hast mich an Dinge gemahnt | Die heimlich in mir sind, | Du warst für die Saiten der Seele | Der nächtige, flüsternde Wind' (You reminded me of things | that are secret in me, | You were for the strings of my soul | The nocturnal, whispering wind). In a further letter to Bahr he referred to the episode with George as 'ein symbolistisches Experiment vom anderen Ufer' (a symbolist experiment from the other bank), and explains that he had approached Bahr because he felt the latter would understand without too much explicit detail. 'Ich habe Sie in der ersten Verlegenheit um Hilfe rufen wollen, weil Sie der einzige sind, dem gegenüber ich mir die lange Vorexplication erspart hätte' (I wanted to call you for help at first, because you are the only one with whom I would have spared myself the long preliminary account). He was, he writes, 'weniger beunruhigt als peinlich berührt; und hoffe Sonntag schon den letzten Bericht "vom anderen Ufer" über dieses symbolistische Experiment erhalten zu können' (less alarmed than embarrassed; and I hope on Sunday to be able to get the last report "from the other side" about this symbolist experiment). Whether George became familiar with the term, or the term had already gained a currency in spoken German at this time, or Hofmannsthal was picking up on George's own imagery of 'the opposite shore', or the usage is simply fortuitous, seems unclear. However, this interchange in written letters seems to clearly pinpoint the origin of the expression. See the online Redensarten-Index, <https://www.redensarten-index.de/suche.php? Suchbegriff=~~vom%20 anderen%20Ufer%20sein&bool=relevanz&gawoe=an&spo=rart_ou&spi=rart_varianten_ou> [accessed 14 March 2020].

81. Adorno, *Noten zur Literatur*, p. 531: 'Georges Verfall zur krampfhaft nationellen Positivität rühre daher, daß er den Trieb zum anderen Geschlecht, und damit zum Anderen schlechthin, in

sich unterdrückte und endogamisch bei dem sich beschied, was ihm so glich wie die Stimme des unseligen Engels aus dem Vorspiel.' See Lehnen, 'Vorspiel', in Egyptien, *Stefan George — Werkkommentar*, p. 257; Fleming, 'The Secret Adorno', p. 101.

82. Adorno, *Notes to Literature*, p. 445.
83. Fleming, 'The Secret Adorno', p. 101.
84. Rieckmann, *Hofmannsthal und George*, p. 46.
85. Ibid., p. 192.
86. Ibid., p. 89.
87. George–Hofmannsthal, *Briefwechsel*, pp. 166–67.
88. See Karlauf, *Stefan George*, pp. 109–12. George, no doubt, used and manipulated those around him — such as Klein — but in this, his ideal-typical *vita*, the recognition of the role of community remains.
89. In, for example, the language of youth, national renewal and 'breakthrough' in the Winfried episode in Thomas Mann's *Dr. Faustus*, set at around the end of the first decade of the century.
90. See Fricker, *Stefan George*, pp. 311–18 for the most detailed, nuanced and sympathetic reading of George's relationship to Nazism among recent commentators. Fricker admits that George did not explicitly reject Nazism, but points out that the refusal to limit the breadth of his imagery and themes represented an indirect rejection. Fricker also notes the extent to which pro-Nazi friends and disciples of George represented the poet after his death. Against figures such as Hildebrandt, however, Ernst Kantorowicz rejected any relationship between George's late poetry and the advent of Nazism (ibid., p. 315).
91. Von Hofmannsthal, *Gesammelte Werke*, I, 124.
92. See Karlauf, *Stefan George*, p. 265.
93. George refers to Fra Angelico, 'der mönch aus Fiesole', in an earlier poem from the *Hymnen*, 'Ein Angelico' (II, 27), as well as in a 1997 letter to Verwey. See Editorial note, V, 114.
94. See Karlauf, *Stefan George*, pp. 261–66.

CHAPTER 3

Damaged Narcissus

The three final volumes of George's poetic life, *Der siebente Ring*, *Der Stern des Bundes* and *Das Neue Reich*, dramatically deepen the engagement with themes of homosexual identity, existential self-doubt and self-discovery explored in the first half of his lyric *vita*, and take us into the controversial territory of narcissistic self-aggrandisement, charismatic leadership and formation of the Bund. In *Der siebente Ring* a homosexual life in the first decade of the German twentieth century moves between lyric self-exploration and discovery and evocation of a sense of 'us'. The poems explore and describe possibilities for a life as a homosexual man needing, seeking and finding the company of other men. *Der Stern des Bundes* offers a redemptive vision of homosexual community through the poetic image of Maximin. In this phase, George's mythology of 'secret Germany' and of the Bund expresses an aspect of the poet's own charismatic narcissism, splitting and projecting the ideal self into powerful poetic images. George will become increasingly preoccupied with the emergent community of the Bund and with his role as prophet and master, a role that reflected charismatic leadership pretensions even as it expressed the wish to create a viable, supportive community of men. With these volumes George deepens his exploration of those themes which associate him with German anti-modernism. These poems contain elements that are deeply questionable in any reading: the mixture of insecurity, grandiosity, charismatic wisdom and the will to power have rendered them precursors of European fascism for many commentators. Without denying these qualities, I argue that while George remained tied to many of the behaviours that he developed in relation to the group of younger men around him until late in his life, the poems themselves tell a different, more complex story. The rest of this analysis is concerned with that story, for in the case of George and his circle over the following decade, life and literature diverge in important ways.

Coming to Terms with the Self: *Der siebente Ring*

Most of the poems in *Der siebente Ring* were written between 1897 and 1904. The volume consists of seven sections, the first two of which, 'Zeitgedichte' and 'Gestalten', build on the socially oriented visionary-prophetic themes we have identified in parts of *Der Teppich des Lebens*. However with the third section, 'Gezeiten', a different note is struck, and even the central section, 'Maximin', focusing on the self-object of George's homosexual-narcissistic fantasy, does not exalt the dead Maximilian to the extent that many commentators suggest. Far from revealing the poet in a state of narcissistic hero-worship based on doctrines of 'aesthetic fundamentalism' and charistmatic leadership, the following sections, 'Traumdunkel' and the 'Lieder', enable a poetic voice whose language of sensibility, nuance, love and passion has reached new levels of maturity. The poems of these sections express fundamental human modes of being and feeling in language that supersedes the personal and individual in its communicative power. In the final section, 'Lieder', short poems, for the most part quatrains, are addressed to figures of George's present and past with intimacy and intensity but little of the animus of earlier poems of this genre.

In the first section of *Der siebente Ring* George adapts the particularly German form of the *Zeitgedicht*, used predominantly by left-wing poets of the nineteenth century such as Heine, Herwegh and Freiligrath to engage with aspects of contemporary society, culture and politics.[1] Böschenstein sees the vehement, critical tone of George's 'Zeitgedichte' as a response to a world in decline. In the opening poem 'Das Zeitgedicht' ('A Poem of my Times'), George aggressively distances himself from his earlier image as aesthete in order to evoke a new generation of warrior-followers:[2]

> Nun da schon einige arkadisch säuseln
> Und schmächtig prunken: greift er die fanfare ·
> Verletzt das morsche fleisch mit seinen sporen
> Und schmetternd führt er wieder ins gedräng. (VI/VII, 6)

> [Now that some few attempt Arcadian murmurs
> And vapid flourishes, he grips the trumpet,
> His spurs torment the flesh that sagged and rotted,
> He clashes on again and heads the charge.] (Morwitz 156)

The poet does not renounce his past: he places it into historical perspective, linking the dynamic of radical self-realization to the revalorization of homoerotic masculinity and the espousal of dramatic change:

> Ihr sehet wechsel · doch ich tat das gleiche. (VI/VII, 7)

> [You see a change, but I have done as always.] (Morwitz 156)

Böschenstein identifies this progression from the idealized image of Fra Angelico's peaceful monastic community of men in 'Das Kloster' to the militant masculinity in 'Hüter des Vorhofs' in *Der siebente Ring*. The redemption of masculinity takes place under authoritarian leadership of an aesthetic-pagan order.[3] This and later poems such as 'Templer' present visions of armed, idealized medieval-feudal *Männerbünde* built on suppressed homoerotic community:

> Wir folgen nicht den sitten und den spielen
> Der anderen die voll argwohn nach uns schielen
> Und grauen wenn ihr hass nicht übermannt
> Was unser wilder sturm der liebe bannt. (VI/VII, 52)

[We do not join the customs and the games
Of those who look askance at us, with suspicion in their eyes,
And terror when their hatred did not overpower
That which with our savage love we caught and held.] (*Morwitz 177)

The relations of lord and liegeman are underpinned by tones of sexual dominance
and submission. Homosexual love and passion masquerade as male bonding and
feudal loyalty in elaborate rituals of belonging and community drawing on the
Männerbünde of past eras. The new nation is a cipher for a homosexual social
structure or *wir-Gefühl*, fusing the revived Germany of right-wing fantasy with
homoerotic community. The result is in line with many of the homosexual fantasies
of the *Männerbund* that would come about after the war. George was a forerunner
in this type of mythopoesis of the resurgent nation as a noxious homosexual fantasy
in which suppressed passion drew on nationalism and misogyny.

In the guise of Dante, soldier-poet in the battle between the Reich and the city
state and lyric voice of the *Vita Nuova*, George discovers a man dishonoured by false
leaders and political defeat, but radicalized by his new self-recognition:

Ich wuchs zum mann und mich ergriff die schmach
Von stadt und reich verheert durch falsche führer (vi/vii, 8)

[Then I became a man who burned with shame
That false leaders had sacked the realm, the city.] (*Morwitz 157)

In poems to German artistic and philosophical figures Goethe (to his 150th
birthday), Nietzsche and Böcklin he finds the protectors of the holy flame 'in kalter
zeit' (vi/vii, 15, 'in a cold time'), precursors of his own role as creative renewers of a
dead present. In these evocations of lord and liege in an ideal past, the homosexual
link remains powerful, in 'Der Minner' ('The Lover', vi/vii, 41), for example,
ending on a powerful statement of subaltern love. Or in 'Manuel und Menes' (vi/
vii, 42) where war is evoked as an alibi of love in the manner of the Theban Band
or other fantasies of homosexual warrior pairs in a powerful projection of idealized
male community with religious underpinnings:

Mein ganzes blut im abend hingeströmt
Für euch Geliebte — o all ihr Geliebten! (vi/vii, 41)

[I streamed my body's blood into the dusk
For you, beloved, O all of you beloved!] (Morwitz 172)

In these poems of the first two sections, 'Zeitgedichte' and 'Gestalten', the *Männerbund* prevails as an expression of ongoing allegiance to past fantasies of homosexual
passion and social validation. However, it is not the poems of homoerotic
subservience that are of primary interest in this collection. It is the poems of the
following sections from 'Gezeiten' ('Tides') onwards that paint a much gentler
picture of George and his passions. The opening poem of the third section,
'Gezeiten', introduces a strikingly different voice and tone. It may have been
inspired by Friedrich Gundolf, but the biographical detail is unimportant. It is a
love poem written by an older man for a younger one and expressing self-doubt as
well as passion before allowing desire to overtake reality:

Wenn dich meine wünsche umschwärmen
Mein leidender hauch dich umschwimmt —
Ein tasten und hungern und härmen:
So scheint es im tag der verglimmt
Als dränge ein rauher umschlinger
Den jugendlich biegsamen baum ·
Als glitten erkaltete finger
Auf wangen von sonnigem flaum.
[...]
Mich hoben die träume und mären
So hoch dass die schwere mir wich —
Dir brachten die träume die zähren
Um andre um dich und um mich ...
Nun wird diese seele dir lieber
Die bleiche von duldungen wund ·
Nun löscht sein verzehrendes fieber
Mein mund in dem blühenden mund. (vi/vii, 67)

[When touched by the breath of my anguish
You float in the swirl of my dreams,
I fumble, and famish, and languish.
When day slowly darkens, it seems
As if a harsh lover were pressing
The supple young tree in embrace,
Or fingers grown cooler, caressing
A downy and luminous face.
[...]
From figment and fancy I bounded
So high that the earth left me free,
But yours was a sorrow you sounded
For others, for you, and for me.
And now you have learned to desire
This soul in its pallor and drouth,
My mouth with its fervour and fire
Is quenched in the bloom of your mouth.] (Morwitz 183)

Similarly in 'Stern der dies jahr mir regiere!' ('Star that shall govern this year!, vi/vii, 69) the lyric voice expresses gentleness and caution, showing nothing of the dominant-subservient relations or aggression of earlier masculinist poems:

Lag doch in jenen schenkenden nächten
Deine wange schon auf meinen knieen
Wenn sich die zitternden melodieen
Rangen empor aus dumpf hallenden schächten!
Folgtest dem spiel von sich streitenden mächten:
Meiner geschicke vergangene gnade
Und meine leiden am fernen gestade
Bis zu der frühwolken rosigem klären ..
Wie auf der schwester verschlungene mären
Lauschte die liebliche Doniazade. (vi/vii, 69)

[Prodigal nights when your forehead lay
Bowed on my knees, when faltering tones

> Breaking from dull subterranean zones,
> Fused into song. You followed the play
> Proffered by forces at feud and at bay:
> Grace I was granted at destiny's hands,
> Sorrow I suffered in far-away lands —
> Followed, while dawn-clouds deepened and glistened,
> Just as beautiful Dunyazad listened
> Long to her sister, twining her tales.] (Morwitz 184)

The voice of these and other poems in 'Gezeiten' is lyrical, personal and intimate in its expressions of homosexual desire, in comparison to the homoerotic masculinism of the 'Zeitgedichte' and 'Gestalten'. This lyrical voice suggests an individual capable of looking beyond the mirrored self-image, potentially a Narcissus healing or healed. What is striking and difficult to reconcile in the work of the late George is not the charismatic-prophetic aspect itself, but rather its co-existence with this lyric-personal aspect which seems so opposed to it. This complex persona co-exists in the two volumes of George's late writing, which surround the prophetic-visionary idealization of *Der Stern des Bundes*. Perhaps we can best explain this with reference to the times and to the particularities of homosexual identity, namely as the expressions of the tensions and conflicts in a homosexual man in the environment of sexual and generational crisis and social upheaval of German central Europe in the early years of the century.

In 'Der Spiegel' ('The Mirror', vi/vii, 75) the speaker sees himself liberated from the mirror which has framed and dominated his life hitherto. The mirroring pond of Narcissus, which reflects his life back to him after every excursion, now lacks the things that make those excursions beautiful, the flowers that feature so strongly in the early poetry. It is a 'shore where nothing blooms' in Morwitz's translation.[4] The beauty of the external world is not reflected back to the narcissistic persona and his narcissistic private world lacks colour and light. And when he brings his wishes, dreams and thoughts to this mirrored world, they seem pale and unfamiliar. This is the state of the homosexual imaginary at the turn of the century, a time when for George and other men the inner world carries nothing of the attraction and allure of the outer world. It is an imaginative-existential world that is at once pale and dark, filled with the bitterness and unhappiness of an unfulfilled existence, the world of the homosexual man who looks out onto a beautiful world but cannot translate it into his own imaginary. But he has become 'bedächtig' ('thoughtful'), aware of the discrepancies in his existence, and bitterness gives way to a sense of euphoria when he realizes that happiness might be within his grasp, even if it has not yet materialized:

> Zu eines wassers blumenlosem tiegel
> Muss ich nach jeder meiner fahrten wanken.
> Schon immer führte ich zu diesem spiegel
> All mein träume wünsche und gedanken
> Auf dass sie endlich sich darin erkennten —
> Sie aber sahen stets sich blass und nächtig:
> ‚Wir sind es nicht' so sprachen sie bedächtig
> Und weinten wenn sie sich vom spiegel trennten. (vi/vii, 75)

[I stumble on at every journey's end
Down to a shore where nothing blooms, and take
My thoughts, and dreams, and wishes there to bend
And gaze at their reflection in the lake,
So they may know themselves at last. But they
Discerned an image always dim and wan.
'Those are not we', they said in musing tone,
And then they wept and slowly went away.] (Morwitz 187)

The world is changing and he will grasp happiness like anyone else. He does so, and throws himself into the waves of passion and surrender to new existence without thought or reflection:

Auf einmal fühlt ich durch die bitternisse
Und alter schatten schmerzliches vermodern
Das glück in vollem glanze mich umschweben.
Mir däuchte dass sein arm mich trunknen wiegte ·
Dass ich den stern von seinem haupte risse
Und dann gelöst mich ihm zu füssen schmiegte.
Ich habe endlich ganz in wildem lodern
Emporgeglüht und ganz mich hingegeben. (VI/VII, 75)

[Bitter and surrounded by the painful shadows
Of the past, I felt happiness hovering around me
All at once in its full glory.
Inebriate within his arms I swayed,
I snatched the star which glittered on his head,
I leaned against his feet and was allayed.
At last and utterly, in savage flares
I flamed, and utter was my self-surrender.] (*Morwitz 187)

The final stanza contains the key to George's crisis of identity at this point, caught between a past in which life was unfulfilled and a future vision of self-gratification. However the confrontation between past and present selves, the former disbelieving, the latter euphoric, does not lead to resolution, but simply to denial and disbelief:

Ihr träume wünsche kommt jetzt froh zum teiche!
Wie ihr euch tief hinab zum spiegel bücket!
Ihr glaubt nicht dass das bild euch endlich gleiche?
Ist er vielleicht gefurcht von welker pflanze ·
Gestört von späten jahres wolkentanze?
Wie ihr euch ängstlich aneinander drücket!
Ihr weint nicht mehr doch sagt ihr trüb und schlicht
Wie sonst: ,wir sind es nicht! Wir sind es nicht!' (VI/VII, 75)

[Come blithely to the lake, my dream, my thought!
How low above the mirror you are bowed.
You still have doubts? Is not your likeness caught?
Perhaps the dancing clouds of autumn move
The glass, or withered tendrils draw a groove?
How anxious one against the next you crowd!
You do not weep, but as at every close
You sigh: 'Those are not we-we are not those!'] (Morwitz 188)

The lyric persona remains caught between two modes of existence: joyless disavowal or denial ('wir sind es nicht') and narcissistic self-gratification. Neither can be resumed into the other, and hence while the persona experiences vicarious passion, he does not find self-knowledge in experience. The antitheses are clear as an unresolved 'either/or' in the sense of immediate sensuous experience (the flowers of external reality) versus critical self-reflection. Each is powerful but pulls in the opposite direction to the other: unrestrained hedonism and existential self-doubt and denial. As neither can yield that which is essential, the lyric persona remains caught in a state of stasis. Self-confirmation comes only through narcissistic identification, which denies and disavows everything other than the self.

The poems of 'Gezeiten' explore feelings and emotions of love, friendship, emotional uncertainty and change, with the exception of the last, 'Lobgesang' ('Song of Praise') which moves in a different direction, addressing a divine figure part Eros, part Dionysus:[5]

> Du bist mein herr! Wenn du auf meinem weg ·
> Viel-wechselnder gestalt doch gleich erkennbar
> Und schön · erscheinst beug ich vor dir den nacken.
> Du trägst nicht waffe mehr noch kleid noch fittich
> Nur Einen schmuck: ums haar den dichten kranz. (VI/VII, 87)

> [You are my lord! When on my path you loom
> In many changing shapes and yet familiar
> And beautiful, I bend my neck before you.
> Now you bear no arms nor garments nor wings,
> All that adorns you is the one clustered wreath
> Around your hair.] (*Morwitz 193)

Like Goethe's Ganymede, George's lyric persona is overwhelmed by the sexual passion of being taken rather than taking, and hence, also as in Goethe's poem, breaking all conventional expectations of heterosexual love-poetry in a male persona or voice. For the lyric persona this figure was gentle, but now is a more visceral figure, associated with nature, intoxication, wild animals and pain:

> Der früher nur den Sänftiger dich hiess
> Gedachte nicht dass eine rosige ferse
> Dein schlanker finger so zermalmen könne.
> Ich werfe duldend meinen leib zurück
> Auch wenn du kommst mit deiner schar von tieren
> Die mit den scharfen klauen mäler brennen
> Mit ihren hauern wunden reissen · seufzer
> Erpressend und unnennbares gestöhn. (VI/VII, 87)

> [He who in the past called you the assuager,
> Had never imagined that your slender finger,
> Your rosy heel could deal such destruction.
> I fling my body back uncomplaining,
> Even when you come with your pack of beasts
> That brand their mark with sharp talons
> And tear open wounds with their fangs, bringing forth from me
> Sighs and unnameable laments.] (*Morwitz 193)

Keilson-Lauritz has pointed to the physicality of the lines, highlighting George's expression, 'Du reinigst die befleckung' ('you cleanse the taint') to imply a sense of redemption of the act of homosexual contact from associations with unclean physicality:[6]

> Kein ding das webt in deinem kreis ist schnöd.
> Du reinigst die befleckung · heilst die risse
> Und wischst die tränen durch dein süsses wehn. (VI/VII, 87)

> [Nothing that weaves in your circle is filthy.
> You cleanse the taint, you heal the gash, and banish
> The trace of tears with your sweet breath.] (*Morwitz 193)

This god cleans and heals, redeeming the homosexual act from the associations of dirt, uncleanliness, contamination and pollution that accompanied it in conventional heterosexual discourse at the time. It is George's most concrete expression of the physical and earthy power of eros, moving beyond even the intimations of physical fulfilment in his earlier works, let alone the spiritualized platonism of earlier poets.

Survival is not certain, but each day brings its own victory, and homage is the smile of the lover:

> In fahr und fron · wenn wir nur überdauern·
> Hat jeder tag mit einem sieg sein ende —
> So auch dein dienst: erneute huldigung
> Vergessnes lächeln ins gestirnte blau. (VI/VII, 87)

> [In threat or thrall, if only we are steadfast,
> Each day shall end in triumph as our service
> To you: the homage renewed,
> A smile surrendered to the starlit blue.] (*Morwitz 193)

The starlit blue ('ins gestirnte blau') brings associations of the 'unverhofftes blau' ('unhoped for blue') of 'Komm in den totgesagten Park', the opening poem of *Das Jahr der Seele*, the collection that intimates the discovery of happiness and fulfilment in the 'totgesagter park' of end-of-the-century Germany. This is a poem about sex, nature and homosexual love.

In an influential reading of the kiss as symbol of the relationship of the self and the other in *Der siebente Ring*, Ernst Osterkamp writes that the lyric persona in 'Lobgesang' opens himself up to the kiss of a time-transcending higher being ('Überzeitlich-Höheren'). However the physicality of the image of the passive speaker throwing his body back in ecstasy to the earthy, passionate god of love does not suggest spiritualized love.[7] Osterkamp de-concretizes and de-sexualizes the imagery of 'Lobgesang'. Similarly, Tina Winzen in the recent major *Werkkommentar* edited by Jürgen Egyptien refers to this poem as an aestheticization of love, ignoring the physicality of the imagery.[8] In fact there is little idealization of love or of the later Maximin-myth in 'Lobgesang'.

Art versus Life: Maximin

George first noticed the thirteen-year-old Maximilian Kronberger in early 1902, saw him again a year later in January 1903, and cultivated his friendship over the following fifteen months. On 15 April 1904 Kronberger died suddenly of meningitis, causing George deep distress.[9] It would be a mistake to assume that this was simply another love-affair between an older man and an adolescent youth (George was in his early thirties and Maximilian had just turned sixteen when he died). The original traumatic emotional-homosexual event for George was not Kronberger, but Hofmannsthal, in whom the older poet hoped to have found a soul-mate. Like Hofmannsthal, Maximilian was handsome and precocious, already frequenting bookshops and literary salons and writing poetry at thirteen. During early 1903 George introduced Maximilian to the circle associated with the *Blätter für die Kunst*. At the same time he established good terms with Kronberger's parents, no doubt aware of their suspicions and remembering the near-disaster with Hofmannsthal a decade earlier. Despite his infatuation, George remained physically distant as well as imperious and demanding in his dealings with Maximilian. Where in the earlier case, the older poet appears to have approached the younger man with passion, in the case of Kronberger, he was careful to maintain his distance physically and to at least appear emotionally detached. The sudden death of Kronberger represented a second traumatic blow to George after the Hofmannsthal affair.

Kronberger's good looks and creative talents (his poetic efforts could be represented as the promise of genius given his age) rendered him a perfect simulacrum of the desired lover, foreshadowed in Hofmannsthal. His early death facilitated his apotheosis as Maximin in George's imagination.[10] In the following year George produced *Maximin: ein Gedenkbuch*, including his own prose 'Vorrede zu Maximin', and several poems that would be included in *Der siebente Ring*, poems by Wolfskehl, Gundolf, and other members of the circle, alongside the poems of Maximilian himself in a volume produced by Melchior Lechter and published in *Blätter für die Kunst* in 1907. In the 'Vorrede' ('Preface') and in *Der siebente Ring* (1907), the poet heralded a new form of collective consciousness, focused on Maximin and imagined in the Bund or covenant of disciples in *Der Stern des Bundes*.[11] Kronberger would exist henceforth in George's poetic mythology as Maximin, unassailed by reality.

Kronberger's death reinforced aspects of George's engagement with his sexuality and determined his psycho-emotional development for the next decade at least. This decade, from 1904 until 1914 was dominated by George's fixation on a transitional image of the self as object, a narcissistic image of himself as both lover and beloved, leader and follower in the divided, displaced and projected images of himself and Maximin. Maximin came to represent George's narcissistic self-identification, 'the point at which he desires to gratify himself in himself' in Lacan's words.[12] Many of the earlier interpretations of George, and some recent ones view George's idealization of Maximin in *Der Stern des Bundes* in terms of religious and cultic mission.[13] However, the progression in George's attachments and attractions from Hofmannsthal to Maximin, to Bernhard von Uxkull-Gyllenband, the inspiration

for the final poem of *Das Neue Reich*, killed in 1918, suggests a different structure
to George's autobiography and to his poetic life.[14]

Since Goethe's invention of what philosopher Wilhelm Dilthey would later
term 'Erlebnisdichtung' ('poetry of experience') German analysis has tended
to exaggerate the links between life and literature.[15] Analysis of George's work
has taken this biographical linkage to a new level. With such preparatory over-
interpretation predicated on George's life, it is little wonder that the short cycle of
poems that follows, 'Maximin', has become a prelude to the apotheosis of the real
Maximilian Kronberger. However closer reading of these poems does not support
such a reading. The 'Maximin' cycle in *Der siebente Ring* is a set of poems written
to the memory of a deceased young man, whom George idealized and fell in love
with — perhaps more in retrospect than during the reality of their brief and prickly
acquaintance over two years between 1902 and 1904. Like earlier poets inspired
by the death of the beloved, these poems use imagery of the eternal as a means of
remembering.

Maximin is not a figment of interpreters' imaginations. However at this point
he is not yet the deified image of the Bund. In *Der siebente Ring* he is still a beloved
memory of a real person. The opening poem, 'Kunfttag 1' ('Advent 1') does not
fulfil the expectations placed on the figure of Maximin by the above interpreters:

> Du an dem strahl mir kund
> Der durch mein dunkel floss ·
> Am tritte der die saat
> Sogleich erblühen liess. (VI/VII, 90)

> [I knew you by the beam
> Which flowed into my dark,
> The step to which the seed
> Replied with sudden bloom.] (Morwitz 194)

In the following 'Kunfttag II' the poet reveals the basis of his imagined love, namely
a lifetime of disappointment with the possibilities for love between men in the
Germany of his time. He looks back on a life of deception and betrayal:

> Als kind sein bild nicht fand ·
> Als jüngling sehnend brach ·
> Der heut die mitte tritt
> Ist satt noch zu vertraun. (VI/VII, 91)

> [The child who failed to find his image.
> The youth broken by longing.
> The one who today is past his middle years
> Has had enough with trusting.] (*Morwitz 194)

In these first three poems of 'Maximin' ('Kunfttag 1–3') we see the origins of
George's fixation as the outcome of disappointment at the failure to find reciprocal
love:

> Wenn solch ein auge glüht
> Gedeiht der trockne stamm ·
> Die starre erde pocht
> Neu durch ein heilig herz. (VI/VII, 92)

[Where such eyes are alight,
The withered branches bud,
The hard earth begins to beat
Again through a sacred heart.] (*Morwitz 195)

The transition takes place *from* homosexual desire for an as-yet undiscovered object *to* the attachment to the memory-image of Maximin. It is achieved through the reinvestment of the self into the memory and the resultant sense of gratification.

Like many of the other youthful homosexual figures in stories from this era, Maximilian died before realizing existential loneliness in a heterosexual world. He is still young, on the cusp of maturity and recognition, but has not experienced the sadness of his older homosexual contemporaries on realizing their existential loneliness. For Freud secondary narcissism develops when individuals turn failed object affection back on themselves. For this reason Maximilian can become Maximin, the repository of George's narcissistic fantasy. He has not experienced disappointment and can become the conduit for the aesthetic re-enchantment of the world, imagined seeing beyond into a land of hope:

Ob du dich auch in finstrem tal verloren ·
Von höhen abgesunken:
Wie du hier stehst bist du erkoren
Ins neue land zu schaun.
Du has vom quell getrunken:
Betritt die offnen aun! (vi/vii, 94)

[Though you have left the hills and wandered far
Down into the dark and wasted valleys,
You have been chosen, just as you stand,
To see into the promised land.
You have drunk of the well,
Now take to the open plains!] (*Morwitz 195)

The kiss of the angel is at once burning, purifying and redemptive:

Gesang des engels tönt ... sein mund
Auf deinem brennt dich rein · (vi/vii, 94)

[The song of the angel resounds.
His mouth on yours burns you clean] (*Morwitz 196)

The transformation of Maximin progresses in these poems from idealized love to adoration. But the language remains that of the love poem, comparable to that of Dante or Novalis. Only later does the adoration of the beloved become the adulation and exultation of the leader — and by that point, Maximin will have become something more and different.

George wrote to his close friend Sabine Lepsius and others of his sadness at Maximilian's death.[16] In the poems 'Trauer I–III' ('Sorrow I–III', vi/vii, 96) we can follow the expressions of grief and its eventual transformation into consolation at the thought of joining Maximilian in death as a process of mourning. Osterkamp views this in terms of a *unio mystica* of man with God via a reading of the 'holy kiss' of i Corinthians 16:20 as a 'kiss of love' (i Peter 5:14) but entirely free of all physicality.[17] Again, however, I would argue that the tone here is not of one exalted mystical union, but rather grief-stricken fixation on the lost object of love. Here we can observe the processes in terms of the workings of grief. The places and objects of Maximilian's life become the objects of veneration and pilgrimage ('Das Zweite: Wallfahrt', 'The Second: Pilgrimage', vi/vii, 100) and the dead youth becomes a watcher and sentinel over the loving living. Redemption will only come later by means of narcissistic self-recursion, not spiritual transcendence.

The poem of grief at the death of the beloved partner is taken for granted as a possibility of heterosexual life and is taken at face value in literary history. Such a poem did not yet exist in the imaginary sphere of the newly constructed homosexual man until George created it. The 'Trauer' ('Mourning') poems are uniquely moving as expressions of homosexual grief addressed to a deceased lover. George hereby achieves both the expression of love and the sorrow of death in the homosexual love poem that he has not achieved in life. This achieves the possibility of expressing love and grief at the same time as giving expression to the sense of unreality and impossibility of homosexual love. The ego ideal is imagined in its plasticity and fullness as a projected identification of the beloved who does not (he is dead) and cannot (he is an image of wish-fulfilment) exist. George furnished the homosexual imaginary in all its fullness with the contents of a potential, but still not possible, life.

Braungart refers to George's grief as a performance for the sake of the circle, a piece of cynical exploitation of feeling in order to bind his disciples more closely to him.[18] Maximilian may never have been the object of love in life that he became as a narcissistic projection in death. And George's anguish is not so much for the departed youth as for his departed youth and the failure to find meaningful response in a hostile world. In this process Maximilian becomes something else, the Maximin who comes to embody not a person, but a figure of narcissistic disappointment and projection, a statement of the failure of life to render an object of love. Nevertheless, the grief is genuine in these and other poems, and the language of love no more instrumental than that of other poets.

In the sub-section 'Auf das Leben und den Tod Maximins' ('On Maximin's Life and Death') George works grief, mourning and depression into something positive, a call to the future, to community and to solace:

> Vereint euch froh da ihr nicht mehr beklommen
> Vor lang verwichner pracht erröten müsst:
> Auch ihr hat eines gottes ruf vernommen
> Und eines gottes mund hat euch geküsst. (vi/vii, 99)

> [Unite in happiness, now that you no longer need blush
> And be uneasy on account of long-gone glory,
> You too have heard the summons of a god,
> And felt a kiss from the mouth of a god.] (*Morwitz 198)

Here, as throughout, the declamatory-prophetic aspect functions in the service of something greater than the poet himself or any of the individuals around him other than the dead Maximin.[19] The emphasis here is on the creation of a community no longer based on the 'long gone glory' of the homosexual heroes and gods of antiquity. The resuscitated Maximin is Patroclus and the heroes of the Theban Band in one, redeemed in an ideal vision of the new homosexual man: a figure of desire, power, validation and passion.

While the deification of Maximilian as the Maximin of the *Stern des Bundes* would come to associate homosexual identity with the messianic-charismatic aura of the Bund, its function is primarily to validate homosexual love and the homo-sexual individual — by no means a superfluous or gratuitous task at this time. In these poems of the transition to the extreme exaltation of Maximin and the linkage of this figure with masculinist militarist and nationalist content shortly before the war in *Der Stern des Bundes*, we can see the lineaments and determinants of the traumatic self-identification of homosexual men at the time.

> Nun klagt nicht mehr — den auch ihr wart erkoren — (VI/VII, 99)
>
> You also were elect, so do not mourn [...] (Morwitz 198)
>
> Du rufst uns an · uns weinende im finstern:
> Auf! tore allesamt!
> [...]
> Was du zu deines erdentags begehung
> Gespendet licht und stark
> Das biete jeder dar zur auferstehung
> Bis du aus unsrem mark
> Aus aller schöne der wir uns entsonnen
> Die ständig in uns blitzt
> Und aus des sehnens zuruf leib gewonnen
> Und lächelnd vor uns trittst. (VI/VII, 103)
>
> [You call on us who weep in dark and anguish:
> Fling all the portals wide!
> [...]
> What strength and light you gave us
> Upon your brief sojourn on earth,
> Let each of us give our all towards your resurrection,
> Your luminous return,
> From all of that which is beautiful
> That constantly flashes within us
> Which became our bodies, born of longing,
> And smiling steps up before us.] (*Morwitz 199–200)

That George's visions would merge with masculinist and nationalist ideology in the conservative reactionary environment is surprising in one sense, less so in another: surprising in the explicit evocation of homosexual attraction which goes beyond the homoeroticism of bonds of fealty and subservience in the earlier poems; less surprising in terms of the context of reactionary-vitalist ideas of the time. George, like so many intellectuals, was attracted by the dogmatic and powerful language of new community in an era of crisis and mixed his message of homosexual love in an increasingly poisonous brew of militarist masculinism.

In the sixth poem on the 'life and death of Maximin', the poet's role changes:

Am dunklen grund der ewigkeiten
Entsteigt durch mich nun dein gestirn (VI/VII, 105).

[And from the timeless depths of eternity
Through me your star emerges.] (*Morwitz 201)

He becomes the rhapsode of his own transformation.

Nun wird wahr was du verhiessest:
Das gelangt zur macht des Thrones
Andren bund du mit mir schliessest —
Ich geschöpf nun eignen sohnes. (VI/VII, 109)

[Now is done what you prophecied:
Succeeding to the power of the throne
Another pact you close with me, and I
Am the child of my own son.] (*Morwitz 202)

It is still a step from this evocation of the exalted, dead youth to the declamatory tones of the opening sections of *Der Stern des Bundes*, George's most problematic work, but the seeds of that change in lyric voice are clearly present.[20]

In the following two cycles of *Der siebente Ring*, 'Traumdunkel' ('Darkness of Dream') and 'Lieder' ('Songs'), George returns to the lyric subjectivity that was introduced in 'Gezeiten' and forms the dominant axis of his poetic life. The poems of 'Traumdunkel' were written between 1902 and 1905 with most written during 1904, roughly over the same period as the poems in 'Maximin'. Adorno registered the rift between ideology and social content in George's work at this time, noting the ways in which the use of language lifted the poems from their ideological bedding. In *Der siebente Ring* an ordering of poetic voices takes place among the cycles.[21]

'Landschaft II' ('Landscape II') is one of George's most beautiful lyric reflections on the difficulties of intimacy, expressed with the power of a folk poem in terms of the German countryside:

Lebt dir noch einmal · Liebe · der oktober
Und unser irrgang unsre frohe haft
Wie wir durch laubes lohenden zinnober
Und schwarzer fichten grünmetallnen schaft
Den und den baum besuchten · stumme gäste ·
Getrennten gangs in liebevollem zwist
Und jedes heimlich horchte im geäste
Dem sang von einem traum der noch nicht ist — (VI/VII, 119)

[Love, does October live for you again,
Our joy in roaming through the sombre maze
Of firs with shafts of green metallic stain,
Through cinnabar of foliage turned to blaze?
As silent guests we visited this tree
And that. I went alone, and so did you,
In loving feud, each listening secretly
To boughs which sang a dream not yet come true.] (Morwitz 207)

The walk into the forest is at once a vision of autumn and an allegory of love, an experience at once absorbing and alienating as each lover listens to a different song of nature as they become lost together. For Theodor Adorno the child picking berries, who shows the lost lovers their way back, is transformed by magic into a figure of folk tale that at the same time eschews all false romanticism.[22]

In 'Nacht' the lovers come together in a kiss of physical, not merely spiritual, union:

> Ist dies dein odem in mir ·
> Luft aus des rausches revier
> Was unsre leiber vermischt ·
> Uns durch das finster verwischt
> In einem schaurigen bund?
> [...]
> Uns: zu zerrinnen bereit
> In einem träumenden Meer. (vi/vii, 121)

> [Your breath in me! Is it this
> Air from the precincts of bliss,
> That has entangled our bodies,
> Woven together by shadows,
> Into a strange oneness?
> [...]
> Us, who are ready to dissolve
> Into an ocean of dream.] (*Morwitz 209)

And in 'Empfängnis' ('Conception') the ecstatic experience of abandonment is imagined by the lyric voice of an adult male giving himself entirely to another in sexual union that also leads to conception ('Empfängnis'), an experience of physical passion as a receptive male. Even Goethe's 'Ganymed' only intimates where George is explicit. Spiritual redemption comes from physical union:

> Schliess mich ein in wolkigem bausche ·
> Nimm und weih mich zum gefässe!
> Fülle mich: ich lieg und lausche! (vi/vii, 128)

> [Enfold me in billowing clouds,
> Take me, consecrate me as your vessel!
> Fill me: I lie and wait.] (*Morwitz 213)

Borrowing from the language of religious mysticism in this secular context, George following Goethe recasts the love poem as a vehicle of homosexual passion.

The 'Lieder' that make up the penultimate cycle of *Der siebente Ring* cover over a decade in terms of composition, from the early nineties (Lieder i–vi in 1892–93) to late 1905 (Lieder i–iii), and include the poem, 'Im windes-weben' ('My question erred ...', vi/vii, 137) which Adorno considered the most irresistible in the German language.[23] This structured cycle creates a continuity in the poet's work from the earliest to the current writings in which hope begins to succeed melancholy, and in which the inexpressible becomes expressed. Of the male lover returned home, the poet writes:

So offen quoll
Die knospe auf dass ich fast scheu sie sah
Und mir verbot
Den mund der einen mund zum kuss schon kor.
Mein arm umschliesst
Was unbewegt von mir zu andrer welt
Erblüht und wuchs —
Mein eigentum und mir unendlich fern. (VI/VII, 143)

[So rich the bud
That almost shyly I withdrew my gaze,
Denied myself
The lips that had already learned to kiss.
My arm enfolds
One who no longer moved by me, has grown
To other worlds,
My own, and yet how far from me, how far!] (Morwitz 219)

What is new in *Der siebente Ring* ('Lieder'), which was intimated but not explicit in the earlier poetry, is the homosexual attraction in its depth and breadth, not merely as a statement of ideal, disembodied or anonymous love, but as disappointment, uncertainty, caution and loss, through to physical passion and ecstatic receptiveness. For the first time a homosexual poet expresses the shades, nuances and tones of love poetry for men to men, reflecting in the lyric mode the potentialities of a life still impossible in the reality of prose. In the final 'Lieder' despair is all that remains for the lover, whose passion has been drowned by the more powerful waves of death. The death of the beloved leads to the final kiss of farewell, and erstwhile friends are distanced as the lover thinks only of his dead loved one:

Die hände die mienen
Erflehn von mir ruh nun ·
Ich frieden vor ihnen ..
Und wach bleibest Du nur. (VI/VII, 162)

[Their hands, their looks
Beseech me to rest now
I shun their advances,
And you alone keep watch.] (*Morwitz 228)

In the following cycle, 'Tafeln' George bids farewell in short, for the most part quatrain-length poems, specifically addressed by name to those friends and associates who have accompanied him this far. The volume ends with a sub-cycle, 'Zum Abschluss des VII. Rings' ('For the End of the Seventh Ring'), of short poems reviving the tone and the prophetic-visionary imagery of the early cycles, of evocations of a world awaiting drastic change and of a lyric subject ready to face a new future:

Da mich noch rührt der spruch der abschieds-trünke
Ihr all! Und eure hand noch wärmt: wie dünke
Ich heut mich leicht wie nie · vor freund gefeit
Und feind · zu jeder neuer fahrt bereit. (VI/VII, 187)

> [Our parting draught! And though the words you say
> Still move, your hands still warm me, yet today
> I feel more free than ever, and inured
> To friend and foe-prepared for any road.] (Morwitz 241)

Der siebente Ring thus operates in two modalities. The first is an aggressively outwardly oriented, object-related ('objekt-bezogen'), heroic-charismatic, visionary mode, influenced by Nietzsche's Zarathustra, which predominates in the early cycles, 'Zeitgedichte' and 'Gestalten'. The second is the passive, inwardly oriented, subject-related ('subjekt-bezogen'), lyric-reflexive and realistic mode, influenced by French symbolist and German romantic folk and nature poetry and expressing itself predominantly in 'Traumdunkel' and the 'Lieder'. These modalities do not represent opposing philosophies or intellectual attitudes. Rather they mirror corresponding aspects in the one voice and may be understood as alternating expressions of the one consciousness, pivoting around the central cycle 'Maximin'. Gert Mattenklott identifies these modalities as two voices in the opposition of Narcissus and Maximin, the former a damaged consciousness seeking self-affirmation, and the latter an idealized alter ego and leader.[24] These iterations of George's lyric voice taken together express an underlying sense of existential loneliness, in which the isolated self is the only point of anchorage in a world lacking reference.

Group Identity and Self-Realization in *Die Aufnahme in den Orden*

In some earlier poems of the *Buch der Sagen und Sänge*, such as 'Der Waffengefährte' with its medieval-chivalric setting, or in the 'Gestalten' section of *Der siebente Ring*, the theme of war and the homoeroticism of the warrior pair and the 'band of brothers' emerges. In the 1901 'Dedicatory drama' ('Weihespiel'), *Die Aufnahme in den Orden* (*Admission into the Order*), which received glowing praise from Hofmannsthal and Wolfskehl, George represents the development from the early idealization of the warrior pair to the nascent Bund. A lost young man seeks entry to an all-male ascetic-monastic order that is bound by the single recognition, that 'change in peace | is the sole duty' ('Wandel in frieden | Ist einzige pflicht', xvIII, 53). The young man is ritually questioned and tested by the group. The names are suggestive of an early Orthodox environment (Chrysostomos, Hermogenes), with the exception of the Latin Donatus, but there is little focus on the religion, and the adjectives of religiosity remain neutral ('heil', 'hehr'). The primary determiners are the motifs of 'peaceful change' and of the order as a 'circle' in which the ego is submerged into the whole.

> Hier bist du nicht dir selbst hier ist dein teil:
> Im kreise fühlen wirken nach dem platze.
> Hier ist verbannt wer eigensüchtig wolle — (xvIII, 53)

> [Here you are not yourself alone but a part:
> Feeling, working in the circle for the place.
> Here is banned whoever selfishly might want.]

Brought into the world in misery ('Ein weib hat sich zum unheil mich geboren'/'A woman bore me to her own misfortune'), the young man's early life is blighted presumably by early sexual experience ('Ein weib war meines frühen unheils schuld'/'A woman was guilty of my early misfortune'). The misogyny suggested by his retelling however seems an alibi for something deeper and more troubling within himself.

> Mich lockt es wo die dunklen wasser schäumen
> O sendet mir den rettenden befehl!
> Die grösste not lenkt meinen lauf –
> Nur wenn mich euer urteil nicht verwerfe
> Geht mir ein weg zu fernerem leben auf. (XVIII, 55)

> [I am drawn to where the dark water foams
> O send me the saving command!
> The greatest need guides my course —
> Only if your verdict does not reject me
> Is there a way for me to live a further life.]

The Grand Master Chrysostomos refuses the boy's request for patronage on the basis that he has not yet truly suffered, and he is likewise refused by Hermogenes because he has not experienced existential fear. The boy has only one more chance, and the youngest of the brothers, Donatus, accepts him as his witness and protector into the monastic circle:

> Der kreis ist der hort
> Der trieb allen tuns
> Ein hehres wort
> Verewigt uns! (XVIII, 58)

> [The circle is the place
> That drives all activity.
> A noble word
> Immortalizes us.]

Little detail is given: a boy has emerged from a disturbed childhood into an adolescence in which he loses his way as a result of experiences and desires that render him a criminal and outsider. His identification in and with all social groupings is lost and he falls into loneliness and despair. The boy needs a group and a friend who will support him in the wake of experiences that hinder him from re-establishing social ties and identifications. Donatus adopts him on the basis of empathy, of existential recognition.[25]

The symbolic grouping suggests what developmental psychologist Erik Erikson refers to as a psychosocial moratorium, namely the state in which the sexually matured individual is 'more or less retarded in his psychosexual capacity for intimacy' and in the psychosocial readiness for adulthood.[26] The moratorium aspect lies in the free role experimentation the young adult may find a niche in some section of his society, in which he 'gains an assured sense of inner continuity and social sameness which will bridge what he was as a child and what he is about to become, and will reconcile his conception of himself and his community's recognition of him'.[27] The adolescent process is completed only when the individual has subordinated his childhood identifications to a new kind of identification, achieved in absorbing sociability and in competitive apprenticeship with and among his age-mates. These new identifications are no longer characterized by the playfulness of childhood and the experimental zest of youth: with dire urgency they force the young individual into choices and decisions which will, with increasing immediacy, lead to a more final self-definition, to irreversible role pattern, and thus to commitments 'for life'.[28]

The group that the youth seeks out is a Christian-ascetic and monastic brotherhood. However, it is defined by acceptance and belonging rather than religious creed, by sublimation of sexual instincts in favour of identification and belonging among men alone. Once the individual has been accepted, the only rules are those of loyalty to the circle and allegiance to the principle of peaceful change. The centrality of this sense of belonging suggests a history of disjunction in all of their lives. The exclusion of past social identifications and the configuration of present stability provides relief for the self traumatized and damaged by its experience of the disjunction between homosexual desire and social judgement. A homoerotic element is present in the figure of the youngest of the brothers, Donatus, who takes the youth under his protection. The role of the Bund in this *Weihespiel* is thus, in Erikson's terms, to provide 'an entirely indispensable support to the ego in the specific tasks of adolescing, which are: to maintain the most important ego defenses against the vastly growing intensity of impulses (now invested in a mature genital apparatus and a powerful muscle system)' and 'to resynthesize all childhood identifications in some unique way, and yet in concordance with the roles offered by some wider section of society ...'[29]

The dynamics of identity, self-validation and belonging that are celebrated in *Die Aufnahme* reflect those of the George Circle underpinning its homoerotic sense of community. There is little sign of jealousy or competition, or of intimacy forming between couples. George's disciples retained their distance from each other even as they found fulfilment in belonging to the group, as is described in *Aufnahme in den Orden*.

> Aus diesem Liebesring, dem nichts entfalle,
> Holt Kraft sich jeder neue Tempeleis
> Und seine eigene — größre — schießt in alle
> Und flutet wider rückwärts in den Kreis. (VIII, 101)

> [And from this ring of love from which nothing is lost,
> Each new templar draws his strength
> And fires it back — greater now — to all his fellows
> Flooding back into the ring.] (*Morwitz 274)

Inasmuch as homosexual feelings were becoming legitimized at this time, they were entering the social imaginary, 'the creative and symbolic dimension of the social world, the dimension through which human beings create their ways of living together and their ways of representing their collective life'.[30] Homosexual values had begun to penetrate the social system of meanings and hence had become part of the individual's *wir-Gefühl* or social consciousness. Homosexuality, that is, became conceivable as something more than unconscious, unarticulated desire. It gained a social ontology in the individual's consciousness and in the process it became social, one of the competing and conflicting categories of social being. During this period of genesis, however, individual *wir-Gefühl* found little resonance or confirmation in broader social environments. The emerging youth movements provided channels for the validation of individual *wir-Gefühl* in group identity. The niche around George provided one model for the resolution of this rupture between ego-ideal and group consciousness. George's lyric-personal autobiography found avid readers among the young men of the *Wandervögel* and other youth groups. Given the receptiveness of these young people to leaders and guides, it is not surprising that George's poetry proved powerfully attractive, especially after he began to formulate his coded messages in terms of the mystique of 'secret Germany', appealing to many who felt dispossessed in social and national terms.

George rejected the identification, 'homosexual'. Nor did he accept Hirschfeld's concept of a 'third sex', or that of 'Freundschaft' associated with Adolf Brand's *Gemeinschaft der Eigenen*. All of these terms were compromised for him by their associations with an existing society that fundamentally rejected the homosexual as a viable identity. Hirschfeld introduced pseudo-science into the debate about homosexuality and Brand's grouping remained dishonest in its self-ascriptions. Neither created a homosexual imaginary in a way that George considered viable or desirable. George rejected these existing models at a time when the symbolic imaginary of the modern homosexual male was not yet formed in any comprehensive sense, and when the determinants of psychosocial development in the German context impelled the emergent homosexual male towards narcissistic identifications in the process of reaching a new model of psychosocial development and sexual maturity. As a result of the Maximin experience George began to espouse a sense of mission beyond the mere discovery and communication of states of personal being. This mission was embodied in the Bund, which represented the disciples grouped around him as the master and as the creator of Maximin, the combined narcissistic self-image of each of them. The poetic fiction of the Bund thus offered a powerful, if flawed, model for the socialization of the homosexual, which had generated a certain level of self-awareness already by 1914, when *Der Stern des Bundes* was published. Yet this also represents a turning point. While some of his disciples would remain bound to the Bund and unable to escape its covenant, George and others eventually moved beyond this vision in various ways during and after the war.

The Conflicted Self of *Der Stern des Bundes*

The tension identified in *Der siebente Ring* between the personal, introspective lyric voice and the voice of the prophetic-charismatic poet-spokesman for the Bund reaches its climax in *Der Stern des Bundes*. This long-awaited volume, coming seven years after *Der siebente Ring* in 1914 shortly before war broke out, is George's most controversial. According to Ernst Morwitz, George's planned title was *Lieder an die heilige Schar* (*Songs to the Sacred Band*), invoking the elite corps of the Sacred or Theban Band. The implied link with George's Bund is clear. It represented to many at the time a call to arms for a new Germany, one which instantiated George as a charismatic-prophetic leader. However, in terms of the poetic life, this role is by no means as clear-cut as is often presented in biographies and commentary. Indeed at this point the issue of voice becomes explicitly problematic. At the centre of this tension are two sides of the historically determined homosexual male in an environment in which self-identity seems possible, but integration into the existing community prohibited.

In Book I of *Der Stern des Bundes* George develops a highly charged language of crisis and destruction of a corrupted dying world, using a powerful lexicon echoing Old Testament, ancient Germanic and classical Greek sources. The voices alternate between a critical and bitter voice, demanding destruction of a world gone astray (VIII, 28), and the prophet pronouncing decline and heralding apocalypse (VIII, 32).

The opening evocation of Maximin is predicated on his belonging to the self-owned group (being part of 'us'), as a handsome, palpably concrete counterpart:

> Da kamst du spross aus unsrem eigenen stamm
> Schön wie kein bild und greifbar wie kein traum
> Im nackten glanz des Gottes (VIII, 8)

> [Then you appeared, a new shoot from our own trunk.
> No image was so fair, no dream so real
> In the naked brilliance of God.] (*Morwitz 244)

He is an image of the transfigured self, an ego-ideal of the charismatic poet — and his followers — adored, but untouchable. The young men were constrained to remain constant in an environment of feudal loyalty, chaste worship and reverence that was modelled on the chivalric Grail legend. Maximin, for example is referred to as the 'heart of the circle', or 'herz der runde', in a striking metaphoric reformulation of the Arthurian 'primus inter pares' (VIII, 15). In providing a positive imaginary of the homosexual as a social being, the poetic idea of the Bund advanced the process of individuation. As an image of unity Maximin represents the self and the other, 'Eines zugleich und Andres' ('at once one and the other', VIII, 9); he is both the alienated self and the desired other, the recognition of the self in the other and vice versa. He thus represents an essential step towards achievement of a sense of *wir-Gefühl*:

> Schon ward ich was ich will. Euch bleibt beim scheiden
> Die gabe die nur gibt wer ist wie ich:
> Mein anhauch der euch mut und kraft belebe
> Mein kuss der tief in eure seelen brenne. (VIII, 10)

> [I am already what I willed. In parting
> Accept a gift which only one such as I can give:
> My breath that shall revive your strength and courage,
> My kiss that shall be branded in your spirit.] (*Morwitz 245)

Maximin's re-appearance is imagined as rebirth, the symbolic transformation of the one into the group. Rebirth is return to life:

Löse mich aus meiner starre
Dass ich auf ins leben taue. (VIII, 61)

[Free me from my wintry bondage,
Let me thaw, and stir, and quicken! (Morwitz 262)

Schilt nicht den leid du selber bist das leid ..
Kehr um im bild kehr um im klang! (VIII, 22)

[[...]   Never
Condemn your grief, for you yourself are grief.
Reverse the symbol and reverse the song! (Morwitz 250)

As a motif, 'death and transfiguration' belongs to the late or neo-romantic canon. It appealed not just to homosexual men as an extreme statement of the desire for release into something at once self and other: it would soon become the anthem of world-weariness and war-readiness in Germany and throughout Europe. Rupert Brooke's war sonnets of 1914, 'The Dead' or '1914 Peace', similarly express the pathos of youthful despair that seeks redemption through dramatic breakthrough into a new and different world:

Now, God be thanked who has matched us with his hour,
And caught our youth, and wakened us from sleeping!
With hand made sure, clear eye, and sharpened power,
To turn, as swimmers into cleanness leaping,
Glad from a world grown old and cold and weary.
(Brooke, 'Peace', in *1914 and Other Poems*, 11)

Brooke, however, was a soldier who lived the dream and died the hero's death. George's image of Maximin's rebirth as the transformation of 'secret Germany' is a fantasy of regeneration expressed as aesthetic transfiguration. However in 1914 it proved fateful as many of the disciples understood it differently, obeying the call to war for the fatherland rather than to 'secret Germany' and the Bund.

Maximilian's Jewish heritage, referred to obliquely in various poems, represents the union of east and west.[31] In a series of further transformations, the oriental sun-god becomes the occidental warrior, the effeminate boy is forged into the warrior adult and the homosexual is transformed into an image of masculinity:

Ist dies der knabe längster sage
Der seither kam mit schmeichler-augen
Mit rosig weichen mädchengliedern
Mit üppigen binden in gelock?
Sein leib ward schlank und straff. Er greift ·
Er lockt nicht mehr · ist ohne schmuck.
Von mut und lust des kampfes leuchtet
Sein blick ... sein kuss ist kurz und brennend. (VIII, 72)

[Is this the boy of common legend,
Who came — they said — with limbs as rosy
And tender as a girl's? With wanton
Wreaths in his locks, with coaxing eyes?
Now he is slim and taut. He takes

And does not ask, is unadorned.
The lust for venture lights his glances,
His kiss is brief and burning.] (Morwitz 265)

The effeminate homosexual of the past longs to become a 'real' man, attractive
as such to other men like himself, and no longer in his own eyes a contemptible
hybrid of male and female. In poems such as this, we can see the genesis of the
homosexual masculinism that rendered the *Männerbund* attractive. The attitudes
may be dated, although they certainly existed until recently. However, it is not the
fantasy of power and revenge that fuels this transformation, but rather the desire to
be considered a man in a world where homosexuals are degraded and humiliated as
perverts, criminals and degenerates and can at best advocate themselves as a hybrid
'third sex'.

In Books Two and Three the apocalyptic tone softens markedly. The poet evokes
his love as an embodiment of light and as 'Gott der frühe' ('God of the dawn', VIII,
71). The pace and tone of the lines are serene and measured. These are love poems,
not expressions of heroic masculinism:

> Du bist für mich solang das loos es fodert
> Mein leben mehr als glück und rausch und lohe
> Bist mir das ganze bist mein innres herz –
> Und solch ein umlauf ist die ewigkeit. (VIII, 58)

> [You are my life as long as fate demands it.
> More than happiness and bliss and glowing heat
> You are my all, my inmost heart,
> And such a cycle is eternity.] (*Morwitz 261)

They are concretely sexual and physical in their adoration of beauty:

> [Ein leib der schön ist wirkt in meinem blut
> Geist der ich bin umfängt ihn mit entzücken:
> So wird er neu im werk von geist und blut
> So wird er mein und dauernd ein entzücken. (VIII, 78)

> [A body that is beautiful incites my blood,
> Spirit that I am, I surround him with bliss:
> So he becomes new in works of spirit and blood,
> So he becomes mine an eternal enchantment.] (*Morwitz 261)

The desire for sexual union is so overpoweringly physical that it is felt as the expression of an original genetic unity despite millennia of separation:

> Wenn meine lippen sich an deine drängen
> Ich ganz in deinem innren oden lebe
> Und dann von deinem leib der mich umfängt
> Dem ich erglühe die umschlingung löse
> Und mit gesenktem haupte von dir trete
> So ists weil ich mein eigen fleisch errate —
> In schreckensfernen die der sinn die misst
> Mit dir entspross dem gleichen königstamm. (VIII, 56)

[When to your mouth, my mouth is pressed in yearning,
Your inner breath impels my every heart-beat,
And then I loose the arms which hold me clasped,
Release your body, fountain of my fires,
And draw away from you with bended forehead,
It is because I feel my flesh confront me:
In pasts too far and dark for thought to gauge,
With you I sprang from the same stem of kings.] (Morwitz 260)

The lyric voice is at once lover and beloved, physically dominant and dominated. The two bodies are tied together into one. Yet this extreme love indicates the ambivalence of that unity, as both loss and discovery of self:

Wo ich mich in dir vernichte ...
Nun bestimmt die höhere sende
Wie ich mich in dir vollende. (VIII, 59)

[Where I destroy myself in you ...
Now a higher force directs
How I fulfill myself in you.] (*Morwitz 261)

Was ist geschehn dass ich mich kaum noch kenne
Kein andrer bin und mehr doch als ich war? [...]
Seitdem ich ganz mich gab hab ich mich ganz (VIII, 65)

[What happened that I almost am a stranger
To my own self, the same yet something more? [...]
But since I gave myself, my self is mine!] (Morwitz 263)

Surprisingly, perhaps, given the focus of so many commentators on George's militarist masculinism, the post-apocalyptic era is not foreshadowed as a global *Männerbund:* on the contrary, it is imagined as pastoral idyll:

Wenn holde freiheit kehrt und holder friede
Dann darf der sang zu allen Mächtigen steigen
Dann dürfen leichte paare in den hainen
Lustwandelnd unbedachte süsse schlürfen. (VIII, 73)

[When gracious peace returns and gracious freedom,
The song again shall rise to all the powers,
And lovers, light of heart, will sport in meadows
And woods, and sip the cup of sweet abandon.] (Morwitz 266)

Germany has been transformed into an idealized southern — Hellenic — landscape. The effect is of dream-like enchantment; it is anything but a Nordic apocalypse:

Da ward mit eins des himmels rasengrüne
Durchleuchtend blau wie in der süder buchten.
Entrückter goldschein machten bäum und häuser
Zum sitz des Seligen ... zeitloses nu
Wo landschaft geistig wird und traum zu wesen. (VIII, 74)

[And all at once the grassy green of heaven
Grew limpid blue like southern bays. A halo
Of gold transformed the trees and roofs to dwellings

> Of the immortals. Timeless flash of Now,
> When landscape turns to spirit, dream to substance.] (Morwitz 266)

In Book 3 the world is transformed by light:

> Von welchen wundern lacht die morgen-erde
> Als wär ihr erster tag? [...]
> Ein breites licht ist übers land ergossen ..
> Heil allen die in seinen strahlen gehn! (VIII, 82)

> [At what wonders does the morning-earth laugh
> As though it were her first day? [...]
> Across the land a wealth of sun is flooded,
> Hail to all who walk in its rays!] (*Morwitz 268)

It is a word, not war or destruction, that creates this new world:

> Das neue wort von dir verkündet
> Das neue volk von dir erweckt. (VIII, 91)

> [The new word proclaimed by you
> The new people awakened by you.] (*Morwitz 271)

The central principle is unity of the part and the whole in an eternal movement of one and all, echoing the legend of the Grail:

> So weit eröffne sich geheime kunde
> Dass vollzahl mehr gilt als der teile tucht
> Dass neues wesen vorbricht durch die runde
> Und steigert jeden einzelgliedes wucht:
> Aus diesem liebesring dem nichts entfalle
> Holt kraft sich jeder neue Tempeleis
> Und seine eigne — grössre — schiesst in alle
> Und flutet wieder rückwärts in den kreis. (VIII, 101)

> [So far may secret lore be discovered:
> That the total counts more than the sum of parts,
> And new being breaks out through the circle
> And raises the strength of every member.
> And from this ring of love from which nothing is lost,
> Each new templar draws his strength
> And fires it back — greater now — to all his fellows
> Flooding back into the ring.] (Morwitz 274)

For the individual poet, not life and death but inclusion in the group is the existential key:

> Im einklang fühl ich keim und welke
> Mein leben seh ich als ein glück. (VIII, 105)

> [I sense accord in bloom and wilting,
> And joy in all I live and do.] (Morwitz 275)

But he and the other members of the Bund, like the Grail community, will go out into the world, spreading the message:

> Entlassen seid ihr aus dem innern raum
> Der zelle für den kern geballter kräfte
> Und trächtiger schauer in das weite land.
> [...]
> Ihr seid im gang getrennt im zweck gesellt. (VIII, 110)
>
> [Now you may venture from the inner space,
> The cell which holds the nucleus of powers
> And life unborn. Before you lies the land.
> [...]
> Your ways divide, your purpose is the same. (Morwitz 277)

And they will return homewards to celebration of the new community:

> Mit kränzen heimwärts zogen mann und maat:
> Hat schon im schönsten gau das fest begonnen. (VIII, 111)
>
> [With wreaths the troops and crews were homeward bound,
> In the fairest regions festivities have begun.] (*Morwitz 277)

The final vision of redemption in the *Schlusschor* is of unification and unity:

> Gottes Band hat uns umschlossen,
> Gottes Blitz hat uns durchglüht
> Gottes Heil ist uns ergossen
> Gottes Glück ist uns erblüht. (VIII, 114)
>
> [God's band has embraced us,
> God's rays have shone through us,
> God's salvation has streamed over us,
> God's happiness has bloomed within us.] (*Morwitz 278)

Regardless of how we read these poems, it is clear that we are in the presence of a master able to draw on every register of the language, play every note and manipulate every association — perhaps to the point where he has fallen under his own spell, losing authenticity for effect, becoming the object of his own genius, believer of his own vision. For the reader, certainly for many readers since the 1960s, this language is suspect, its messianic and prophetic tones presaging Nazism. *Der Stern des Bundes* is generally considered a book of cultic poetry, not only in terms of its hieratic gestures and language, but also in its evocation of an idealized realm. This may be true of Book 1. But as the above analysis demonstrates, the hieratic aspect is exaggerated. The enthusiastic commentaries of the disciples at the time, especially Gundolf, has over-determined the reception of the work both in positive and in negative terms.[32] Adorno's later belief that George sacrificed his heterosexuality to the masculinist homoeroticism of the militarized *Volk* is the perverse logic of the heterosexual, to say the least. Similarly Ernst Osterkamp devotes his study *Poesie der leeren Mitte: Stefan Georges neues Reich* (2010) to showing that George directed his full genius to the political programme of the 'new Germany', and hence that he prepared the way for Nazism. Such critical responses are over-determined by the subsequent history of Germany. They fail to explain the unresolved tensions between the apocalyptic and the idyllic in the work and sacrifice the progression through George's successive volumes to the static ideology of militarist masculism.

For all their language of transcendence and redemption, these poems are a far cry from the demagogic authoritarianism of the epoch which aimed for maximum political reach. The politics of the era certainly generated dangerous charismatic demagogues but George was not one of them. He avoided the political sphere in favour of an aesthetic realm that exploits the language of passionate attachment and secret belonging but has no immediate contact with the world of politics. Moreover, George is writing in a German tradition of visionary poetry that Schiller and Hölderlin had taken to its greatest heights. It has its origins in earlier Christian religious poetry and in the classical tradition of nostalgic evocation of better times in eras of upheaval. Essential to this tradition was the tension between the real and the ideal, expressing the longing for the regeneration rather than of wholesale destruction of a world that has lost its way. In *Der Stern des Bundes* only the wished-for realm of perfection is evoked. The destruction that will bring this about is accepted — as is the case in many futuristic scenarios — and there is no sense of nostalgia. The disillusionment, regret and bitterness of a disappointed god and the extremism of an Old Testament prophet colour the first book, but there are no bloodied heroic warriors, no cataclysmic war or slaughtered hordes. Indeed Book 2 moves through the evocation of physical love and adoration directly to post-apocalyptic pastoral in Book 3. Like the language of other leading writers of the time — Hofmannsthal, Rilke, Mann or Trakl — it is the expression of a crisis-consciousness, and belongs generically with the fantasies of upheaval, breakthrough and rebirth that typically accompany eras of crisis. Though many of these poems have interpreters bristling with horror, they are no more threatening than a video-game, full of overblown imagery and inflated passions, but played out entirely in the imagination, reflecting unresolved sexual energies and power fantasies, not political programmes or ideological fixations.

The lyrical-personal humanism of the poet's seeking of knowledge, self-understanding and self-affirmation as a homosexual man exists in dynamic tension with the attraction to a charismatic-prophetic vision of masculine redemptive community — the former oriented towards personal individuation, the latter toward narcissistic self-affirmation. The poetry expresses the positive dialectic of the traumatized Narcissus and the youthful god: of the individual modern homosexual seeking a way forward through engagement with the narcissistic ideal. The dynamic tension between the searching lyric self (George's poetic voice) and the overwhelming self-object (the evocation of Maximin) survives even in this most extreme of George's volumes.

The thesis that George's charismatic leadership of the Bund was underwritten by pathological narcissism is scarcely tenable other than through a selective reading of *Der Stern des Bundes*. An aspect of this work certainly verges on fixation and stasis, on narcissism as a self-referential loop from which the ego cannot escape. Overall, however, the conflict between narcissistic self-affirmation and generative self- and group-exploration is the crucial dynamic factor counteracting fixation. There is much more to the late work than merely an 'esoteric doctrine of redemption'.[33] Even the most extreme of George's poetic statements of messianic narcissism cannot be reduced to the one-dimensional programme of reactionary anti-modernism, predicated on the poet's narcissistic personality as suggested by Breuer, Osterkamp and others.

Apostle of Narcissus

Rieckmann notes that the figure and the topos of Narcissus were part of homo-erotic discourse at the turn of the century, although in Freudian theory it dates only to around the end of the first decade.[34] The figure of Narcissus appears throughout George's oeuvre from the early self-mirroring of *Die Fibel* and the role-play of *Algabal* through the growing sense of insufficiency of the narcissistic self in *Der siebente Ring* to the troubled dialectic of the wounded youth and the youthful god of *Der Stern des Bundes*. David, Mattenklott and others have long identified the tension in George's poetic voice between intimacy and domination.[35] More recently, however, the unitary thesis of George's pathological narcissism has come to dominate discussion in the wake of Breuer's account of George's 'aesthetic fundamentalism'.

In Freud's terminology narcissism results when the libido fails to find objects in the external world and begins to reinvest the self.[36] Freud accepts that the diversion of libidinal energy back to the self is a legitimate stage 'in the regular course of human sexual development', and that narcissism can function as 'the libidinal complement to the egoism of the instinct of self-preservation, a measure of which may justifiably be attributed to every living creature'.[37] Homosexual men particularly seemed to Freud to experience narcissistic states, as a result of the failure of the ego to attain object love and the resultant flow of libido energies back to the self. Freud's image of libidinal balance between the ego and the other, flowing backward to the self if thwarted in its orientation outward, describes the situation of these men at this time in Germany and in their individual lives. Their libidinal investments had proved transitory, unfulfilling and damaging as they were identified socially as perverts, deviants and criminals and rewarded with personal unhappiness. Even Adorno, no great friend to homosexual men, considered narcissism in terms of the ego's libidinal solution to the existential problem raised by the contradiction between the claims of the libido and the need for self-preservation in a society in which libido and self come into conflict.[38]

As a typical characteristic of homosexual men of this time, narcissism is not *constitutive*: it was *contingent* upon socio-historical circumstance. The failed dynamic of development had left these men self-dependent, disappointed and unsure of their place in the world. The inability of the self to trust the sexual other resulted in failure of discharge of libido and the regression of libidinal energies in adolescence and early adulthood in narcissistic states.[39] The result was external disillusionment and inward descent.

George rendered this narrated life influential and paradigmatic for young homosexual men by tying their lives as lonely outsiders into that of an ideal who represented both the embodiment of their sexual longings and desires, and a narcissistic image of self-fulfilment and self-perfection. The figure of Maximin in

Der siebente Ring and *Der Stern des Bundes* offers resolution of this cleavage in the poetic consciousness. Through the projection of the ego ideal as the beloved other, Maximin brings together subject and object as 'self-object', thereby resolving the tension in the narcissistic libido between self-love and object love.

In *Ästhetischer Fundamentalismus*, Stefan Breuer put forward the argument that George instrumentalized aestheticism in the service of the principle of charismatic domination. He thereby created a hierarchy of followers who shared his fixated pathological narcissism and experienced redemption from their group spiritual-psychological crisis through the narcissistic 'mirror image' of George's poetic-redemptive creation, Maximin.[40] In this reading, George's narcissistic personality enabled the turn inward from engagement with the world in favour of an idealized world of the self. However Breuer's analysis focuses on the charismatic personality and its influence at this time, reading George entirely in biographical and sociological terms. In literary terms George mirrored himself into his poetry, generating a powerful homosexual imaginary that influenced and moved young men beyond anything they had previously encountered in their lived experiences or their reading imaginations.

George may have confided to Hofmannsthal that he could see no way forward after finishing *Algabal*, but he had in fact found a beginning, not an end. In the works that followed he began to reflect back onto the world the very conditions of that world that made homosexual life so difficult. In his poetry George searches for and reconstructs the parts of himself that have been broken by the ego wound. The poet thereby began to release himself — and his readers — from those conditions by creating a new imaginary realm of shared experiences and dreams in the lyric mode. We must abandon Breuer's reading of homosexuality as the consequence of narcissistic fixation, and open our interpretative faculties to the tensions, the emphases and the intimations of this volume as a whole. There is no reason to assume that change and development must cease at the point of strongest expression of the narcissism of the poetic voice. If we understand homosexuality as a sexual orientation that, like heterosexuality, guides the individual from childhood through adolescence to adult object love, in which narcissistic phases or stages can both aid and impede the progress (i.e. in line with the work of Kohut and other post-Freudian theorists), we can view *Der Stern des Bundes* in a different light from that of aesthetic anti-modernism. The poetry expresses the positive dialectic of the traumatized Narcissus and the youthful god: of the individual modern homosexual seeking a way forward through engagement with the narcissistic ideal. Even at the high point of George's evocation of Maximin as the youthful god, the imagery of Narcissus and of watery self-reflection represent the counter-force of the thinking, feeling individual. George's path forward would move beyond the detours and potential dead-ends of narcissistic self-idealization and charismatic leadership towards a recognition of homosexual object-love as an end in itself.

The backshadowing of George in terms of later Nazi developments in Germany has screened these aspects from view. The aestheticization of the nation in imagery of youth and rebirth appealed to many young men in the crisis years between *c.* 1907 and 1914, enabling a bridging of social differences and a merging of identities, for

Jews and homosexuals as well as others. George's Bund enabled the expression of a particular type of homoeroticism and nationalism, a new *Gemeinschaft* through a process that could scarcely take place through established social contacts or political parties.[41] Homosexual men may have approached the *Männer-* and *Jünglingsbünde* of the early decades of the century in the hope of realizing their fantasies of acceptance, companionship and love but by the 1920s they would be disabused of this fantasy unless they turned to political Nazism themselves. For most of George's disciples by that time, the fantasy had run its course: by the time of George's death they were in danger of persecution by Nazi thugs.

Notes to Chapter 3

1. Klussmann, 'Ästhetische Imperative in Zeitgedichten von Stefan George', p. 443.
2. Böschenstein, 'Stefan Georges Spätwerk als Antwort auf eine untergehende Welt', p. 1.
3. Ibid., pp. 3–4.
4. Marx and Morwitz, *The Works of Stefan George*, p. 187.
5. See Winzen, 'Gezeiten', in Egyptien, *Stefan George — Werkkommentar*, p. 411; Keilson-Lauritz, 'Übergeschlechtliche Liebe als Passion', p. 150.
6. See Keilson-Lauritz, 'Übergeschlechtliche Liebe als Passion', pp. 150–51; cf. Rieckmann, *Hugo von Hofmannsthal und Stefan George*, pp. 70, 189, 90.
7. Osterkamp, 'Die Küsse des Dichters', pp. 83–84.
8. Winzen, 'Gezeiten', in Egyptien, *Werkkommentar*, p. 412.
9. On George and Kronberger, see Egyptien, *Stefan George: Dicher und Prophet*, pp. 242–66; Karlauf, *Stefan George*, pp. 342–60; Norton, *Secret Germany*, pp. 326–28, and Kauffmann, *Stefan George*, pp. 134–35. According to both Norton and Karlauf, George noticed the thirteen-year-old Maximilian Kronberger in March 1902 in Schwabing and sometime later asked to accompany him to a professional photographer, along with his sister Johanna, to have a portrait made. The following year George visited Munich again and encountered Maximilian by chance; they met up the following day, again with Karl Wolfskehl, to see the photograph that George had had made the previous year. During 1903 Maximilian attended various social events at which George was present and visited his apartment. He died suddenly of meningitis at the age of 16 on 15 April 1904. There is no evidence of sexual advances of any sort; indeed, the relationship was brief and relatively superficial in terms of their contact with each other.
10. On the brief and uneasy relationship between George and Maximilian Kronberger, see in particular Karlauf, *Stefan George*, pp. 344–49.
11. George, *Tage und Taten*, SW, XVII, 61–66.
12. Lacan, *Four Fundamental Concepts*, p. 257; Norton, *Secret Germany*, pp. 343–44.
13. Hildebrandt, 'Agape und Eros bei George', p. 84; Goldsmith, *Stefan George*, p. 35; Böschenstein, 'Stefan Georges Spätwerk als Antwort auf eine untergehende Welt', pp. 7, 9 and passim; Bisno, 'Stefan George's Homoerotic Erlösungsreligion, 1891–1907', p. 38 and passim.
14. Goldsmith, *Stefan George*, p. 33, suggests that George fell in love with both Ludwig Klages and Alfred Schuler during the late 1890s.
15. The concept was used by Wilhelm Dilthey in *Das Erlebnis und die Dichtung* to describe a phenomenon present in German literature since the Middle Ages and finding its high point in the lyric output of Goethe. See Sauerland, *Diltheys Erlebnisbegriff*, esp. pp. 12–13. Edith Landmann discusses George's use of the expression 'Erlebnisausdruck', *Gespräche mit Stefan George*, p. 87; See George, *Der Stern des Bundes*, SW, VIII, 119. George was influenced by the recent publication of the newly discovered late hymns of Hölderlin; indeed the editor of the Hölderlin edition, Norbert von Hellingrath, himself a member of George's circle, first noted this influence, although most of the Bund poems were completed before the late hymns were brought to George's attention (editors' comment, *Der Stern des Bundes*, SW, VIII, 118).

Nevertheless, the influence of Hölderlin's style is noticeable and Hellingrath's comment has considerable validity, even if George was only familiar with the earlier Hölderlin at this stage. In the ideal evocations of a perfected group consciousness of *Der Stern des Bundes*, George had aimed, according to his friend Edith Landmann, to supplant the poetry of experience (Goethe's model of 'Erlebnisdichtung') with the experience of language ('Spracherlebnis'), the other great tradition of German poetry that reached a high point with the late Hölderlin's transcendental-idealist lyric style. George for Landmann signals a change in poetic thinking away from the hypostatized 'Spracherlebnis' of *Der Stern des Bundes* back towards a poetry of experience.

16. See Karlauf, *Stefan George*, pp. 348–50.
17. Osterkamp, 'Die Küsse des Dichters', p. 85.
18. Braungart, *Ästhetischer Katholizismus*, p. 289.
19. See Braungart, 'Kult, Ritual und Religion bei Stefan George', p. 257.
20. Ibid., p. 258.
21. Adorno, *Noten zur Literatur*, p. 64.
22. Ibid., p. 65.
23. 'Lieder' II, *SW* VI/VII, 137. See Adorno, *Noten zur Literatur*, p. 66.
24. Mattenklott identifies the tension between these opposed voices in the oeuvre. Mattenklott, *Bilderdienst*, p. 177. For Mattenklott the damaged youth, Narcissus, represents the poet's recognition of modernist suffering and alienation. However, the search for healing and wholeness finds resolution in the idealization of Maximin, whose values presage Nazism, albeit for the readers of the time. As part of this interpretation Mattenklott recognizes the claim to existential and linguistic authenticity in the early work (ibid.).
25. The names perhaps suggest that the boy is received out of a sense of charity, 'giving' implicit in the name Donatus, as opposed to words and language (Chrysostomos) or birth and position (Hermogenes).
26. Erikson, 'The Problem of Ego Identity', p. 66.
27. Ibid.
28. Ibid.
29. Ibid., pp. 66–67.
30. Thompson, *Studies in the Theory of Ideology*, p. 6.
31. Like Gundolf, Morwitz and other members of the Circle, Maximilian was Jewish. But as these lines suggest in reference to the Bund members' Germanic and Jewish origins, there is none of the language of biological racism that would become central to Nazism.

> Blond oder schwarz demselben schooss entsprungne
> Verkannte brüder suchend euch und hassend
> Ihr immer schweifend und drum nie erfüllt! (VIII, 41).

> [Fair-haired or dark, the selfsame womb begot you.
> Each hates and seeks and does not know his brother,
> And always roams and never is fulfilled.] (Morwitz 256)

32. See David, *Stefan George: Sein Dichterisches Werk*, p. 285; Goldsmith, *Stefan George*, p. 35; Osterkamp, 'Die Küsse des Dichters', pp. 76–77; Bisno, 'Stefan George's Homoerotic Erlösungsreligion', pp. 37–55; Braungart, 'Kult, Ritual und Religion bei Stefan George'.
33. Ibid., p. 17, 'Medien einer esoterischen Heilslehre'.
34. Rieckmann, *Hugo von Hofmannsthal und Stefan George*, p. 57.
35. David, *Stefan George: Sein Dichterisches Werk*, p. 194; Mattenklott, *Bilderdienst*, p. 177.
36. Freud would further distinguish between the primary narcissism of the infant, which is overcome during the early stages of development, and the secondary narcissism of the adult, which is the *re-investment* of libidinal energies in the self.
37. Freud, 'On Narcissism', pp. 65–66.
38. Adorno, 'Sociology and Psychology', pp. 86–89; see also Grubner, 'Narcissism in Cultural Theory', p. 51.
39. 'A damming up of the libido which no object-cathexis can completely overcome' (Laplanche and Pontalis, *Vocabulary of Psychoanalysis*, pp. 255).

40. Breuer, 'Ästhetischer Fundamentalismus', p. 239.
41. See Reichardt, *Faschistische Kampfbünde*, p. 355.

CHAPTER 4

The Healing of Narcissus

War and Crisis

By 1914, when *Der Stern des Bundes* appeared, George's lyric exploration of a homosexual man's life had reached a crisis just as Germany found itself on the threshold of war. George was in a potentially compromised situation. On the one hand he loathed the *bürgerlich* Germany of the Second Empire and had made public his longing for a new age to take its place. On the other, he disdained the war and its nationalist jingoism. His poetic vision of apocalypse and rebirth of the new society around the Bund scarcely related to the current political crisis. Modern war had little in common with the idealized feudal-chivalric images of battle that George evoked as part of the mythology of the new beginning. George had idealized war as feudal combat and heroic battle in earlier poems such as 'Traum und Tod', the final poem of *Der Teppich des Lebens*:

> Glanz und ruhm! so erwacht unsre welt
> Heldengleich bannen wir berg und belt
> Jung und gross schaut der geist ohne vogt
> Auf die flur auf die flut die umwogt. (v, 85)

> [Glow and fame, so our world awakens,
> Like heroes we subdue cliff and bay,
> And the mind, young and great, without constraint
> Views the plain and the surrounding sea.] (★Morwitz 154)

But 1914 brought a rupture between aesthetic vision and political reality. The Bund did not represent in any political sense the core of a national movement of change, and George's reactionary political mythology had only attracted a small coterie of young men around him. Given George's narcissistic disengagement with political realities throughout this period, there is little credible evidence to suggest any progression from the aesthetic rituals and habituses of the Bund into concerted political action. The visions and fantasies of Maximin, the Bund, 'Secret Germany' and '*das neue Reich*' remain narcissistic configurations of an inner world in which all is possible, even the rebirth of the poet himself and the formation of a group of men around him as their centre. The component of homosexual self-imagining essential to George's Bund overshadowed any political programme of aesthetic fundamentalism.

His rejection became more concrete and personally felt as war broke out and his beloved disciples turned their backs on 'secret Germany' in order to fight for a cause that he spurned. This support of the war and of the *real* German nation versus the *ideal* 'secret Germany' represented the first large-scale desertion by figures who had been part of his inner sanctum.[1] While the process lasted years in many cases, and while George provided these renegades with a way back to him, he was unable to countenance open betrayal. His bitterness in 1914 against the Germans, the French, and all involved parties led to contemptuous tirades, but it was in the poems of the crucial years from 1914 until around 1920 that George gave expression to the deep changes that the war brought about for himself.

The war came to represent everything that George had heralded but had not been able to deliver to his disciples. It unified the German people, transforming 'the dismembered and separated body parts into a single people, a single body, and a holy one at that'.[2] For some members of the Bund it manifested a sense of oneness and a supersession of individual alienation with which George's individual charisma could not compete. The war, that is, represented the repressed narcissitic parent-image, the psychological experience of wholeness, totality and omnipotence which George had heralded and embodied, and which had been awaiting the moment of redemptive release.[3] The war relegated George to the role of mere prophet, a superseded figure, no longer prophet and messiah in one. He had become dispensable. He would never reassert his authority or charismatic significance to the same extent as in the years before the war.

The war thus proved a watershed, fragmenting the Bund and leading to the departure of disciples. The Bund as a model of homosexual affection, attraction and even love had become unsustainable. It had provided the individual at an important stage of development with a set of objects and values onto which to project homoerotic energies, and with which to identify. However these projective identifications ultimately reinforced rather than resolved the narcissistic loneliness of the individual. The youths and young men who identified with George's lyric persona and who received the poet's idealization of the youth-hero-leader Maximin as ego ideal were faced with the option of stepping out to realize and fulfil that ideal or of failing to do so. The Bund was not a place in which object love was imagined (i.e. the transference of their affections to a male other) even to other members of the Bund. Love was directed only to the poet and master/prophet, or, after 1904 to the alter ego and ego-ideal, Maximin. Some moved beyond this, with wartime experiences providing resolution where the Bund had not.

Looking back to the pre-war years, Thomas Mann caught the spirit of the time in the 'Winfried' episode in chapter fourteen of *Doktor Faustus*. His young seminarians discuss youth, manliness and national renewal or 'breakthrough' as they lie in the hay-loft of a barn at night on a rural *Wanderung*. Homoerotic bonding is linked to the broader issues of the nation, social change, violence and masculinity. The seductive power of the war for young Germans, when it finally broke out, indicates the nature and limits of the Bund. It was, after all, only one of many different groupings with its origins in the youth movement, that appealed to the generations born after around 1890. Dirk von Petersdorff writes that the circular dynamic of the Bund as a 'Gesamtseele' cannot suffice in the long term. 'Anyone who parallels Redeemer, Poet and Conqueror must at some point also say who is to be healed and what is to be conquered.' George cannot do this because 'he can no longer find any starting points or materializations for his position'.[4] The war did so for many of his adherents, but not just for them: it appealed to young and old as a promise of national regeneration in that hot August of 1914.

George's model may have provided the individual at an important stage of development with a set of objects and values onto which to project homoerotic energies, and with which to identify. However, these projective identifications ultimately reinforced rather than resolved narcissistic loneliness. The idealization of the Bund hindered these young men from finding object love, that is, from transferring of their affections to a male other, or even to the others of the group. Those who had found a sense of stability and homosexual identity through George's poetry now encountered difficulty in escaping the self-referential mode in order to move on towards sexually fulfilling relationships with others like themselves. The war and the opportunity to merge with the greater national whole represented a crisis that brought George's ideal crashing down within a year of the publication of *Der Stern des Bundes* — at least for its creator. The encounter with the reality of war was a shock from which neither George nor many of his disciples would recover. There was no possibility of return to the pre-war symbolism of Maximin and 'secret Germany'.

In the final volume, *Das Neue Reich*, the effect of the war is palpable as the poet attempts to negotiate a path between the flawed mysticism of the Bund and the recognition of loss. The war brought home to George the imperfections of his ideal and an awareness of failure. *In Das Neue Reich* he engaged with existential disappointment and in doing so came to recognize and express object-love alongside self-love as the core experience of the homosexual individual. This volume represents the poet's ongoing journey from the grandiose visions of the idealized alter ego to a new reckoning with aspects of his life as he relinquishes or at least distances himself from aspects of his past. He does not renounce the journey, but he recognizes that the destination is different. George's response to the war in poems such as 'Der Krieg' and 'Einem jungen Führer im Ersten Weltkrieg' does not merely express an early and far-sighted criticism of the German enthusiasm for the war and bitter castigation of his contemporaries. It also represents a form of self-criticism that moved the poet beyond the model of narcissistic adulation of Maximin to object love for his homosexual community. Though by no means a clear or decisive break, *Das Neue Reich* charts an uneven process of disenchantment and reckoning with his earlier aesthetic imaginary, brought on by war and the loss of men whom he loved.

Friendship, Love and Self-Acceptance: *Das Neue Reich*

Das Neue Reich was finalized and published in 1928, fourteen years after the previous volume, *Der Stern des Bundes*, and only five years before George's death. It contains work dating from before the war (in the case of 'Goethes lezte nacht in Italien' from around 1908) along with poems written between 1914 and the post-war period up until shortly before publication. The title, the structure and the selection of poems have been the topic of much discussion since the volume's publication. I would suggest that here, as elsewhere in George's *oeuvre*, the selection and ordering is an essential part of the narrative, a literary strategy of looking back, of identifying the moments in which the dream began to fade, and of gathering that which remained — a process in which George recognized both the end of his dream of a 'new Germany' and the truth of his life as a homosexual in its final stages. As the volume draws to a close, prophetic grandiosity has long given way to a sober reckoning with the poetic myth.

If *Der Stern des Bundes* is George's most negatively received work, this final volume is his most contested. Commentators past and present have written copiously on the vision of the 'Kingdom Come' in Morwitz's striking translation of the title. Some have identified a unified vision, but they are relatively few (Morwitz and Ockenden); others have registered the aporias, the incongruity between title and content and the unevenness of the content. At the time of publication the work generated opposed responses even from those close to George.[5] For George's most faithful disciple, Ernst Morwitz, *Das Neue Reich* heralded a new era of creative flexibility, breaking with the 'architectonically closed' structures of the earlier works, especially *Der Stern des Bundes*.[6] Morwitz uses the metaphor of the bridge, 'suspended over a broad, deep current' to explain the tensions and unevenness alongside the unity of intention, leading to the 'New Empire' of the title.[7] For all his insight and sensitivity to George's language, however, Morwitz remains a disciple, using the vocabulary of Georgean mysticism but failing to recognize George's engagement with the new post-war reality. Yet Ernst Glöckner, a member of George's closest circle during the wartime years, condemned it as a 'collection of leftovers, augmented with trivialities'.[8]

Claude David suggests that poetry had fulfilled its function for George by the 1920s, and that he abandoned it in order to pursue his pedagogical programme and to act as 'Seelsorger' for those around him.[9] This final volume was merely a collection of whatever was left over or published in the *Blätter* during the previous two decades.[10] Writing in 1968, Hans-Georg Gadamer also noted the looser structure of *Das Neue Reich* and the broadening of style and tone, as well as a return to George's earlier ambivalence of voice.[11] He identifies a tension between the 'being-for-others [...] and the being-for-himself of the great individual who has always been lonely'.[12] A 'tone of renunciation, restraint, unknowing and suffering makes itself felt, in contrast to the gestures of melancholy and sadness of the early volumes, or to the harder, sparer and more austere late work'.[13] In this volume George 'no longer stylizes himself in the role of the unrecognized redeemer who knows himself. He does not know himself.'[14] Von Petersdorff finds self-doubt, scepticism and insecurity, and confirms Gadamer's identification of a weakening in the force of determination that had defined George's earlier work, concluding that 'one can no longer speak of a 'New Empire'.[15]Many commentators since then have agreed that the proclaimed empire of the title disappears from view, indicating unevenness, loss of resolve and waning of poetic powers.[16] Karlauf devotes over five of his nine pages on *Das Neue Reich* to the title alone, which for him as for Osterkamp and Mattenklott, was a sinister anticipation of the Third Reich.[17]

Where earlier commentators make a convenient separation at around the time of *Der siebente Ring* between the early aestheticist poet and the late dogmatic leader, both Bernhard Böschenstein and Ernst Osterkamp follow Gert Mattenklott in subsuming the poetry entirely into the reactionary politics, reading the volume as George's culminating statement of intent.[18] The origins of this type of interpretation lie with the younger 'third generation' of disciples — men such as Ernst Morwitz, Robert Boehringer, Ludwig Thormaehlen, Kurt Hildebrandt and others — who increasingly came to speak on behalf of George during the 1920s and who propagated the mythology in one form or another after his death. Some of these, including Thormaehlen and Hildebrandt, would later become committed Nazis. To a certain extent the poet became a victim of his own earlier success as age, illness and disillusionment wore him down. However even the influential interpretation by Willi Koch in the year of George's death subsumes the poetry into a mystical cult of vitalism and rebirth around the figure of Maximin. While not overtly political, Koch's reading nevertheless renders George a type of prophet for an age of despair.[19] This type of interpretation, combined with the profiling of George as a Nazi before his time by a sector of the disciples, impacted on reception of *Das Neue Reich* and the poetry as a whole in the politically charged context of the 1968 student movement (of which both Mattenklott and Osterkamp were members). The ambivalences of the early Lukács, Benjamin, Adorno and Gadamer were not shared by these commentators as they divided the German literary tradition into precursors and opponents of Nazism.

It is certainly difficult to discern clear lines in *Das Neue Reich*, especially after the formal uniformity of *Der Stern des Bundes*. However, as we have seen, even that latter work includes lyric reflection alongside bombastic glorification of the Bund. In *Das Neue Reich* George's two voices continue to be heard. The poems which echo the prophetic-charismatic extremes of *Der Stern des Bundes* express the seductions of homoerotic dominance and the ongoing dream of a homosexual male community. Yet it is the other voice which now comes to the fore, the lyric voice of the flawed individual, Narcissus, who comes to recognize himself and find a point of resolution which is neither negation of the past nor projection into the future.

It is ultimately too simplistic to interpret all forms of anti-modernism simply as precursors of Nazism. The truth of the era lies in the diversity of its attempts to find alternatives to a past that was perceived to be dead. Not all attempts at recovery of life were fascist: some were liberationist movements, such as the youth movement or the various forms of sexual and women's liberation movements. Most took on aspects of politics, whether of the left or the right, that were potentially dangerous.

To view them simply as precursors of Hitler is to reduce a complex period of crisis to black and white. George's images of exultant young men in landscapes of sun and sea represents a realization in poetry of a homosexual imaginary. It is neither fascist in essence nor a *Männerbund* of Nazi warriors in Sombart's sense, even if the crisis environment of Weimar brought it — like so much else of the period — into the orbit of Nazism.[20]

The Homosexual Vision of 'Goethes lezte Nacht ...'

The long opening poem 'Goethes lezte Nacht in Italien' ('Goethe's Last Night in Italy') is the earliest in *Das Neue Reich*, having likely been composed some time between 1905 and 1908 in the period in which George was producing the works that would be included in *Der siebente Ring* and *Der Stern des Bundes*. 'Goethes lezte Nacht' imagines the poet on his last night in Rome (22 April 1788) before returning to Germany after almost two years away. Goethe had sought Italy in desperation after a decade of ambition and frustration at the court of Saxe-Weimar:

> Unter euch lebt ich im lande der träume und töne
> In eueren domen verweilt ich · ehrfürchtiger beter ·
> Bis mich aus spitzen und schnörkeln aus nebel und trübe
> Angstschrei der seele hinüber zur sonne rief. (IX, 9)

> [I lived among you in the land of dreams and sounds.
> In your cathedrals I lingered with reverent prayers,
> Till from the nebulous gloom, the fretwork, and turrets,
> My soul cried out in torment to the sun.] (*Morwitz 281)

Goethe had left Germany in 1786 at the age of thirty-seven, on the verge of middle age. He was still a product of the Lutheran-pietistic culture of the north, although he had rebelled against German emotional and intellectual constriction during the first decade in Weimar. In Italy he discovered the warmth, sensuality and colour of southern Catholic culture, and devoted himself to scientific research, writing, art and travel, written up later in the *Italian Journey*. In his own reading, the Italian experience led to a rebirth of identity and revival of creativity, leading to the completion of important previously unfinished works, such as *Iphigenie* and *Faust, Part 1*. The syntax of 'Bis mich [...] | Angstschrei der seele hinüber zur sonne rief' conveys the desire for recognition as well as change. The cry of the soul brings liberation into life with the recognition of light and warmth. George imagines Goethe bringing the ideas for these new works back with him to a changing Germany:

> Heimwärts bring ich euch einen lebendigen strahl · (IX, 9)

> [Now I bring home to you a living beam,] (*Morwitz 281)

George's Goethe has experienced southern light, above all, in Italy, as the afterglow of antiquity, where he sees 'wesen wandeln im licht | [...] und durch reste der säulen der Seligen reigen' (IX, 8, 'creatures moving in light [...] | And through the broken columns the dance of the blessed', Morwitz 280). In the first stanza the poet remembers the gleaming Mediterranean, the deep blue of the night and, less expectedly, the appearance of the 'Heiliges Paar':

> Aus den büschen tritt nun das Paar .. vor dem Bild
> Mitten im laub-rund · leuchtender marmor wie sie ·
> Tun sie noch immer umschlungen den grossen schwur.
> Mächtig durch der finsteren bräuche gewalt
> Heben sie nun ihre häupter für herrschaft und helle. (ix, 8)

> [Now the two emerge from the grove .. before the image
> Circled with leaves · gleaming marble like them ·
> Still embraced they make the great pledge.
> Mighty through the power of dark customs, they lift
> Their heads with the promise of rule and radiance.] (*Morwitz 280)

The Greek lovers and champions of freedom against tyranny, Harmodius and Aristogeiton ('Das Paar'), are the point of reference for a large part of this first stanza. Goethe presumably had seen the statue of them in the national museum in Naples.[21] Known as the 'Tyrannicides' in writings of Thucydides and Herodotus, Harmodius and Aristogeiton became symbols of democracy and of homosexuality in ancient Athens after the assassination of the tyrant Hipparchus in 514 BC. They introduce the theme of southern light, warmth and homosexuality in *Das Neue Reich*, all of which Goethe had experienced in Italy, particularly among homosexual artists and expatriates such as Winckelmann in Rome at the time.[22] Goethe, departing Italy, glimpses the lovers and tyrannicides in their eternal pledge, at once sexual and political, as the bringers of a new era. The pallid antique figures of earlier homosexual desire are reimagined as living, not dead, statues, realizing themselves in movement, not stasis.

This poem belongs with those written sometime between 1905 and 1909, which were included in the two earlier volumes, *Der siebente Ring* and *Der Stern des Bundes*. But the imagery of antiquity and male heroism is very different. The homosexual lovers are not associated with George's mythology of 'secret Germany', the 'neues Reich' or Maximin; on the contrary, they are symbols of radical liberation from tyranny in the ancient Greek context and they are individual lovers, not members of a homoerotic-charismatic Bund. They are the bringers of a new order in which homosexual love and political emancipation from tyranny are pre-eminent. For this reason it is difficult to accept Osterkamp's reading of this poem simply as a reiteration of earlier prophecies, or even as jingoistically nationalist, given the homage paid to the 'heilige[r] Boden' of classical Greece and Italy as sources of historical, political and intellectual influence in lines 13–36. Moreover the description of the Rheinland in the fourth stanza, referring to Goethe's visit to Bingen, George's birthplace, in 1814, evokes the southern influence of the culture of wine which has passed across the 'römische[...] Walle' of the river Rhine.[23] This imagery binds north and south, Germanic and Romance and hearkens back to George's own experience as a Rhinelander, an early admirer of Mallarmé and French symbolism, and a translator into German of romance languages:

Heimwärts bring ich euch einen lebendigen strahl ·
[...]
Nehmt diesen strahl in euch auf — o nennt ihn nicht kälte! —
Und ich streu euch inzwischen im buntesten wechsel
Steine und kräuter und erze: nun alles · nun nichts ..
Bis sich verklebung der augen euch löst und ihr merket:
Zauber des Dings — und des Liebes · der göttlichen norm. (XI, 9)

[Now I bring home to you a living beam
[...]
Open yourself to this beam! Do not call it cold!
And I shall scatter you quartzes, and simples, and metals,
Colourful sequence suggesting now nothing, now all,
Till your eyes are opened and you can see the magic
Which lurks in bodies and things, the divine norm.] (*Morwitz 281)

George's rejection of the millennial promises of Christianity begs comparison with his own evocation of a youthful god in Maximin:

Sich bekehren zur wildesten wundergeschichte
Leibhaft das fleisch und das blut eines Mittlers geniessen ·
Kniend im staube ein weiteres tausendjahr
Vor einem knaben den ihr zum gott erhebt. (IX, 10)

[They will believe in the wildest of miracle-legends,
Taste with their senses the body and blood of an intermediary,
Then for another millennium kneel in the dust,
Bowed to a boy whom you have enthroned as a god.] (*Morwitz 281)

The difference lies however in the nature of the promised national redemption. The millennial hopes of an infantile and slavish Christianity are juxtaposed with the vision of physical redemption in the here and now.

The final stanza returns to the imagery of ancient Greece and to the 'noble pair' of lovers 'Sind es die schatten der sehnsucht · lieblich und quälend' ('Are these the shadows of yearning, lovely and vexing?' (IX, 10, Morwitz 282). This stanza imagines a Germany in which the physical and the spiritual, the active and the contemplative are united, a Germany perhaps under the 'tyranny of Greece' in Butler's phrase, but not one in which Christian asceticism, pre-fascist ideology, or even German nationalism is in evidence.[24] This open, Hellenized and European Germany is hardly an advertisement for Hitler before his time; nor does the voice reverberate with the prophetic tones of Goethe as precursor to George as herald of the 'neues Reich'.[25] Hence I cannot accept Osterkamp's verdict on the poem, summarized by Zanucchi as 'a nationalistic-biological distortion of the universalist educational program of Weimar Classicism'.[26]

The poem is a dramatic monologue in the sense that it portrays Goethe's thoughts on leaving Italy. Osterkamp's suggestion that George represents Germany's great poet as a precursor to himself is based on flimsy evidence such as the coincidence of dates between the appearance of the 'Vollständige Ausgabe letzter Hand', the finalized version of the complete works shortly before Goethe's death (1827–30), and George's *Das Neue Reich* a century later.[27] There is little in the text itself to justify this reading of Goethe's departure from Italy and the antique past as the symbolic heralding of the German century of the Nazi-homosexual Bund. George's Goethean elegy to the Italy he is leaving behind seems rather an attempt to preserve ancient values in the present and unite north and south, than to overcome and separate them.[28] The promise is palpable in Goethe's vision for his nation, but it is the hope for a future that builds on antiquity. Even at this stage in George's poetic development, before *Der siebente Ring* and *Der Stern des Bundes*, it is a promise that does not exaggerate 'heroic' values to foreshadow Nazism.

'Goethes lezte Nacht in Italien' was written when George was still infatuated with the idea of Maximin and the cult of the Bund. But this poem also already evidences the attraction of an alternative homosexual model in the pair of ancient lovers, combining heroic masculinity with homosexual identity and reducing the Bund to the pair. The longstanding love of southern culture is not infused with a new bellicose nationalism, but rather represents a merging of north and south that is closer to Winckelmann than to Hitler. It is not hard to see why this poem found no place in earlier collections, despite its origins in the years immediately following the death of Maximin. While 'Goethes lezte Nacht in Italien' shares some of the millennial-visionary tones of the earlier volumes, national redemption is imagined through the historical pair, not the single narcissistic ego-ideal. The redemptive nationalism may render this poem unappealing and dated, but it is not militarist masculinism. The historical lovers are idealized as the forerunners of a free Germany, but Osterkamp's reading of pre-Nazi political content is over-determined by later history and fails to account for the actual forces at work in George's poetry. In reading the pair of lovers as warriors he overlooks the antagonistic tone of homosexual self-assertion projected into these figures, the product of a suppressed identity at the point of emergence. It may not be an attractive image of homosexuality, but it is present and it is not simply aggressive nationalist masculinism.

In Germany, unlike Britain or France at this time, the notion of homosexuals as the modern-day embodiments of the 'erhabenes Paar' (IX, 10), linking them with ancient figures such as Harmodius and Aristogeiton, the Theban Band, or Achilles and Patroclus, had the potential to develop in three different directions. It could move, firstly, towards greater self-liberation and release from socially, culturally and historically determined forces of identification through imaginative construction of social roles; secondly towards the instrumentalization of the youth movement under the alibi of Greek pederasty as a cover for paedophile exploitation; or thirdly towards the instrumentalization of homoerotic libido in the service of a specific ideology of masculinism — also an offshoot of figures associated with the youth movement, such as Wyneken and, later, Blüher. This latter direction was, to be sure, constructed as a socially validated force, building the national community. But in fact it represented a dangerous option for those men who saw it in the first instance as a means of finding male company in a homoerotic environment. After the First World War, this movement became increasingly nationalist and militarized in the right-wing *Männerbund* groups, and by the late 1920s the homoerotic elements were being eradicated in the name of emergent Nazism. The first of these directions opened up the possibilities of a homosexual imaginary and a reconception of the potential life-span of homosexual men, the latter two represented developments incompatible with Western understandings of sexual orienation and identity. But of course history provides a clarifying lens: at the time these lineaments were not so clear.

Hölderlin's Transfigured Germany

The newly discovered late works of Friedrich Hölderlin exerted a powerful influence on George at this time. Norbert von Hellingrath became a member of George's circle around 1908, brought out his edition of Hölderlin's Pindar translations in the Verlag der Blätter für die Kunst in 1910, and began publishing a full edition of Hölderlin's works in 1912. He was killed at Verdun in 1916. By this time, according to sources such as Klaus Mann, Max Kommerell and Walter Benjamin, Hölderlin's poetic image of Germany was the most important influence alongside Plato for the Circle and for academic youth in general.[29] In 'Hyperion I–III', written between 1911 and 1914, George reflects Hölderlin's transfigured language of contemporary alienation and imaginative identification with Hellas as a pre-Christian culture in which body and soul have not yet been divided. And again, while George's themes of heroic death and the Reich are evoked towards the end of 'Hyperion III', it is in the service of love, not war:

> [...] LIEBE GEBAR DIE WELT . LIEBE GEBIERT SIE NEU. (IX, 14)
>
> [[...] Love engendered
> The world and Love shall kindle it again.] (Morwitz 285)

And if the god of the last line, around whom the circle is closed, is a figuration of Maximin, it is as the deity of a circle of loving men, that defines the new Reich. While the sentiments may not be palatable or agreeable for a modern audience, the context of a homosexuality still unspoken and lacking any sort of positive social validation renders these sentiments and ideas comprehensible. George's Bund has much more to do with the nineteenth-century idealization of Greek homosexuality as the only socially acceptable form of public attestation than with the post-war men's groups. Yet George insists on the physical component of love, where other early advocates (including the figures associated with the *Gemeinschaft der Eigenen* and with the homoerotic youth movement including Blüher) insisted on platonic (i.e. non-physical) love of one sort of another. Whether this was hypocritical or not (i.e. whether they in fact refrained from male-male sex) is irrelevant. The issue was to express the physical relations between men, thereby contributing to the ongoing dynamic of homosexual identity at this time. George speaks to homosexual men, among others, and in this he is unique. He is not primarily interested in advocating rights and hence had little interest in figures such as Magnus Hirschfeld or in debates about decriminalization or public acceptance.

In comparing Hölderlin's evocation of an ideal future through the feminine image of Diotima to George's masculine Maximin in *Hyperion* I–III, Osterkamp

THE HEALING OF NARCISSUS 157

identifies George's transformation of the sphere of (female) freedom and individual self-determination into (male) dominance and hierarchy.[30] However the evocation of an adored masculine other does not evoke subservience to a warrior myth for a homosexual audience. Rather, the valorization of homosexuality through idealized images of historical masculinity enables a self-confirmation that was otherwise unavailable for a homosexual imaginary that had until this point been negatively determined by the medical, legal and criminal spheres. As many post-war men's groups showed their true colours and merged with the Nazi movement, many homosexual men, including writers and intellectuals who had dallied with the far right, would realize that this promise of homoerotic fulfilment could prove a fatal mistake.

The poems of 'Kinder des Meeres' were written before the outbreak of war in early 1914, addressing young men from George's past and present in an elegiac mode, expressing affection and the recognition of lives lived partly in and partly out of his orbit:

Einst mir verehrt und gastlich · dann gemieden
Vergelten nun die vielgesichtigen wogen
Die lange scheu? [...]
Seefahrend heil und sucht des abenteuers
Reisst dich — den heftigen zauber frommer tage —
Aus unseren augen auf das fernste meer. (IX, 16)
Versippter uns durch der gemeinschaft brauch
Wirst bald du fahren · unsrer hut entzogen ·
Macht-rühmlicher! Aus deinem edlen hafen
In welches neue land auf welch ein meer? (IX, 18)

[Once I revered you as my host — then shunned you.
Is this the vengeance for my long evasion,
[...]
A sailor's luck and hunger for adventure
Sweep you, the startling spell in days of fervour,
Beyond our ken and to the furthest sea. (Morwitz 286)
More kin to us through common rites of life,
Your quest begins, and wrested from our keeping
— Greater in force — you leave your noble harbour
To seek what other land, what other sea?] (Morwitz 287)

The adolescent boy on the verge of manhood had become central to homosexual literature by this time, for example in Mann's Tadzio or Mackay's Fenny Skaller. In George these figures are described with a sense of integrity and alterity, and with affection. The controlling, manipulating voice of the prophet and master of *Der Stern des Bundes* is absent. George's fascination appears to be with adolescence or early manhood as a moment on the threshold of life. There is none of the lubriciousness that characterized the writing and illustrations of other homosexual publications of this era, for example Brand's journal *Der Eigene*:

Sorglosen gangs schleppst du geheime kette
Entziehst dich uns und gibst nur froh vertraun

Dass das geweihte blut der licht-gehaarten
Noch pulst in süss unsinnigem verschwenden. (IX, 16)

[Though free of care, you seem to drag a chain,
Elude us, and yet strengthen our belief
That those with hair as fair as light still squander
Their priceless blood in sweet and senseless spending.] (Morwitz 286)

The discovery of homosexual orientation and its social significance lends these poems an elegiac quality. Looking back, the poet recognizes that this was the last experience of a life uncomplicated by the loneliness, self-castigation and social exclusion of the self-accepting homosexual, or the hypocrisy and dissembling, self-hatred and unfulfilment of the married or closet homosexual.

The fourth of these poems, 'Nachklang' ('Echo'), was written by Ernst Morwitz, copying George's vocabulary and style in response to the three earlier poems, and extending the argument of promise and loss as a form of counterpoint in which he, the 27-year-old disciple, finds what they have lost. This quartet reveals a new aspect of the lyric voice, letting the others go their ways, not seeking to control or return them. The inclusion of Morwitz's epilogue is telling too, in its combination of devotion (to the man and his style) and adoption of the role of disciple and judge. Nowhere in this collection is George's opacity of intention more evident than in the inclusion of this poem by his favoured disciple. Was this simply a recognition of Morwitz's services and success in copying his vocabulary and manner? Or did it signal a recognition on George's part of the role that his disciples were taking on in relation to him? If the latter is the case, the inclusion suggests relinquishment of the control that was his hallmark. In the following poem, 'Der Krieg', one of the most important in the volume, the sources of such resignation might be found.

The Killing of Young Men in 'Der Krieg'

The outbreak of war led to a redefinition of the relationship between the poet, the lyric autobiography, and the socio-literary phenomenon propagated by members of the Circle. The long poem, 'Der Krieg' ('The War', IX, 21), written sometime before mid 1917, breaks with the charismatic self-idealization that reached a high point in *Der Stern des Bundes*, and brings about a reconnection and re-engagement with German reality.[31] The power of the poem derives from the tension between the homosexual poet's distress at the deaths of young men and the socio-politics of imperialist German nationalism. The tensions between war and the ideal of the Bund which underpin this poem mark a new — and final — threshold in George's lyric life after the homoerotic transcendental idealism of *Der Stern des Bundes*. George is unable either to cut himself off from contemporary reality (as he had before the war) for an itinerant life as master-poet, seer and charismatic leader, or to engage with the reality of the new Germany other than in terms of personal distress and public castigation. The engagement with the war, brought on by the enlistment and suffering of many of the disciples (particularly Percy Gothein and Bernhard von Uxkull-Gyllenband), obliged George to review his relationships in human terms rather than in the idealized language of *Der Stern des Bundes*. Edith

Landmann reports his comment in November 1923: 'Als [...] die Rede auf den Krieg kam, meinte er, Teile von ihm seien an der Front gewesen.'[32]

'Der Krieg' begins with a citation from canto seventeen of Dante's *Paradiso* (George's translation), recounting Dante's indictment of his native town and the words of Cacciaguida, Dante's ancestor, who foretells the poet's banishment from his Florentine homeland.[33] Cacciaguida tells his mortal guest that the demands of conscience must override those of patriotism: 'Do not resort to lies | let what you write reveal all you have seen [...] Though when your words are taken in at first they may taste bitter, but once well-digested | they will become a vital nutriment.' This preface sets up an authoritative precedent for George's criticism of Germany and, by replacing Dante's 'menzogna' ('lies') with 'Schmucke' ('false ornamentation') unites the moral with the aesthetic.[34] George's bitterness towards the national bonding that took place with the outbreak of war is powerfully expressed in the extended simile of the Germans as savage animals, used to turning on each other, but running as a pack when disaster strikes:

> Wie das getier der wälder das bisher
> Sich scheute oder fletschend sich zerriss
> Bei jähem brand und wenn die erde bebt
> Sich sucht und nachbarlich zusammendrängt:
> So in zerspaltner heimat schlossen sich
> Beim schrei DER KRIEG die gegner an ..
> (George, *Das Neue Reich*, SW, IX, 22)

> [As jungle beasts, which slink away or snarl
> At one another in their greed to rend,
> Seek company and huddle in a flock
> When forests are ablaze, or mountains quake,
> So in our country, split to factions, foes
> United at the cry of war.] (Morwitz 290)

The war is a response to inner fragmentation ('in zerspaltner heimat') and innate savagery, not external forces. National identity is merely a moment of hitherto unknown empathy ('eingefühl'), confusion and apprehension ('verworrnes ahnen') among the different strata, making them forget the emptiness and banality of the national past. 'Das volk [...] sah sich gross in seiner not' ('The nation saw itself as great in its need'). This, not '*das neue Reich*', is German reality.

Poets as different as Rilke, Trakl and Heym had written of the war in terms of sublime terror, apocalypse and redemptive destruction.[35] However George in 'Der Krieg' distinguishes clearly between wartime destruction and human redemption:

> [...] kein triumf wird sein ·
> Nur viele untergänge ohne würde ...
> [...]
> Der selbst lacht grimm wenn falsche heldenreden
> Von vormals klingen der als brei und klumpen
> Den bruder sinken sah · der in der schandbar
> Zerwühlten erde hauste wie geziefer ..
> Der alte Gott der schlachten ist nicht mehr. (IX, 24)

> There will be no victory,
> But only downfalls, many and inglorious ..
> [...]
> He who saw his comrade crushed to pulp and fragments,
> Who lived the life of vermin in the broken
> And desecrated earth, must laugh with anger
> At speeches once heroic, now deceitful.
> The ancient god of battles is no more.] (*Morwitz 291)

The battles of the past, idealized in the earlier poetry, fought according to the rules of ancient warfare belong to an imaginary sphere that no longer obtains. George pillories Paul von Hindenburg as the man who saved the Reich but cannot save the Germans from themselves or young men from the murderous fantasies of their elders:

> Wo zeigt der Mann sich der vertritt? Das Wort
> Das einzig gilt fürs spätere Gericht? (IX, 24)
>
> [Where is the man who stands for all? And where is
> The only word that holds on Judgment Day?] (Morwitz 292)

Even in its metaphorical extremes this language does not render human destruction sublime. Sublimity remains for George in the reality of the young men who are killed, not in the mode of their deaths:

> Heilig sind nur die säfte
> Noch makelfrei verspritzt — ein ganzer strom. (IX, 24)
>
> [The only ichors that are sacred
> Are those which, still unstained, are spent in floods.] (Morwitz 291)

For the 'hermit on the mount', the voice of the poem, the war is nothing new:

> Was euch erschüttert ist mir lang vertraut·
> Lang hab ich roten schweiss der angst geschwitzt
> Als man mit feuer spielte .. meine tränen
> Vorweg geweint .. heut find ich keine mehr.
> Das meiste war geschehn und keiner sah .. (IX, 22)
>
> [What grips you now — I knew it long ago!
> Long have I sweated blood of anguish while
> They played and played with fire. I exhausted
> My tears before and I have none today.
> The thing was almost done and no one saw.] (Morwitz 290)

The self-stylization of the poet-hermit is given deeper resonance through the echoes from Old and New Testament, breaking any simple identification with Nietzsche's Zarathustra for an older, more stable topos of prophetic scorn.[36] He cannot feel in this conflict as they do, as he has foreseen it all. The earlier events of the century, the Morocco crisis of 1905 and the sabre-rattling of the increasingly belligerent states, had prepared him to expect the worst, even if he was alone in his knowledge. And yet the phenomena of this war pale beside the greater evil of 'mord am Leben selbst' ('the killing of life itself'). The culture of death and the destruction of the nation's young men is a crime that George holds not against the foreign enemy, but against the everyday *Bürger*, men and women alike who have thrown the country into the fervour of war. Against the rhetoric of national glory is the reality of the glazed eyes and dismembered bodies ('verglasten augen and zerfeztem leib') of sons and nephews. Yet they too, the young and the followers, are guilty, since they, 'the youngest and most precious' ('die jüngsten | Der teuren') have participated of their own accord: 'Sie wissen was sie treibt und was sie feit' ('They know what drives, what renders them immune!'). Of the disciples, Salin, Gothein, Thormaehlen, Wolters, Morwitz, Hildebrandt, Heyer, Hellingrath, and the two Boehringer brothers enlisted; even Wolfskehl tried to enlist but was rejected on account of his poor eyesight. Gundolf enthusiastically corresponded with George about the war and eventually also was drafted.[37] For George this represented a betrayal of the life-affirming 'secret Germany'. The power of the poem arises from the poet-prophet's bitterness at the failure of his nation which has thrown itself into war and despoiled the aesthetic-ideological goal of the Bund as the imagined core of a new, better Germany.[38]

Commentators have been quick to seize upon aspects of the poem such as the use of the expression 'Blut-Schmach', literally 'blood-disgrace'. According to the editorial commentary, 'Blut-Schmach' signifies 'blood guilt as murder of members of one's own people'.[39] Norton translates it as a racist term, 'miscegenation', which seems exaggerated to say the least.[40] The evocation of a cycle of civilizational purity and decline in this poem is neither new nor surprising in the intellectual context of the time. Thomas Mann, for example, refers to 'the Asiatic danger' in a group discussion with Erich von Kahler in May 1919 and the motif is present in the cholera advancing from the east in *Death in Venice*.[41] However the term seems rather to refer to the disgrace of the killing of young German men in a war unleashed by their Kaiser himself.

The criticisms of George's reactionary stance neglect the tension overall between contempt and pain that brings out the poem's greatest lines. The effect of the poem results from the cognitive dissonance that the war brought about by war in this writer who had adopted the pose of prophet and charismatic leader in *Der Stern des Bundes*. J. P. Stern has commented that 'Der Krieg' shows George at his best and his worst as a poet and ideologue.[42] However it is not the ideological coherence of the poet-as-Zarathustra that is central to this poem. Rather it is the tensions between this earlier prophetic role and the reality of the war that render this poem problematic and interesting in terms of George's development. 'Der Krieg' is not an apocalyptic vision of redemptive terror, but a barrage of scorn and castigation from one who, unlike most of his contemporaries, had never supported the war, even in its beginnings. The stance has something of the lofty denunciation of the disillusioned poets of Rome, Catullus, Horace or Persius, castigating the failures of their day through thundering evocations of the grandeur of the past. The poem has moments of grandiosity, to be sure. But the tone of hurt comes from the heart, revealing a man who can no longer maintain his stance of aesthetically distanced contempt. George had long hated the Germany that generated the war. But he had been able to detach himself during peacetime, occupying an aesthetic existence as charismatic leader of a tiny group of young men. The war took from him not only his closest advisers, friends and lovers; it also robbed him of the pretention to autonomy. His aestheticism, which reached a high point in *Der Stern des Bundes*, focussing on the idealized homoerotic relationship symbolized in Maximin, was brought down by the forces of German *bürgerlich* normality that he had scorned for so long. In 'Der Krieg' he recognizes that his project to create an aesthetic myth of a new Germany has failed.

Where Rilke transfigured the war in sublime metaphors celebrating August 1914 in his *Fünf Gesänge* (*Five Songs*), George was torn between myth and tragedy, his charismatic role foundering on the reality of the war and the mutilation of the young men he loved:

> Wie faulige frucht
> Schmeckt das gered von hoh-zeit auferstehung
> In welkem ton. [...]
> Keiner der heute ruft und meint zu führen
> Merkt wie er taste im verhängnis · keiner
> Erspäht ein blasses glühn vom morgenrot. (IX, 25)

> [The withered cant
> Of zenith and a resurrection savours
> Of rotted fruit. [...]
> Not one who summons now and thinks he governs,
> Knows that he gropes about in doom, and no one
> Can see the palest flicker of a dawn.] (Morwitz 292)

In the final stanzas the poet saves the memory of 'secret Germany' as an aesthetic unity of Greece and Germany, a pastoral vision 'wo der traum noch webt' ('where the dream still weaves'):

> Zu schön als dass dich fremder tritt verheere:
> Wo flöte aus dem weidicht tönt · aus hainen
> Windharfen rauschen · wo der Traum noch webt
> Untilgbar durch die jeweils trünnigen erben ..
> Wo die allblühende Mutter der verwildert
> Zerfallenen weissen Art zuerst enthüllte
> Ihr echtes antlitz .. Land dem viel verheissung
> Noch innewohnt [...] (IX, 26)

> [Too beautiful for alien feet to ravage,
> Where groves are harps for winds, where in the osiers
> A flute resounds, and where the dream still weaves,
> Although your children always try to rend it,
> And where the radiant mother of white peoples
> Now fallen and turned wild, first showed
> Her true face, O land, still hiding
> So great a promise [...]] (*Morwitz 293)

This evocation of an ideal Germany reveals the depth of George's loss.

The poem ends with a striking juxtaposition of the images of Germanic, Greek and Judeo-Christian cultures. Tyr, driver of the storm-clouds and herald of the

'Längste[r] Winter', is imagined alongside the crucified Christ; the mutilated Wotan hangs from Yggdrasil, and the sun-god Apollo whispers the secret of the future to his Germanic brother, Baldur:

> 'Eine weile währt noch nacht ·
> Doch diesmal kommt von Osten nicht das licht'. (IX, 26)
>
> [For a while there will be night
> But this time light will not come from the east...] (Morwitz 294)

Whether this is a message of hope, or not, is unclear, but the master of the future is he who can adapt to the times, not the prophet clinging to the past:[43]

> Sieger
> Bleibt wer das schutzbild birgt in seinen marken
> Und Herr der zukunft wer sich wandeln kann. (IX, 26)
>
> [He is the victor
> Who harbours the protective image within himself,
> And he who can change is Lord of worlds to come.] (*Morwitz 294)

This final recognition of his own obsolescence — as a prophet of the eternal, not a lord of transience — is, as J. P. Stern remarks, 'a strange conclusion'.[44] Yet it is in accordance with the unresolved tensions of the poem, in which past achievements and present loss are juxtaposed. The dream of 'secret Germany' and the vision of the homoerotic Bund is set against the mutilation of the young men's bodies in the modern imperial war ('brei und klumpen'), the perversion of the ideal of the nation, and the transformation of the charismatic poet-leader into the bitter voice of disillusionment. For von Petersdorff, 'Der Krieg' shows the full extent of the destruction of George's dream of a restoration of the mental oneness of individual and society.[45] For George, therefore, the war is not conceived as an agent of rebirth. On the contrary, it introduces an era of change, of a modernity that would destroy his poetic dreams of revival. George's war breaks once and for all the hope of linking history to the dream of a new nation.[46]

The Healing of Narcissus

'Der Krieg' embodies many of the tensions between past and present, ideology and feeling, self- (narcissistic) and other-oriented (object-centred) libido. Further poems in this collection revise earlier ideational constructs and memories. Self-doubt and scepticism take the place of the prophetic omniscience of parts of Der Stern des Bundes and of the adventurous self-exploration that characterized Das Jahr der Seele and Der Teppich des Lebens. However, there is also something new which Claude David identified early, if in problematic terms, namely a quality of freedom, generosity and grace after the tension of Der Stern des Bundes.[47] For David, George's decision to quit writing with this volume was based on the belief that art had lost its self-justification.[48] David identifies a new aspect in the mature George, a commitment to the men and youths around him that has divested itself of the prophetic, demanding and hortatory tones of the earlier work.[49] While the tone of

Der Stern des Bundes is still perceptible, it is muted and lacking conviction; no longer claiming a confident, unified world view or utopian vision. The poet's task in 'Der Dichter in Zeiten der Wirren' dedicated to Bernhard Count Uxkull, is framed in more modest terms:[50]

> Der Sänger aber sorgt in trauer-läuften
> Dass nicht das mark verfault · der keim erstickt.
> Er schürt die heilige glut die über-springt
> Und sich die leiber formt · er holt aus büchern
> Der ahnen die verheissung die nicht trügt
> Dass die erkoren sind zum höchsten ziel
> Zuerst durch tiefste öden ziehn dass einst
> Des erdteils herz die welt erretten soll ..
> Und wenn im schlimmsten jammer lezte hoffnung
> Zu löschen droht: so sichtet schon sein aug
> Die lichtere zukunft. (IX, 29–30)

> [But in a mournful age it is the poet
> Who keeps the marrow sound, the germ alive.
> He stirs the holy flame that leaps across
> And shapes the flesh, he gathers from the books
> Of the ancestors the tidings that do not deceive
> That those elected to the highest goal
> Begin by passing through the wastelands, that once
> The heart of this continent shall redeem the earth.
> And when the final hope has almost perished
> In sternest grief, his eyes shall already see
> The coming light.] (*Morwitz 296)

The vocabulary of the poet's role is drawn from the same aesthetic-mythic sphere as earlier, but the aims here are modest, ultimately merely to retain the memory for the better future of the new Reich.

> Ein jung geschlecht das wieder mensch und ding
> Mit echten maassen misst · das schön und ernst
> Froh seiner einzigkeit · vor Fremdem stolz ·
> Sich gleich entfernt von klippen dreisten dünkels
> Wie seichtem sumpf erlogner brüderei (IX, 30)

> [A young generation that again has honest standards
> For the measure of men and things, who fair and grave
> Rejoice in their oneness, feel pride among strangers
> Avoid the rocks of brazen boasting
> And the morass of false brotherhood.] (*Morwitz 296–97)

And while the terminology of the 'neues Reich' with which George ends the poem had become politicized by 1917/18 when this poem was written, it was by no means under sole ownership of the political far right; it remains here a term drawn from George's poetic vocabulary, reactionary-romantic to be sure, but not prefiguring Nazism. Holding George responsible for the Nazis' appropriation of the swastika or the terminology of the 'Reich' makes little sense in historical terms. George refused throughout the 1920s to change the images and expressions that he had been using for decades before the Nazis came along. This was signalled later in his choice of Morwitz, whose Jewish ancestry rendered him anathema to the Nazis, to reject in his name all honours by the Nazi state, including the Presidency of the Prussian Academy of the Arts. The poem, 'Einem jungen Führer im Ersten Weltkrieg' similarly eschews militarist or nationalist language as it addresses a young soldier devastated by the experiences of war, returning to peace-time life. This poem is striking for its empathy with the soldier who participated in a war that George had staunchly opposed.

Large parts of these poems are made up of condemnation, even vituperation, of the state of things, registering a level of engagement with external social and political reality that is rare in the earlier poems. In 'Geheimes Deutschland' the poet is awakened from his state of aversion to the present to find the inner truth again of the 'heilige heimat' ('holy homeland') and the original promise of the figure of Maximin. ('Da stand ER in winters erleuchtetem saal' (IX, 47, 'In winter he stood in the candle-lit hall', Morwitz 306). Yet this poem, for all its desire to return to the idealized dreams of *Der Stern des Bundes*, is an elegy inspired by a dream vision of Pan, a symbol of the natural order buried deep within all of us. In the following stanzas the poet remembers various figures from his past, beginning with Maximilian as a young man in 1904 in Fasching costume. This is not Maximin, the German hero and self-object of *Der Stern des Bundes*. George's memory moves across diverse friends and associates from his past, including Hans von Prott, Ernst Glöckner, Saladin Schmitt, Karl Wolfskehl, and Berthold Vallentin.[51] Underpinning each of these memories is the poet's recognition that meaning is to be found inside, in the 'secret Germany' of these young men, not in their external present:

> Wer denn · wer von euch brüdern
> Zweifelt · schrickt nicht beim mahnwort
> Dass was meist ihr emporhebt
> Dass was meist heut euch wert dünkt
> Faules laub ist im herstwind
> Endes- und todesbereich:
> Nur was im schützenden schlaf
> Wo noch kein taster es spürt
> Lang in tiefinnerstem schacht
> Weihlicher erde noch ruht —
> Wunder undeutbar für heut
> Geschick wird des kommenden tages. (IX, 49)

> [Who then, who of you brothers
> Doubts, unshocked by the warning,
> That what most you acclaim, what
> Most you value today is
> Rank as leaves in the autumn-wind,
> Doomed to perdition and death!
> Only what consecrate earth
> Cradles in sheltering sleep
> Long in the innermost grooves,
> Far from acquisitive hands,

> Marvels this day cannot grasp
> Are rife with the fate of tomorrow.] (*Morwitz 307)

The southern influences of Goethe's *Italian Journey* and Arnold Böcklin's neo-romantic modernism, as well as the voice of the mocking satyr, Silenus, in Nietzsche's *Birth of Tragedy* are perceptible in the cloven hoof, and the 'Mittagsschreck' ('midday terror') in both 'Geheimes Deutschland' ('Secret Germany', IX, 46–49) and 'Der mensch und der drud' ('Man and Faun', IX, 54–56). In each case, the primeval spirit of nature warns the poet that he who forgets the magic of life will die: 'Nur durch den zauber bleibt das leben wach' ('Only by magic is life kept awake', IX, 56). Essential to these poems is the explicit or tacit recognition that the war has changed everything, putting an end to the fantasy of Maximin and the Bund and opening the ageing poet's eyes to truths about himself and his life.

Similarly in the 'Gebete' ('Prayers'), 'Geheimes Deutschland' ('Secret Germany'), and 'Burg Falkenstein' George revisits the past, but not in the spirit of conservative revival or political reactionary modernism, despite the overblown language of some of these works. These poems are, as von Petersdorff and others point out, written in a quite different spirit from that of anti-modernist defiance.[52] They accept the passing of life and time, and hope lies deep still in the sleeping imagination, not in the politics of the future.

Eckhart Grünewald defines George's 'secret Germany' as a vision of inner unity, sometimes used for the George Circle, sometimes as a nostalgic or utopian evocation of the nation itself.[53] George himself used it in 1922 as the title for the poem which questions his future-utopian vision of Germany. Here too, there is a tone of *apologia pro vita mia*, of a man relinquishing past hopes and dreams as he looks back over a life in which the scaffolding had come to overshadow the structure. In poems such as 'Der mensch und der drud' ('Man and Faun') George explores the individual's relationship to nature in less loaded anti-modern terms than in earlier evocations of pre-modern life. In this poem, the faun represents those chthonic forces of nature that George had, paradoxically, repressed in order to build the ideology of aesthetic homosexuality. The faun is still a rebarbative figure, with the dialogue form indicating the ongoing opposition of nature and consciousness. For the poet, however, the recognition of nature in the figure of the faun is significant: it suggests a new willingness to face the raw forces which opposed everything his aestheticism stood for.

In the middle section of verses to the living and to the dead, George continues the theme of reminiscence and memory, surveying those who were important to him, the men both dead and alive who were the focus of his life. Divested of the obsolete imagery of warrior and secret nation, this poetry celebrates the lives of those whom George loved. The 'Sprüche an die Toten' ('Verses to the Dead') open with bitter recrimination of the failure of Germans to have liberated themselves from 'the shackles of bondage' (IX, 90). But the Germanic imagery of 'Walstatt' (battlefield) and 'Helden' (heroes) ends here.

This theme of reckoning with the past is new to *Das Neue Reich*. The self-doubt and self-exploration of the early volumes and the narcissistic-charismatic self-idealization of *Der siebente Ring* and *Der Stern des Bundes* are superseded by a sense of fragility and vulnerability, even frailty and failure. The voice of the ageing poet is at once weaker and more convincing in its lack of bombast. These poems approach other human beings — friends or loved ones — with lyric depth and a penetrating subtlety that is incompatible with his earlier language of Wagnerian hyperbole. The individual poems express human, not divine, sadness and personal failure. The opening poem of the 'Sprüche an die Toten', addressed to the 27-year-old Heinrich Friedemann who died in Polish Masuria in 1915, for example, is tender and personal:

> Leicht wie ein kind ein vogel · froh im wahne
> Im aug schon die bestimmung gingst du fort ..
> Du ein entrückter schon bein abschiedswort ..
> Als ersten deckt dich · freund · die schöne fahne. (IX, 91)

> [Blithe as a child, a bird, joyful in your belief
> You left us, friend, your fate was in your eye,
> And you — away before you said goodbye —
> Were first to fall, the gallant flag your shroud.] (*Morwitz 333)

The poem dedicated to 'Walter W' (Walter Wenghöfer) who took his own life in 1918 similarly extends a 'negative capability' to this poet whom George had known since around 1904 and addressed in an earlier poem, 'Einem Dichter' in *Der siebente Ring* (VI/VII, 172). Wenghöfer's imaginative response to the world of Watteau competed with and compensated for the depression and failure in his lived life:[54]

> Schwermütiger tanz der täuschend leicht-gesinnten
> In zarter zier mit rosen-bausch und -falte
> Da leben leztesmal sich band und ballte:
> Dort war mein reich .. doch war es — liegt weit hinten.
> Wo ist ein halt noch heut wo eine stütze? (IX, 91)

> [Their mournful dance whose lightness was pretended!
> The puffs of dainty satin, pink and frilled!
> They were the last whose lives were linked and filled.
> This was my world — it was — but now is ended.
> Where can I find a footing, where a prop?] (*Morwitz 334)

The relationship and the sense of failure of the poet is powerfully conveyed in 'Wolfgang', dedicated to Wolfgang Heyer who went missing in action in 1917:

> Was soll ich deinem stummen blick erwidern?
> Ich gäbe gern dir mehr zum abschied mit .. (IX, 92)

> [How can I reply to your silent gaze?
> Would that I could give you more for your farewell ..] (*Morwitz 334)

These short poems celebrating shared life with past friends are generous and affectionate. The bombastic self-glorification of Maximin and the grandiosity of the 'neues Reich' have evaporated, leaving the poet with nothing more than the memories. These are some of George's most open and forgiving poems, softening the hard tones of the earlier inflexible and demanding master. Amongst the living, new figures emerge; for example 'M', identified only by an initial (probably Ernst Morwitz), as someone loved and appreciated for his otherness in the 'Sprüche an die Lebenden':

> Versunkner träumer ward nun ein begleiter
> Der aus dem zwielicht strebt zum vollen licht ·
> Er schreitet neben mir gelöst und heiter
> Und netzt mit tau das kindliche gesicht. (IX, 83)

> [The sunken dreamer now becomes a comrade,
> Striving from the grey of dawn to light's fullness,
> He walks beside me relaxed and cheerful,
> And gently bathes his childish face with dew.] (*Morwitz 329)

Von Petersdorff points to the grief expressed in the short poems to dead friends such as Friedemann, Wenghöfer, Heyer and others.[55] Here too, the march of modernity has rendered the poet's ideology of return meaningless. For von Petersdorff George's radical anti-modernism has left him cast adrift, with no means of positioning himself even linguistically in spiritual-affective or historic-geographical terms.[56] I draw different, although not incompatible, conclusions from George's expressions of grief, anger and loss of earlier certainties.

The final, longer poem of the section, 'Victor ★ Adalbert', was written shortly after George heard of the double suicide of the two young deserters Bernhard von Uxkull-Gyllenband and Adalbert Cohrs at the end of July 1918. According to Karlauf, this affected George more deeply than anything else during the war years. Karlauf cites Ernst Glöckner's letter to Ernst Bertram:

> Adalbert und Bernhard sind beide tot. Da sie es nicht mehr in Deutschland aushielten — sie sollten getrennt werden, jeder sollte wieder zu seinem Regiment zurück — unternahmen sie einen Fluchtversuch nach Holland, der missglückte.[57]

> [Adalbert and Bernhard are both dead. Since they couldn't stand it any longer in Germany — they would have been separated as each was obliged to return to his regiment — they tried to escape to Holland but failed.]

The two were picked up near the border and both shot themselves rather than undergo trial for desertion.[58] 'Victor ★ Adalbert' is a dialogue between the two immediately before their suicide. Adalbert foresees his own death at the front as well as Germany's loss; Victor tries to convince him to live, but to no avail. He resolves to die alongside his partner. Unlike 'Der Krieg' it does not focus on the carnage and brutality of war, but rather on the desperation of the situation and the pair's loyalty and inseparability. Karlauf refers to it as a 'heroic interpretation' in which Victor's love is such that he puts Adalbert's fate above his own, like the dioscuri Castor and Pollux.[59] George avoids the reality of the abject misery of the pair as their reason for desertion. The poem is, after all, about homosexual love. Victor chooses death over life without his lover. This represents a threshold in George's self-understanding, since it is about the love of two men for each other, not for an idealized self-object or cultic figure:

[Ich] bleibe treu dem schwur der uns verbunden
Im jünglingsjahr den immer wir besiegelt ..
Ich bin untrennbar mit dir . seis auch schuld ·
Und wenn nach deinem schicksal du beschlossen
Durchs dunkle tor zu gehen: so nimm mich mit! (IX, 96)

[[I] Believe in all that holds for you and keep
The vow we made when we were adolescent
And often have repeated since. I cannot
Live on without you, impious though it be.
So if you choose the gate of dark, obeying
Your destiny in this, then take me too!] (Morwitz 337)

In the earlier poem to the dead Walter W. (IX, 91) the suicide represents the end of meaning in the wartime context:

Wo ist ein halt noch heut wo eine stütze?
Die pfosten faulen alle angeln rasseln
Bald wird im morschen bau die flamme prasseln.
Was ist zu tun für uns? was not was nütze? (IX, 91)

[Where can we find a footing where a prop?
The hinges creak and all the rafters crumble,
Soon in the brittle house the flames will tumble,
What shall we do? How can we help or stop?] (Morwitz 334)

In 'Victor ★ Adalbert' the poet attempts to give meaning to the death of his beloved Uxkull-Gyllenband and Cohrs by showing loyalty to be based on love. This is the final poem in the 'Sprüche an die Toten', leading to section three, 'Das Lied' ('The Song') in which the personal register of autobiographical intimacy gives way to folk-songs of elemental power about states of love, all with the exception of 'Das Lied' (1910) and 'Schifferlied' ('Sailor's Song', 1914) written after the end of the war in 1918 and 1919, with 'Der lezte der getreuen' ('The Last of the True') 'Das licht' ('The Light') and 'In stillste ruh' ('Through deepest rest') written in 1928.

The folk-song motif of the return in 'Das Lied' communicates the existential significance of experience. A young man finds himself back in his village after seven years in the magic forest, a wise simpleton whose only listeners are the children with their lives still before them. As an allegory of the poet's experience it is unmistakeable. 'Schifferlied' takes the lyric voice of the departed sailor, drowned at sea, at once remembering and foreseeing his lover's grief. Here too, the curious mixture of retrospectivity and presence suggests a life which is given meaning by, but has released itself from, the past. In 'Seelied' ('Sea Song') an old woman, materially secure but lonely, finds joy only in the daily sight of a passing child. The simple promise of the future in this poem as elsewhere in the collection, does not depend on the Bund, 'secret Germany', or the revival of the 'new empire', but simply on a child's existence. Aided on the wayside by a man she has long admired, 'die törichte pilgerin' ('the foolish pilgrim') foretells that she will only be remembered by him for having been helped. The lyric voice is the man's, who recognizes in retrospect the truth of the woman. Recognition and knowledge come long after experience has passed. In 'Der letzte der getreuen' ('The Last of the Faithful') the king will not return, but the passionate loyalty of the 'last of the faithful' is no less significant for the loss of its object:

> Und kehrt er nie mehr hier zurück
> Holt er mich nicht zu seinem dienst —
> Gibt mir nur EINES ziel und sinn:
> Mit meinem könig sterben! (IX, 106)

> [And if he never should return
> Nor summon me to serve him there,
> My only thought and aim is: die
> When he, my king, is dying.] (Morwitz 342)

In 'Das Wort' ('The Word') knowledge is limited to cultural experience and memory. The foreign jewel that the traveller brings with him remains unnamed and hence without significance. As in 'Das Lied', the knowledge he brings back can find no meaning in his own land. Is this the fate of the ageing poet?

> Wunder von ferne oder traum
> Bracht ich an meines landes saum
>
> Und harrte bis die graue norn
> Den namen fand in ihrem born –
>
> Drauf konnt ichs greifen dicht und stark
> Nun blüht und glänzt es durch die mark ...
>
> Einst langt ich an nach guter fahrt
> Mit einem kleinod reich und zart
>
> Sie suchte lang und gab mir kund:
> 'So schläft hier nichts auf tiefem grund'
>
> Worauf es meiner hand entrann
> Und nie mein land den schatz gewann ...
>
> So lernt ich traurig den verzicht:
> Kein ding sei wo das wort gebricht. (IX, 107)

> [I carried to my country's shore
> Marvels and dreams, and waited for
>
> The tall and twilit norn to tell
> The names she found within her well.
>
> Then I could grasp them, they were mine,
> And here I see them bloom and shine ...
>
> Once I had made a happy haul
> And won a rich and fragile jewel.
>
> She peered and peered: 'No symbol lies
> Below', she said, 'to match your prize'.
>
> At this it glided from my hand
> And never graced my native land.
>
> So I renounced and came to know:
> Where the word fractures the thing does not exist.] (*Morwitz 343)

Here George expresses his sense of having brought into words, uniquely in the German language, something that did not previously exist other than in his mind. For von Petersdorff this poem epitomizes the enigma at the core of this poet, expressing anti-modernism in terms of a radical modernism, negating the Platonic doctrine of ideas and placing language before thought.[60] If poetic ideas do not find words they are lost. Von Petersdorff interprets this to mean that the lyrical voice loses that which it discovers unless it finds a linguistic form.[61] As a result, the lyric voice must surrender that material back to the prelinguistic realm. However there are ambiguities here, as Heidegger pointed out, in the understanding of the prelinguistic material of the poem.[62] The opening alternatives in 'Das Wort' make the point that *unless* the poet finds words for his poetic ideas, they will be lost. The Norn can find no adequate symbol in language for the poet's find. She sees it but finds no name for it. It does not exist because existence in human reality requires intersubjective meaning. If the word 'love' for example, fragments, then love does not exist. That which is subjective and individual, unique to him, must find expression but existing words fragment under the strain of representation. Von Petersdorff notes the emergence of themes of failure and lack of certainty for the first time in George's poetry in 'Das Lied', a major change to the hieratic self-confidence of *Der Stern des Bundes*. He attributes this to George's recognition of the contradictions in his poetic-visionary stance.[63]

'Das Wort' is a plea for the totality of George's *oeuvre*, in which he for the first time brings words, expressions and images to the life of a homosexual man as a narrated trajectory with its own symbolic imaginary, which had been created in the volumes from the *Bücher* and the *Fibel* onward. George had also tried to realize ideas that could find no adequate words — for Maximin and the Bund as the core of the new Empire, for example — and had failed. After the war he recognized the truth of the words, 'so schläft hier nichts auf tiefem grund', and learned to relinquish those dreams that found no adequate expression ('So lernt ich traurig den verzicht: | Kein ding sei wo das wort gebricht'). Late in his poetic life, long after the deaths of the men he loved, George despaired of finding words for his experience. But indeed by this time he had created and populated a world for homosexual men. He did so through the creation of a narrated poetic life of experiences and images. Had he not tried to put these poetic ideas into words, there would ultimately have been no change to the mute anonymity of homosexual men in Germany. George's symbolic imaginary was neither ideal nor perfect, but it represented possibility and it furnished a world of images that were uniquely accessible and relevant to those homosexual men whose sexual orientation was still lacking a viable social identity and a shared sense of world, self and other. The 'wunder von ferne oder traum' found words and broader social life, even if the 'kleinod reich und zart' remained unspoken, George's concession that some dreams remained undreamt just as others were dreamed for many.

The last three poems of the collection — and of George's lyric life — date from the final writing decade, from 1918 to 1928. During this period George reached a level of acceptance of himself and his life, and his writing achieved the spare perfection of the greatest poetry. Each poem creates a single image. 'Das Licht' is the light of Hellas, the earliest symbol of homosexual freedom to love in works from *Der Teppich des Lebens* onward. In the past it had been dim for some and for others had burned bright; now it shines for all in this most inclusive of George's lyrics. The light itself however remains impersonal: meaning is found only in personal experience as those it illuminates struggle to come to terms with its equanimity. George, too, is no longer the prophet/Maximin: the lyric voice joins the ranks of the followers. Maturity lies in acceptance:

Wir wären töricht · wollten wir dich hassen
Wenn oft dein strahl verderbendrohend sticht
Wir wären kinder · wollten wir dich fassen –
Da du für alle leuchtest · süsses Licht! (IX, 109).

[We should be fools to let our hatred touch you,
When often with your blaze you threaten blight,
We should be children if we tried to clutch you
Because you shine for every one, sweet light!] (Morwitz 344)

In the penultimate poem, 'In stillste ruh' (1928), the narrative of life is condensed into the recognition of creative destruction. The stable soul is thrown into panic by the vision of the unexpected. Nature is neither predictable nor gentle:

In stillste ruh
Besonnenen tags
Bricht jäh ein blick
Der unerahnten schrecks
Die sichre seele stört
So wie auf höhn
Der feste stamm
Stolz reglos ragt
Und dann noch spät ein sturm
Ihn bis zum boden beugt
So wie das meer
Mit gellem laut
Mit wildem prall
Noch einmal in die lang
Verlassne muschel stösst (IX, 110)

[Through deepest rest
Of ordered day
A glance has flashed
That rouses to alarm
Undreamed the tranquil soul.
Just as on heights
The moveless tree
Looms firm and proud,
And late a tempest bends
It downward to the ground.
Just as the tide
With strident sound,
With savage lunge,

      Once more into the long
      Abandoned sea-shell thrusts.] (Morwitz 344)

Existence shatters the soul's security. And while the robust tree is finally toppled, the modest sea-shell achieves a victory against the elements. The ageing poet hears the sound of the sea again in the 'lang | Verlassene muschel' ('the long | Abandoned sea-shell') and the shock of life is remembered through the empty shell. Thrown up by the sea, it will resound with the ocean long after the storm is over. In this poem life reverberates as the only remaining memory; there is nothing more.

    In the final poem, 'Du schlank und rein wie eine flamme' ('You like a flame, pure and slender'), inspired in July 1918 by the death of Bernhard von Uxkull-Gyllenband, George creates a testament to love and to presence. The opening similes of the flame, the spring, and the breeze, and the fragility of the adjectives, 'schlank' (slender), 'rein' (pure), 'zart' (tender), 'geheim' (hidden), 'licht' (light) and the verb, 'begleitest' (you are a companion), render this a gentle and tender spirit, something quite different from the deified Maximin in *Der Stern des Bundes*. Moreover the erotic content, 'Du kühler wind du heisser hauch [...] ich küsse dich mit jedem duft' (ix, 111, 'You cool of wind, you breath of blaze [...] I kiss you in every scent', Morwitz 345) is secondary to the comforting presence of the beloved. The musical variation of the first stanza in the last abcd/cdab renders a cyclical sense of homecoming in the other which is unique in George's oeuvre. This closing re-orientation towards the poetry of experience of an old man revisiting the value-systems of a lifetime must be read in the light of the opening poems: the evocation of Goethe on the verge of his return to Germany, smitten with the experience of southern sensuality, and Hyperion's late recognition that 'Liebe gebar die Welt' ('Love engendered the world').

    This final poem of the collection, and of George's poetic *vita*, is a love-poem in which the lesson is learned and passed on: in the end, all that is left is love. There is nothing of Maximin, the Bund or the earlier charismatic-prophetic grandiosity, only the recognition of the physical and emotional truth of loving another man. While many have recognized the beauty of this poem, few have drawn attention to the way in which the language of homosexual love functions in its evocation of youthful masculinity, creating a unique set of metaphors in the corpus of European love poetry. This poem cannot be mistaken for a heterosexual love poem: the evocation of male love is powerful and unparalleled, expressed in elegant imagery of natural occurrence, of a flame at once warm and slender, of morning light, of vigorous development, simplicity, decorum, transparence and purity. The loved one is always present, leading the way through night and darkness, surrounding the lyric persona as a gentle force of nature:

      Begleitest mich auf sonnigen matten
      Umschauerst mich im abendrauch
      Erleuchtest meinen weg im schatten
      Du kühler wind du heisser hauch (ix, 111)

      [Companion me in sunny meadows,
      Encompass me in evening haze,

> And where I go, you shine through shadows,
> You cool of wind, you breath of blaze.] (Morwitz 345)

The final stanza, rearranging the lines of the opening stanza, renders these images equivalent in weight. No line begins or ends the stanza and all are interchangeable, suggesting the eternally moving and eternally changing aspect of the loved one. The poem finishes where the poet began. Bernhard von Uxkull-Gyllenband's tragic suicide is transfigured into images of a perfect and untouched nature as a gesture of love.

Das Neue Reich does not present a united programme, nor was it intended to at this late stage in George's life. The underlying tenor is the acceptance of the loss of earlier certainties; not merely about the people and environments of the pre-war years, but of beliefs that had seemed unshakeable. The few early poems which appear to celebrate warrior values, national war and a neo-feudal 'neues Reich' express bitterness, not conviction. Maximin, the Bund and even 'secret Germany' recede into the background of this volume, present as echoes but lacking the conviction and power of earlier works. Two dominant themes emerge: the love and care for the men around the poet-persona especially in the wake of the war, and the value of loyalty. Motifs and tonalities of the earlier prophetic George continue to reverberate, but the volume as a whole cannot be reduced to ideology. The aristocratic value of loyalty, which had found expression in the veneration of feudal allegiance in earlier poems, finds a more profound level of expression as faithfulness in *Das Neue Reich*. The lyric dialogue of Victor and Adalbert does not dwell on the horror or the tragedy, but reimagines the historical facts simply in order to focus on the young men's courage and loyalty to each other at the end. The final section, 'Das Lied', returns to the poet's origins in German folksong. The neo-romanticism of this section expresses the core of George's lyric existence, rivalling the poetry of Goethe and the late Heine in depth and immediacy. It is here we see how little remains of Maximin, 'secret Germany' or the 'neues Reich'.

Change comes about in this volume, but not in the sense of transformation or mythic rebirth. The inclusion of past and present in this collection suggests fragmentation of history and the present, but does not lead to despair. On the contrary, the outcome is a recognition of what is important in George's life — as a man and a homosexual who loved the men around him. All that remains is the simple expression of 'Das Lied', words of love, affection and caring, nothing else. The final poem, 'Du schlank und rein', is the most beautiful love poem in German from a man to a man. In the place of the damaged, problematic language of Maximin and the Bund, the language of these final poems reaches a level of simplicity and purity that has been inherent in his poems from the beginning, but is here brought to its most reduced form, a transparent foil over the archetypes of German lyric.

George's Homosexual Imaginary

In George's early volumes, lyric openness to the other was present as social desire. It became subsumed into the vision of Maximin and the Bund in *Der siebente Ring* and *Der Stern des Bundes*, as images of a flawed ideal of homosexual strength and courage. In *Das Neue Reich* a counter-movement is unmistakeable. George's commitment to his circle is ongoing, but in a different spirit. The earlier ideational frameworks appear increasingly fragmentary and uncertain. They are remnants from the past, reflections, memories and reverberations of a world gone by:

> euer preis
> Tönt in der meergeraubten muschel brausen
> Die dort ein knabe in die ferne blickend
> Zum ohr hebt · lauschend ernst im feuchten wind. (IX, 19)

> [your praises surge
> Within the hollow shell the sea abandoned,
> The shell a boy holds to his ear,
> Heeding its sound in the damp wind.] (*Morwitz 288)

The lyric voice of this imaginary life breaks the earlier trajectory that moved from *Der siebente Ring* to *Der Stern des Bundes* and abandons the mythology of the Bund and Maximin for something more profound. The poet stays committed to the bodies and souls of the men around him — but in a spirit of care, not of leadership. In this final collection George has abandoned the role of pedagogue and prophet. A new sobriety has taken over, a sense of himself as an ageing man who has finally come to understand what is important and what is not. The imagery of the sea, elemental and eternal, is evoked as memory of past experience by the wanderer hearing the sounds of the waves in the shells he picks up on the beach.

The unevenness of this final volume connotes not the abandonment of poetry, but rather the abandonment of his pre-war self, and his new dedication to the figures of past and present. Moreover the lack of unity suggests loss, even fragmentation, as the old world breaks up and a new lyric world moves to take its place. Poems in this volume rate among George's best, revealing the poet's return to his roots in the 'long-forgotten genre of the Volkslied', to connect and engage with those he has come to recognize that he has loved.[64]

The relinquishment of earlier ideational and ideological material is accompanied by the poet's recognition of intimacy and of the emotional relationships with the men around him. The core of this experience is love, something that George's earlier poetry had lacked, despite its evocation of the homoerotic ideal. The early poems were instead about self-discovery, and the focus on Maximin and the Bund marked a narcissistic stage in George's self-validation. But these were not the beginning or the end of his poetic journey. In this sense David's early appraisal rings true, namely that the poet is divesting himself of constraints, and discovering freedom and emotional generosity in this late volume.

George's late works reflected the German sense of crisis and dramatic change during the first two decades of the century. In particular the messages emanating from *Der Stern des Bundes* were carried more widely by younger followers such as the Stauffenberg brothers, Ludwig Thormaehlen and Kurt Hildebrandt after the First World War. But for George the poet, as we have seen in re-reading *Das Neue Reich*, this message had become superseded by history and self-understanding.[65] It is a mistake to allow the poetry to be subsumed under the politics of the Weimar years or the emergence of National Socialism, or to be determined by the ongoing advocacy of the disciples. The importance lies in the processes of recognition and acceptance of homoerotic feelings, in the prevarications and the pretexts of the early volumes, the increasingly outspoken revelation of homosexual attraction and identity, the hope for redemption of *Der Stern des Bundes* and the final late acknowledgment of object-oriented love in *Das Neue Reich*. These are the elements of George's poetry that render it so moving as an aesthetic documentation of the process of coming to self-understanding and, equally importantly for those homosexual men reading George, as the creation, population and elaboration of a modern homosexual imaginary, an imagined lifeworld which embraced the social alongside the individual, creating a vibrant and living *wir-Gefühl* in the intersubjective spaces of lyric poetry where there had been none before.

The contours of an individual life rarely fit the neat outlines of theory. George's life is no exception. His lyric life, traced out in the volumes of verse, is a record and an exploration, but not a model, of a homosexual man's experiences in and responses to his place and his time. *Das Neue Reich* represents a stage of life in which the past outweighs the present. The load of memory is heavy. Maximin, the disciples, living and dead, the poet's hopes and dreams, the Mediterranean and the Rhineland, 'secret Germany' and the war, pre-modern past and present modernity, nature and human consciousness are the themes of this final volume. But one theme stands out above the others.

The last poems of *Das Neue Reich* bring the generic forms of German poetry, the *Lied*, the ballad and the love song, to bear on the homosexual experience, merging the homosexual imaginary with the wider social imaginary and bringing social existence to private experience. Fresh, hesitant and tentative, these lyrics of the final section focus on the beloved other, describing and evoking the objects of George's love, in particular the dead Bernhard von Uxkull-Gyllenband. These poems do not break with the past: they are heavy with it still. But the transformation of the poetic voice is unmistakeable as George moves to a new level of awareness, freeing himself of former ballast, no longer requiring fealty in order to express love. The simple love lyric suffices after all for the last and greatest of his poems. 'Du schlank und rein' is the first and last true love poem in George's work. It is not conventional, it is not addressed to a transfigured grandiose self or to the boy-god Maximin. It is an evocation of a beloved other, the poet's engagement at the end of his created life with a man whom he loved. There is no political agenda or ideological framework other than the articulation of love.

Das Neue Reich is the fitting end to George's lifelong mission. It is not a culmination of his earlier prophetic-charismatic ethos. Rather it is a recognition of failure. In the failure of the prophet lies the redemption of the man. The mission founders on the rocks of its creator's human affections. *Das Neue Reich* is the chart of that wreckage, but the final poems, like Leopardi's 'il naufragar m'è dolce in questo mare', convey the tragic beauty of self-recognition.[66] Love came late to George's poetic life, and acceptance came even later. Stefan George ended his lyric *vita* with a statement of refusal: refusal to mask his true self. It was a late, problematic and damaged recognition of his own humanity, and it came about only after the deaths of those he loved. But it ended with one of the greatest love poems in the language. His life had consisted in the creation of a myth and a mystique, which in the end lay in ruins around a simple fact of human existence: love for another man.

Notes to Chapter 4

1. George used the term '*First* World War' ('Erster Weltkrieg') at a time when others for obvious reasons simply referred to 'the war'. For him it was the first of the future cataclysms that would strike Germany and Europe. His late preface to *Der Stern des Bundes* (added in 1928) makes clear that any reception of the war in terms of the utopian symbolism of the poetry is a misunderstanding ('misverständnis'), and he exhorts his followers to seek revelation and resolution of the precipitous rush of world events ('die sich überstürzenden welt-ereignisse') in the 'unknown world of mystery and proclamation' ('unbekannte welt des geheimnisses und der verkündung') rather than in the Verdun and on the Somme. But it was too late. The work was misunderstood as a 'breviary of an almost popular sort' ('brevier fast volksgültiger art'), he added bitterly. ('Vorrede' to the 1928 edition of *Der Stern des Bundes*, SW, VIII, 18.) The homosexual imaginary of the Bund was engulfed by the broader national imaginary of Germany at war.
2. Breuer, *Ästhetischer Fundamentalismus*, p. 76.
3. Ibid.
4. Petersdorff, 'Als der Kampf gegen die Moderne verloren war', p. 335.
5. Karlauf, *Stefan George*, p. 577.
6. Morwitz, *Die Dichtung Stefan Georges*, p. 153.
7. Ibid..
8. Cited in Karlauf, *Stefan George*, p. 577.
9. David, *Stefan George: Sein Dichterisches Werk*, p. 338.
10. Ibid., p. 345. Despite this, *Das neue Reich* contained some of the poet's best work for David. Like Morwitz, David stresses the theme of continuity in change alongside the signs of tension and upheaval, reading the lack of coherence in terms of a new sense of maturity, concluding that George 'finally achieved grace and freedom' in this final volume despite its weak architecture and slim dimensions (ibid., p. 337). George, that is, has found freedom from the mission of the earlier works, enabling him to experience the 'hope and confidence' or 'assuredness' of poetic and personal maturity: the more thoughtful and human tone is attributable to experiences of the wartime, to which many of the most important poems relate, as well as to the maturity of old age *per se*. The men in George's life are no longer simply subsumed into their role as disciples: the person rather than the heroic role is the essential quality (ibid., pp. 346–47, 351).
11. Gadamer, 'Der Dichter Stefan George', p. 36. 'Indessen zeigt der letzte Gedichtband *Das Neue Reich*, der offenbar eine Sammlung in das strenge Gefüge des vorigen Bandes nicht einzufügender Gedichte mit neueren Gedichten vereinigt, die ganze Schwingungsweite des Georgeschen Tones [...]'
12. Ibid.
13. Ibid.
14. Ibid., p.37. '[George] stilisiert sich damit keineswegs in die Rolle eines unerkannten Heilands, der das von sich weiß. Er weiß sich nicht'.
15. Petersdorff, 'Als der Kampf gegen die Moderne verloren war', pp. 341–44.
16. Ibid., p.341. The term 'neues Reich' originated in a poem by Karl Wolfskehl from 1895 and had belonged to the vocabulary of the circle for decades. George was unlikely to bow to political events at this stage of his career by abandoning this term because of the new associations of the title, despite the concerns of friends such as Edith Landmann. Karlauf, *Stefan George*, p. 577. See Osterkamp, *Poesie der leeren Mitte*, pp. 36–37. In poems such as 'Der Brand des Tempels',

or 'Viktor ★ Adalbert' von Petersdorff finds 'tried and tested models of world interpretation to be disturbed and broken' as George reveals 'an astonishing openness to insecurity and new experience', diminishing or abandoning his earlier authority and now showing a weakening of resolve, scepticism regarding the redemptive validity of 'secret Germany', and 'uncertainty regarding the lyric voice that was earlier characterized by sovereign superiority' (von Petersdorff, 'Als der Kampf gegen die Moderne verloren war', p. 351 and *Fliehkräfte der Moderne*, p. 130). Von Petersdorff locates *Das Neue Reich* in the ideational context of George's anti-modernism, as a late and bleak rejection of the present in which the earlier promise of the romanticized past is missing. The source of George's disillusionment lies in the tension between ideological anti-modernism and the recognition of the ongoing processes of modernism (von Petersdorff, 'Als der Kampf gegen die Moderne verloren war', p. 336). In this post-war scepticism about the possibility of regeneration and rebirth, the messianic title becomes highly ironic as George recognizes 'the irrelevance of his aesthetic fundamentalism' (ibid., p. 340). Thus there is no dawning of a new age to be seen in this final volume. The poet recognizes his own remoteness and obsolescence as the voice of the charismatic prophet fragments into the 'questions and exclamations' of the ageing poet (ibid., p. 337). George's loss of certainty and authority expresses recognition of the failure of his reactionary modernist programme, or aesthetic fundamentalism in Breuer's term. It results in a loss of bearings, an anarchic position which has lost its roots in tradition and has not found any orientation for the future (ibid., p. 325, 340–44).

17. Karlauf, *Stefan George*, pp. 577–82. See Mattenklott, *Bilderdienst*, p. 177; Osterkamp, *Die Poesie der leeren Mitte*, p. 25; see also Zanucchi, 'Ernst Osterkamp, *Poesie der leeren Mitte*', p. 107.

18. Böschenstein recognizes the heterogeneous and uneven quality of *Das Neue Reich* in terms of the poet's recognition of a world in decline, compared to the formal structure of *Der Stern des Bundes* and despite the 'claim to closure' ('Geschlossenheitsanspruch') implicit in the title, but nevertheless identifies continuity of theme from *Der Stern des Bundes* and the preceding work. (Böschenstein, 'Stefan Georges Spätwerk als Antwort auf eine untergehende Welt', p. 8). However, it is Osterkamp's *Poesie der leeren Mitte: Stefan Georges Neues Reich* (2010) that represents the major redirection of analysis since Breuer, claiming to restore the poetry to its rightful place as the focus of study of the poet. Osterkamp aims to resolve the interpretative impasse between the early aestheticist and the later dogmatist by revealing the consistency of the worldview. The para-religious, cultic and national-ideological elements persist unbroken from the early works where they are first established to the late works after *Der siebente Ring*, as the poetic voice transforms itself into the charismatic prophet of the New Reich. For Osterkamp George put his poetic genius into the service of a political programme, producing in this final volume a 'vision of a complete historical renewal under the rubric of an imperial utopia' both sustaining and sustained by his narcissistic-charismatic personality (Osterkamp, *Poesie der leeren Mitte*, p. 25). The late work in particular instrumentalizes contemporary commentary, prophetic proclamation, mythology and history, theology and sexuality in the 'metapolitical desire for world renewal' through the agency of poetry (ibid., pp. ix, 19–20). In their time these works were received as a form of 'esoteric secret doctrine', but for today's readers their hieratic and prophetic tones ring empty and false (ibid., p.16, 18). The extremism of the late works is merely indicative of the ageing poet's inflexibility of attitude. Where Glöckner and others saw fragmentation and loss of orientation, and Morwitz a new phase of creativity, Osterkamp finds consistency of ideational content, but not aesthetic quality (ibid., p.24–25). Osterkamp observes that the title is one of the most ambitious in the history of German poetry, but given the unevenness of the volume, it is nothing more than an 'emergency covering, thrown hastily over a textual storage space and covering all sorts of very different things' (ibid., p. 24, 'ein thematisches Notdach, das eilig über einen viel Unterschiedliches versammelnden Textspeicher geschlagen wurde'; see also Karlauf, *Stefan George*, p. 577). Yet he argues both ways regarding George's artistic-totalitarian ambitions. On the one hand, all of the poems are subservient to the ideological claims of the Neues Reich; on the other, they are a mixed bag of uneven tone, address and quality. In fact Osterkamp interprets only four of the poems in detail. The selected poems were written before the war and do indeed echo the prophetic tones of their era. But at this point they still primarily express the seductions of homoerotic dominance, the ongoing dream of a homosexual community of men. Osterkamp exaggerates the ideological aspects

on the basis of extrinsic readings in terms of the dogma of the Bund at its peak between 1907 and 1914, the era of Maximin as the god of the new age and mystical force directing its every thought, attitude and expression (ibid., p.126). And yet Maximin scarcely appears in *Das Neue Reich* other than by extension of George's evocation of an idealized youth.

19. Koch, *Stefan George*, p. 93.
20. Nicolaus Sombart refers to George as the 'high priest' of the *Männerbund*, 'Männerbund und politische Kultur in Deutschland', p. 161. For Sombart the *Männerbund* as described by Blüher and Bäumler represented a particularly German form of homosexual identity. It was characterized by misogyny, preservation of masculinity through separation of the sexes after adolescence, and initiation rites involving infliction of pain alongside male–male sex in order to establish a hierarchy of masculinity. However, Sombart fails to distinguish between homosexuality as a sexual orientation gaining a modern social voice, and the homoerotic libido which can be harnessed and controlled within all-male groups. The conflation of the categories of homosexuality, homoeroticism and homosociality obscures what it was that rendered these environments attractive to homosexual men in the absence of other male sexual environments in this early environment of self-determination and self-identification.
21. See Editorial Note, IX, 130.
22. Winckelmann was murdered only several months after Goethe left Italy. See Aldrich, *The Seduction of the Mediterranean*, p. 54.
23. This line perhaps echoes Goethe's own lines from *Hermann und Dorothea* set at the time of the French revolutionary army's advance towards the Rhine in the early 1790s, in which Hermann's father, the innkeeper, exclaims: 'ich konnte nicht denken, daß bald sein liebliches Ufer | Sollte werden ein Wall, um abzukehren den Franken' ('I could not think that soon its lovely shore | should be a wall to stop the Franks', 'Kalliope', ll. 193–94).
24. See Butler, *The Tyranny of Greece over Germany*, pp. 1–8 and passim.
25. See Zanucchi, 'Ernst Osterkamp, *Poesie der leeren Mitte*', p. 108, where Goethe in the poem is referred to: 'in die Rolle des Vorläufers [...], der dazu verurteilt ist, an der Grenze des neuen Zeitalters zu verharren, das nur George verkünden kann'.
26. Zanucchi, 'Ernst Osterkamp, *Poesie der leeren Mitte*', p. 109, 'eine nationalistisch-biologistische Verzerrung des universalistischen Bildungsprogramms der Weimarer Klassik'; see Osterkamp, *Poesie der leeren Mitte*, p. 113.
27. Osterkamp, *Poesie der leeren Mitte*, p. 83.
28. Ibid., p. 85.
29. See Karlauf, *Stefan George*, pp. 406–09.
30. Osterkamp, *Poesie der leeren Mitte*, p. 147.
31. According to Morwitz 'Der Krieg' was written between 1914 and 1916, see Zeller, *Stefan George*, p. 262.
32. 'When [...] talk turned to the war, he said it was as though parts of him had been at the Front'. Landmann, *Gespräche mit Stefan George*, pp. 66, 123.
33. Stern, *The Dear Purchase*, pp. 228–30, cites the translation of E. H. Plumptre, *The Divina Commedia and Canzoniere*, 5 vols (London: Isbister, 1886), III, 129 .
34. Stern, *The Dear Purchase*, p. 230.
35. For a comprehensive overview of George's attitudes to the war at this period, see Egyptien, 'Die Haltung Georges und des George-Kreises zum 1. Weltkrieg', pp. 205–06. For George's contemporaries, see Heym, 'Krieg', 1911; Rilke, 'Fünf Gesänge', 1914; Trakl, 'Groddek', 1914.
36. Cf. Editorial Note, IX, 139.
37. Norton, *Secret Germany*, pp. 521–36; Zeller, *Stefan George*, pp. 261–64. Norton comments scathingly on George's criticisms of those disciples who could not accept the grinding misery of wartime service, particularly Gundolf (*Secret Germany*, pp. 540–44). However, there was a great deal of wounded narcissism in George's response here as elsewhere in his relations with his friends and followers. In fact, the war and the loss of the young men he loved took a considerable toll on his health (ibid., pp. 532–41). The poems themselves tell a different story, particularly the 1922 masterpiece, 'Geheimes Deutschland', and the final poem of *Das Neue Reich*, written in 1918 after George heard the news of Bernhard von Uxkull's suicide. His final poetic statement, 'Du schlank und rein wie eine flamme', was dedicated to Uxkull.

38. See Zeller, *Stefan George*, p. 262 for George's letter of 5 October 1914.

39. Editorial Note, IX, 140, 'Blutschuld als Mord an Angehörigen des eigenen Volkes'. See Landfried, *Stefan George*, pp. 217–20; Wuthenow, 'Weltverhängnis', p. 116, Ockenden, 'Kingdom of the Spirit', pp. 92–93.

40. Norton, *Secret Germany*, p. 547; see Ockenden, 'Kingdom of the Spirit', pp. 92–93.

41. George's model of civilizational purity divides the world broadly into the 'white' Judaeo-Christian and Greek civilization, and the 'yellow' and 'black' Asian and African civilizations respectively. The other races are not necessarily inferior, only incompatible. This scheme is a far cry from later theories and practices of racial extermination. That George was not antisemitic is clear from his passion for Maximilian Kronberger and his deep friendships with Karl Wolfskehl, Friedrich Gundolf and Ernst Morwitz, his closest disciples (Norton, *Secret Germany*, p. 534). For Mann's 'die asiatische Gefahr', see Mann, *Tagebücher 1918–1921*, p. 233.

42. Stern, *The Dear Purchase*, pp. 228–38.

43. See Egyptien's positive reading of these lines in 'Die Haltung Georges und des George-Kreises zum 1. Weltkrieg', pp. 210–11.

44. Stern, *The Dear Purchase*, p. 237.

45. von Petersdorff, 'Als der Kampf gegen die Moderne verloren war', p. 331.

46. Ibid., p. 332.

47. David, *Stefan George: Sein Dichterisches Werk*, p. 337.

48. Ibid., p. 338.

49. Ibid.

50. George used the shortened form of the name, Uxkull, in this dedication and in the accompanying note to the final poem of the collection, 'Du schlank und rein wie eine flamme'. The full family name was Uxkull-Gyllenband.

51. See Editorial Note, IX, 151–53.

52. von Petersdorff, 'Als der Kampf gegen die Moderne verloren war', pp. 325–266.

53. Grünewald, *Ernst Kantorowicz und Stefan George*, p. 76; Wolfskehl, 'Die Blätter für die Kunst und die neuste Literatur', pp. 14–15; von Hellingrath, 'Hölderlin und die Deutschen', pp. 124–25. See also Karlauf, *Stefan George*, p. 409.

54. See Karlauf, *Stefan George*, pp. 338–40 and Editorial Notes, VI/VII, 230 and IX, 169.

55. von Petersdorff, 'Als der Kampf gegen die Moderne verloren war', p. 326.

56. von Petersdorff, 'Als der Kampf gegen die Moderne verloren war', p. 347.

57. Cited in Karlauf, *Stefan George*, p. 478.

58. Karlauf notes that only 48 arrests were made for desertion during the war, and that only some of these were executed, of whom none were officers. The implication is that deserters such as Cohrs and Uxkull-Gyllenband were tacitly given access to guns in order to commit suicide while under arrest, and hence escape the ignominy of court martial and execution. Karlauf, *Stefan George*, p. 478.

59. Ibid., p. 479.

60. von Petersdorff, 'Als der Kampf gegen die Moderne verloren war', p. 347.

61. Ibid.

62. See Heidegger, *On the Way to Language*, p. 140.

63. von Petersdorff, 'Als der Kampf gegen die Moderne verloren war', pp. 326, 341.

64. David, *Stefan George: Sein Dichterisches Werk*, p. 345.

65. Ruehl reports that Stauffenberg's decision 'to defy and, eventually, kill Hitler seems to have been inspired by Georgean notions such as heroism, nobility of spirit, the Master's belief in a decisive, redemptive *Tat*, and his original insistence that the mission of the Secret Germany was to stand in opposition to the "public" Germany.' Hence, for Ruehl, George's influence 'inspired others not just to renounce, but to actively and heroically resist' Nazism. Ruehl, 'Aesthetic Fundamentalism in Weimar Poetry', p. 260.

66. Leopardi, *Canti*, p. 103. This is the final line of Leopardi's great poem of reflection on loneliness and his desire to experience the ocean of existence around him, for 'foundering is sweet in such a sea'.

BIBLIOGRAPHY

ADORNO, THEODOR WIESENGRUND, 'George und Hofmannsthal: Zum Briefwechsel', *Gesammelte Schriften*, X/1: *Kulturkritik und Gesellschaft I, Prismen* (Frankfurt a.M.: Suhrkamp, 1977), pp. 195–238

—— 'The George–Hofmannsthal Correspondence, 1891–1906', in *Prisms*, trans. by Samuel and Shierry Weber (Cambridge: MIT Press, 1981), pp. 187–226

—— *Noten zur Literatur* (Frankfurt: Suhrkamp, 1981)

—— *Notes to Literature*, ed. by Rolf Tiedemann and trans. by Shierry Weber Nicholsen (New York: Columbia University Press, 1992)

—— 'Sociology and Psychology' (Part II), *New Left Review*, 47.1 (1968), 79–97

ALDRICH, ROBERT, *The Seduction of the Mediterranean: Writing, Art and Homosexual Fantasy* (London: Routledge, 1993)

ALTMAN, DENNIS, *Homosexual Oppression and Liberation* (Harmondsworth: Penguin, 1973)

ANDERSON, BENEDICT, *Imagined Communities: Reflections on the Origin and Spread of Nationalism* (London: Verso, 2006)

ARNOLD, HEINZ LUDWIG, ed., *Stefan George*. Munich: text + kritik, 168 (2005)

AURNHAMMER, ACHIM, WOLFGANG BRAUNGART, STEFAN BREUER, and UTE OELMANN, eds, *Stefan George und sein Kreis: Ein Handbuch* (Berlin: De Gruyter, 2012)

BACHOFEN, JOHANN JAKOB, *Das Mutterrecht: Eine Untersuchung über die Gynaikokratie der alten Welt nach ihrer religiösen und rechtlichen Natur*, ed. by Hans-Jürgen Heinrichs (Frankfurt a.M.: Suhrkamp, 1975)

BEACHY, ROBERT, *Gay Berlin: Birthplace of a Modern Identity* (London: Vintage, 2015)

—— 'The German Invention of Homosexuality', *The Journal of Modern History*, 82.4 (2010), 801–38

BENJAMIN, WALTER, 'Rückblick auf Stefan George: Zu einer neuen Studie über den Dichter', in *Gesammelte Schriften*, III, ed. by Rolf Tiedemann and Hermann Schweppenhäuser (Frankfurt a.M.: Suhrkamp, 1972), pp. 392–99

—— 'Über Stefan George', in *Gesammelte Schriften*, II/2, ed. by Rolf Tiedemann and Hermann Schweppenhäuser (Frankfurt a.M.: Suhrkamp, 1977), pp. 622–24

BENN, GOTTFRIED, 'Rede auf Stefan George', in *Essays und Aufsätze, Gesammelte Werke*, ed. by Dieter Wellershoff (Frankfurt: Zweitausendeins, 2003), p. 1035

BERGER, DEMIAN, 'Theodor W. Adornos Stefan-George-Rezeption: Eine dialektische Literaturbetrachtung', *Weimarer Beiträge*, 66.2 (2020), 212–20

BERNSTEIN, MICHAEL ANDRÉ, *Foregone Conclusions: Against Apocalyptic History* (Berkeley: University of California Press, 1994)

BISNO, ADAM, 'Stefan George's Homoerotic Erlösungsreligion, 1891–1907', in *A Poet's Reich: Politics and Culture in the George Circle*, ed. By Melissa S Lane and Martin Ruehl (Rochester NY: Camden House, 2011), pp. 37–55

BLAZEK, HELMUT, *Männerbünde, eine Geschichte von Faszination und Macht* (Berlin: Links, 2001)

BLÜHER, HANS, *Die Rolle der Erotik in der männlichen Gesellschaft: Eine Theorie der menschlichen Staatsbildung nach Wesen und Wert*, ed. by Hans Joachim Schoeps (Stuttgart: Klett, 1962)

—— *Werke und Tage: Geschichte eines Denkers* (Munich: List, 1953)

BOEHRINGER, ROBERT, *Mein Bild von Stefan George*, 2 vols (Munich: Kupper, 1951)

BORCHARDT, RUDOLF, *Aufzeichnung Stefan George betreffend*, ed. by Ernst Osterkamp, Schriften der Rudolf-Borchardt-Gesellschaft (Berlin: Verlag für Berlin-Brandenburg, 2015)

BÖSCHENSTEIN, BERNHARD, JÜRGEN EGYPTIEN, BERTRAM SCHEFOLD, and WOLFGANG GRAF VITZTHUM, eds, *Wissenschaftler im George-Kreis: Die Welt des Dichters und der Beruf der Wissenschaft* (Berlin: De Gruyter, 2005)

—— ' "Magie in durftiger Zeit" — Stefan George: Junger — Dichter — Entdecker', *George Jahrbuch*, 1 (1996/97), 7–22

—— 'Stefan Georges Spätwerk als Antwort auf eine untergehende Welt', In *Stefan George: Werk und Wirkung seit dem Siebenten Ring*, ed. by Wolfgang Braungart, Ute Oelmann, and Bernhard Böschenstein (Tübingen: Niemeyer, 2001), pp. 1–16

BOZZA, MAIK, *Genealogie des Anfangs: Stefan Georges poetologischer Selbstentwurf um 1890*, Castrum Peregrini, NF, Bd. 9 (Göttingen: Wallstein 2016)

BRAUNE, JOAN, *Erich Fromm's Revolutionary Hope: Prophetic Messianism as a Critical Theory of the Future* (Rotterdam: Sense Publishers, 2014)

BRAUNGART, WOLFGANG, UTE OELMANN, and BERNHARD BÖSCHENSTEIN, eds, *Stefan George: Werk und Wirkung seit dem ,Siebenten Ring'* (Tübingen: Niemeyer, 2001)

BREUER STEFAN, *Ästhetischer Fundamentalismus: Stefan George und der deutsche Antimodernismus* (Darmstadt: Wissenschaftliche Buchgesellschaft, 1995)

—— 'Ästhetischer Fundamentalismus und Eugenik bei Kurt Hildebrandt', *Wissenschaftler im George-Kreis: Die Welt des Dichters und der Beruf der Wissenschaft*, ed. by Bernhard Böschenstein, Jürgen Egyptien, Bertram Schefold and Wolfgang Graf Vitzthum (Berlin: De Gruyter, 2005), pp. 291–310

—— *Ästhetischer Katholizismus: Stefan Georges Rituale der Literatur* (Tübingen: Niemeyer, 1997)

—— 'Kult, Ritual und Religion bei Stefan George',in *Kunst und Religion*, ed. by Richard Faber and Volkmar Krech (Würzburg: Königshausen & Neumann, 1999), pp. 257–73

—— *Stefan George und die Jugendbewegung* (Stuttgart: Metzler, 2018)

—— ' "Was ich noch sinne und was ich noch füge/Was ich noch liebe trägt die gleichen züge": Stefan Georges performative Poetik', in *Stefan George*, ed. by Heinz Ludwig Arnold, *Munich: text + kritik*, 168 (2005), 3–18

BROKOFF, JÜRGEN, 'Macht im Innenraum der Dichtung: Die frühen Gedichte Stefan Georges', in *Die Souveränität der Weltliteratur: zum Totalitären der klassischen Moderne 1900–1933*, ed. by Uwe Hebekus and Ingo Stockmann (Paderborn: W. Fink, 2010), pp. 415–32

BROOKE, RUPERT, *1914 and Other Poems* (London: Sidgwick & Jackson, 1915)

BRUNOTTE, ULRIKE, *Zwischen Eros und Krieg: Männerbund und Ritual in der Moderne* (Berlin: Klaus Wagenbach, 2004)

BRUNS, CLAUDIA, ' "Ihr Männer seid Männer!" Maskulinistische Positionen in der deutschen Homosexuellenbewegung zu Beginn des zwanzigsten Jahrhunderts: Zwischen Revolution und Reaktion', in *Politiken in Bewegung: Die Emanzipation Homosexueller im 20. Jahrhundert*, ed. by Andreas Pretzel and Andreas Weiß (Hamburg: Männerschwarm Verlag, 2017), pp. 28–31

—— 'The Politics of Masculinity in the (Homo)Sexual Discourse (1880–1920)', *German History*, 23.3 (2005), 306–20

—— *Politik des Eros: Der Männerbund in Wissenschaft, Politik und Jugendkultur (1880–1934)* (Vienna: Böhlau, 2008)

BUTLER, ELIZA MARIAN, *The Tyranny of Greece over Germany: A Study of the Influence Exercised by Greek Art and Poetry over the great German Writers of the Eighteenth, Nineteenth and Twentieth centuries* (Cambridge: Cambridge University Press, 1935)

BUTLER, JUDITH, *Bodies That Matter: on the Discursive Limits of 'Sex'* (New York: Routledge, 1993)

—— *Gender Trouble: Feminism and the Subversion of Identity* (New York: Routledge, 1999)

CERULO, KAREN A., 'Identity Construction: New Issues, New Directions'. *Annual Review of Sociology*, 23 (1997), 385–409

CROMPTON, LOUIS, '"An Army of Lovers": The Sacred Band of Thebes', *History Today*, 44.11 (1994), 23–29

COOLEY, CHARLES H., *Human Nature and the Social Order* (New York: Scribner's, 1902)

CORNWALL, MARK, *The Devil's Wall: The Nationalist Youth Mission of Heinz Rutha* (Cambridge, MA: Harvard University Press, 2012)

DAHLKE, BIRGIT, *Jünglinge der Moderne: Jugendkult und Männlichkeit in der Literatur um 1900* (Cologne: Böhlau, 2006)

DAUB, ADRIAN, 'From Maximin to Stonewall: Sexuality and the Afterlives of the George Circle', *The Germanic Review*, 87 (2012), 19–34

—— '"Ein Blitz, Für Uns": Stefan George's Queer Dynasty', *Deutsche Vierteljahrsschrift für Literaturwissenschaft und Geistesgeschichte*, 90 (2016), 135–59

DAVID, CLAUDE, *Stefan George: Son Œuvre poétique* (Paris: Bibliothèque de la société des études germaniques, 1952)

—— *Stefan George: Sein Dichterisches Werk* (Munich: Carl Hanser Verlag, 1967)

DERKS, PAUL, *Die Schande der heiligen Päderastie: Homosexualitat und Öffentlichkeit in der Deutschen Literatur 1750–1850* (Berlin: Verlag Rosa Winkel, 1990)

DIETRICH, HANS [HANS DIETRICH HELLBACH], *Die Freundesliebe in der deutschen Literatur* (Berlin: Männerschwarm Verlag, 1966. Reprint d. Ausg. 1931)

DIMASSA, DANIEL, 'Stefan George, Thomas Mann, and the Politics of Homoeroticism', *German Quarterly* 86/3 (2013), 311–33

DOKTOR, FREDERIK, *Die Eulenburg-Affäre und die Genese des modernen Homosexualitätskonzepts* (Bielefeld: Transcript Verlag, 2021)

DOMEIER, NORMAN, 'The Homosexual Scare and the Masculinization of German Politics before World War I', *Central European History*, 47.4 (2014), 737–59

DÖRR, GEORG, *Muttermythos und Herrschaftsmythos: Zur Dialektik der Aufklärung bei den Kosmikern, Stefan George, Walter Benjamin und in der Frankfurter Schule* (Würzburg: Königshausen und Neumann, 2019), pp. 279–375

DOUGHERTY, RICHARD, *Eros, Youth Culture and Geist: The Ideology of Gustav Wyneken and its Influence Upon the German Youth Movement* (Madison: University of Wisconsin Press, 1978)

DÜRHAMMER, ILIJA, *Geheime Botschaften: Homoerotische Subkulturen im Schubert-Kreis, bei Hugo von Hofmannsthal und Thomas Bernhard* (Vienna: Böhlau, 2006)

DURZAK, MANFRED, *Zwischen Symbolismus und Expressionismus: Stefan George* (Stuttgart: W. Kohlhammer, 1974)

EGYPTIEN, JÜRGEN, *Stefan George: Dichter und Prophet* (Darmstadt: Theiss, 2018)

—— 'Die Haltung Georges und des George-Kreises zum 1. Weltkrieg', in *Stefan George, Werk und Wirkung seit dem 'Siebenten Ring'*, ed. by Wolfgang, Braungart, Ute Oelmann, Bernhard Böschenstein (Tübingen: Niemeyer, 2001), pp. 197–212

—— 'Herbst der Liebe und Winter der Schrift: Über den Zyklus "Nach der Lese" in Stefan Georges *Das Jahr der Seele*', *George-Jahrbuch*, 1 (1996/97), 23–43

—— 'Entwicklung und Stand der George-Forschung 1955–2005', in *Stefan George*, ed. by Heinz Ludwig Arnold, *Munich: text + kritik*, 168 (2005), 105–22

—— *Stefan George — Werkkommentar: Studien und Interpretationen Zu Sämtlichen Dichtungen und Übertragungen* (Berlin: De Gruyter, 2017)

ELIAS, NORBERT, *Die Gesellschaft der Individuen* (Frankfurt/M.: Suhrkamp, 1987)

—— *What is Sociology?* (London: Hutchinson, 1978)

EPSTEIN, STEVEN, 'A Queer Encounter: Sociology and the Study of Sexuality' (1987), in *Queer Theory/Sociology*, ed. by Steven Seidman (Oxford: Blackwell, 1996), pp. 145–67

ERIKSON, ERIK H., *Childhood and Society* (Harmondsworth: Penguin, 1975)

——'The Problem of Ego Identity', *Journal of the American Psychoanalytic Association*, 4 (1956), 56–121

ESCHENBACH, GUNILLA, *Imitatio im George-Kreis* (Berlin: De Gruyter, 2011)

FALETTI, HEIDI E., *Die Jahreszeiten des Fin de Siècle: Eine Studie über Stefan Georges Das Jahr der Seele* (Bern: Francke, 1983)

FLEMING, PAUL, 'The Secret Adorno', *Qui Parle*, 15.1 (2004), 97–114

FOUCAULT, MICHEL, *The History of Sexuality*, I: *An Introduction*, trans. by Robert Hurley (Harmondsworth: Penguin Books, 1981)

FRANK, LORE, and SABINE RIBBECK, *Stefan-George-Bibliographie 1976–1997*. Mit Nachträgen bis 1976. Auf der Grundlage der Bestände des Stefan-George-Archivs in der Württembergischen Landesbibliothek (Tübingen: Niemeyer, 2000)

FRANZ, MARIE-LOUISE VON, *Puer aeternus: Ewiger Jüngling und kreativer Genius* (Küsnacht: Verlag Stiftung für Jungsche Psychologie, 2002)

FREUD, SIGMUND, 'On Narcissism: An Introduction', in *Pelican Freud Library*, XI: *On Metapsychology*, (Harmondsworth: Penguin, 1984), pp. 59–98

FRICKER, CHRISTOPHE, *Krise und Gemeinschaft: Stefan Georges 'Der Stern des Bundes'* (Frankfurt a.M.: Klostermann 2017_

——*Stefan George: Gedichte für Dich* (Berlin: Matthes & Seitz, 2011)

——'Stefan Georges Gedicht 'Geheimes Deutschland: Ein politisches Program?', in *Stefan George: Dichtung, Ethos, Staat: Denkbilder für ein geheimes europäisches Deutschland*, ed. by Bruno Pieger and Bertram Schefold (Berlin: Verlag für Berlin-Brandenburg, 2010), pp. 131–63

FRIEDEMANN, HEINRICH OTTO, *Platon: Seine Gestalt* (Berlin: *Blätter für die Kunst*, 1914)

FRIEDLAENDER, BENEDICT, *Die Renaissance des Eros Uranios: die physiologische Freundschaft, ein normaler Grundtrieb des Menschen und eine Frage der männlichen Gesellungsfreiheit: in naturwissenschaftlicher, naturrechtlicher, culturgeschichtlicher und sittenkritischer Beleuchtung* (Berlin: Verlag 'Renaissance' (Otto Lehmann), 1904)

GABBARD, GLEN O., and HOLLY CRISP-HAN, 'The Many Faces of Narcissism', *World Psychiatry*, 15 (2016), 115–16

GADAMER, HANS-GEORG, 'Der Dichter Stefan George', in *Poetica: Ausgewählte Essays* (Frankfurt a.M.: Insel Verlag, 1977), pp. 7–38

GEORGE, STEFAN, *Sämtliche Werke in 18 Bänden*, ed. by Georg Peter Landmann and Ute Oelmann under the auspices of the Stefan George Stiftung (Stuttgart: Klett-Cotta, 1982–2012) (*SW*)

GEORGE, STEFAN, and HUGO VON HOFMANNSTHAL, *Briefwechsel zwischen George und Hofmannsthal*, ed. by Robert Boehringer (Munich: H. Küpper, 1953)

GEORGE, STEFAN, and STÉPHANE MALLARMÉ, *Briefwechsel und Übertragungen*. Hg. und eingeleitet von Enrico De Angelis. Mit einem Nachwort von Ute Oelmann (Göttingen: Wallstein 2013) (= Castrum Peregrini, NF, Bd. 5)

GEUTER, ULFRIED, *Homosexualität in der deutschen Jugendbewegung* (Frankfurt/M.: Suhrkamp, 1994)

GLOCKNER, ERNST, *Begegnung mit Stefan George* (Heidelberg: Lothar Stiehm, 1972)

GOLDSMITH, ULRICH K., 'The Renunciation of Woman in Stefan George's *Das Jahr der Seele*', *Monatshefte*, 46.3 (1954), 113–22

——*Stefan George: A Study of His Early Work* (Boulder: University of Colorado Press, 1959)

——*Stefan George* (New York: Columbia University Press, New York 1970)

GREENBERG, DAVID F., *The Construction of Homosexuality* (Chicago: University of Chicago Press, 1988)

GROPPE, CAROLA, *Die Macht der Bildung: Das deutsche Bürgertum und der George-Kreis 1890–1933* (Cologne: Böhlau, 2001)

GRUBNER, BERNADETTE, 'Narcissism in Cultural Theory: Perspectives on Christopher Lasch, Richard Sennett, and Robert Pfaller', *Frontiers of Narrative Studies*, 3.1 (2017), 50–70

GRÜNEWALD, ECKHART. *Ernst Kantorowicz und Stefan George: Beiträge zur Biographie des Historikers bis zum Jahre 1938 und zu seinem Jugendwerk Kaiser Friedrich der Zweite.* Wiesbaden: Franz Steiner, 1982.

GUERRA, GABRIELE, '"Herr der Wende" und "erkrankte welten"': Wirklichkeit des Apokalyptischen und Erwartung des Eschatologischen bei George und in seinem Kreis 1914–1917', *George-Jahrbuch*, 11 (2016/17), 157–70

GUNDOLF, FRIEDRICH, and FRIEDRICH WOLTERS, eds, *Jahrbuch für die geistige Bewegung* 1912 (Berlin: Verlag der Blätter für die Kunst, 1912)

HAMECHER, PETER, 'Der männliche Eros im Werke Stefan Georges', *Jahrbuch für sexuelle Zwischenstufen*, 14 (1914), 10–23

HARRIS, JOSEPH C., 'Love and Death in the *Männerbund*: An Essay with Special Reference to the Bjarkamál and The Battle of Maldon', in Joseph C. Harris, *'Speak Useful Words or Say Nothing': Old Norse Studies*, ed. by Susan E. Deskis and Thomas D. Hill, Islandica 53 (Ithaca: Cornell University Library, 2008), pp. 287–317

HEFTRICH, ECKHARD, *Stefan George* (Frankfurt a.M.: Vittorio Klostermann, 1968)

HEIDEGGER, MARTIN, *On the Way to Language*, trans. by Peter D. Hertz (London: HarperCollins, 1982)

HELLER, AGNES, 'Cosmopolitanism as Philosophy, Refuge and Destiny', in *After Thoughts: Beyond the 'System': Political and Cultural Lectures by Agnes Heller*, ed. by John Edward Grumley, Social and Critical Theory, 24 (Leiden: Brill, 2019), pp. 43–51

HELLINGRATH, NORBERT VON, *Hölderlin, zwei Vorträge: Hölderlin und die Deutschen; Hölderlins Wahnsinn* (Munich: H. Bruckmann, 1922)

HERF, JEFFREY, *Reactionary Modernism: Technology, Culture and Politics in Weimar and the Third Reich* (Cambridge: Cambridge University Press, 1984)

HETHERINGTON, KEVIN, 'The Contemporary Significance of Schmalenbach's Concept of the *Bund*', *Sociological Review*, 42.1 (1994), 1–25

HEWITT, ANDREW, 'Die Philosophie des Maskulinismus', *Zeitschrift für Germanistik*, NF 9 (1999), 36–56

HEYM, GEORG. "DER KRIEG". *Dichtungen und Schriften.* Vol. 1, Hamburg: Ellermann, 1960. P. 347.

HILDEBRANDT, KURT, 'Agape und Eros bei George', *Deutsche Vierteljahrsschrift für Literaturwissenschaft und Geistesgeschichte*, 28 (1954), 84–101

——*Erinnerungen an Stefan George und seinen Kreis* (Bonn: H. Bouvier, 1965)

——*Das Werk Stefan Georges* (Hamburg: Hauswedell, 1960)

HOFMANNSTHAL, HUGO VON, *Gesammelte Werke in zehn Einzelbänden*, I: *Gedichte, Dramen* (Frankfurt a.M.: Fischer, 1979)

IMMER, NIKOLAS, 'Mit singender statt redender Seele: Zur Nietzsche-Rezeption bei Stefan George und seinem Kreis', in *Friedrich Nietzsche und die Literatur der klassischen Moderne*, Ed. by Thorsten Valk (Berlin: De Gruyter, 2009), pp. 55–86

INFANTE, IGNACIO, *After Translation: The Transfer and Circulation of Modern Poetics Across the Atlantic* (New York: Fordham University Press, 2013)

JAEGER, HANS, 'The Works of Stefan George by Olga Marx, Ernst Morwitz'. [untitled review], *Monatshefte*, 45–46 (1953), 391–93

JAEGER, WERNER, *Paideia: Die Formung des griechischen Menschen* (Berlin: De Gruyter, 1936)

——*Paideia: The Ideals of Greek Culture* (Oxford: Blackwell, 1946)

JUNGMANN, FRITZ, 'Autorität und Sexualmoral in der freien bürgerlichen Jugendbewegung', in *Studien über Autorität und Familie: Forschungsberichte aus dem Institut für Sozialforschung*, ed. by Max Horkheimer, vol. 5 (Lüneburg: Dietrich zu Klampen Verlag, 1987; reprint of the 1936 Paris edn), pp. 669–705

KANTOROWICZ, ERNST, 'Das Geheime Deutschland: Vorlesung, gehalten bei Wiederaufnahme der Lehrtätigkeit am 14. November 1933'. Robert L. Benson, and Johannes Fried, eds. *Ernst Kantorowicz*: Erträge der Doppeltagung Institute for Advanced Study, Princeton / Johann-Wolfgang Goethe-Universität, Frankfurt. (Frankfurter Historische Abhandlungen, Band 39.) (Wiesbaden: Franz Steiner Verlag, 1998), pp. 77–93

KARLAUF, THOMAS, *Stefan George: Die Entdeckung des Charisma* (Munich: Blessing, 2007)

KAUFFMANN, KAI, *Stefan George: Eine Biographie* (Göttingen: Wallstein 2014)

——'Von Minne und Krieg: Drei Stationen in Rudolf Borchardts Auseinandersetzungen mit Stefan George', *George-Jahrbuch*, 6 (1006–2007), 55–79

KEALY, DAVID, JOHN S. OGRODNICZUK, SIMON M. RICE, JOHN L. OLIFFE, 'Pathological Narcissism and Maladaptive Self-Regulatory Behaviours in a Nationally Representative Sample of Canadian Men', *Psychiatry Research*, 256 (2017), 156–61

KEILSON-LAURITZ, MARITA, *Die Geschichte der eigenen Geschichte: Literatur und Literaturkritik in den Anfängen der Schwulenbewegung am Beispiel des Jahrbuchs für sexuelle Zwischenstufen und der Zeitschrift Der Eigene* (Berlin: Verlag Rosa Winkel, 1997)

——*Kentaurenliebe: Seitenwege der Männerliebe im 20. Jahrhundert* (Berlin: Männerschwarm Verlag, 2016)

——'Maske und Signal — Textstrategien der Homoerotik', in *Literaturwissenschaftliche Beiträge zum Internationalen Kongress 'Homosexuality, Which Homosexuality?', Amsterdam 1987*, ed. by Maria Kalveram, and Wolfgang Popp (Essen: Verlag Die Blaue Eule, 1991), pp. 63–75

——'Stefan George's Concept of Love and the Gay Emancipation Movement', in *A Companion to the Works of Stefan George*, ed. by Jens Rieckmann (Rochester, NY: Camden House, 2005), pp. 207–30

——'Tanten, Kerle und Sandale: Die Geburt des 'modernen Homosexuellen' aus den Flügelkämpfen der Emanzipation', in *Homosexualität und Staatsraison in Deutschland: Männlichkeit Homophobie und Politik in Deutschland 1900–1945*, ed. by Susanne zur Nieden (Frankfurt a.M.: Campus, 2005), pp. 81–99

——'Übergeschlechtliche Liebe als Passion: Zur Codierung mannmännlicher Intimität im Spätwerk Stefan Georges', in *Stefan George: Werk und Wirkung seit dem Siebenten Ring*, ed. by Wolfgang Braungart, Ute Oelmann and Bernhard Böschenstein (Tübingen: Niemeyer, 2001), pp. 142–55

——*Von der Liebe die Freundschaft heißt: Zur Homoerotik im Werk Stefan Georges* (Berlin: Verlag Rosa Winkel, 1987)

KENNEDY, HUBERT, 'Research and Commentaries on Richard von Krafft-Ebing and Karl Heinrich Ulrichs', *Journal of Homosexuality*, 42.1 (2002), 165–78

——*Ulrichs: Life and Work of Karl Heinrich Ulrichs, Pioneer of the Modern Gay Movement* (Boston: Alyson, 1987)

KIEFER, DR. O., 'Der Eros bei Stefan George', *Geschlecht und Gesellschaft*, 14.7 (1926), 301–09

KIESEL, HELMUTH, 'Stefan Georges Kriegstriptychon: Über die Gedichte "Der Krieg", "Der Dichter in Zeiten der Wirren", "Einem Führer im ersten Weltkrieg" und "Wenn einst dies geschlecht sich gereinigt von schande"', *George-Jahrbuch*, 11 (2016/17), 109–32

KLUSSMANN, PAUL GERHARD, 'Ästhetische Imperative in Zeitgedichten von Stefan George', in *Weltseitigkeit: Jörg-Ulrich Fechner zu Ehren*, ed. by Dirk Kemper (Munich: Fink, 2014), pp. 443–51

——'Stefan George', in *Deutsche Dichter des 20. Jahrhunderts*, ed. by Hartmut Steinecke (Berlin: Erich Schmidt Verlag, 1994), pp. 59–73

KOCH, WILLI, *Stefan George: Weltbild, Naturbild, Menschenbild* (Halle/Saale: Max Niemeyer Verlag, 1933)

KOEBNER, THOMAS, *Unbehauste: Zur deutschen Literatur in der Weimarer Republik, im Exil und in der Nachkriegszeit* (Munich: Text + Kritik, 1992)

KOHLENBACH, MARGARETE, 'Walter Benjamin, Gustav Wyneken and the Jugendkulturbewegung', in *Counter-Cultures in Germany and Central Europe: From Sturm und Drang to Baader-Meinhof*, ed. by Maike Oergel and Steve Giles (Oxford: Peter Lang, 2003), pp. 137–53

KOLK, RAINER, *Literarische Gruppenbildung: Am Beispiel des George-Kreises 1890–1945* (Berlin: De Gruyter, 1996, repr. 2012)

KORNAK, JACEK, 'Judith Butler's Queer Conceptual Politics', *Redescriptions: Political Thought, Conceptual History and Feminist Theory*, 18.1 (2015), 52–73

KÖSTER, ROMAN, WERNER PLUMPE, BERTRAM SCHEFOLD, and KORINNA SCHÖNHÄRL, eds, *Das Ideal des schönen Lebens und die Wirklichkeit der Weimarer Republik: Vorstellungen von Staat und Gemeinschaft im George-Kreis* (Berlin: De Gruyter, 2012)

KRAFT, WERNER, *Stefan George* (Munich: Text und Kritik, 1980)

KRÖHNKE, FRIEDRICH, ' "Wandervogel" und "Homosexuellenbewegung": Zum erotischen und literarischen Ideenkreis der Jugendbünde 1890–1933', in *Der Eigene: Ein Blatt für männliche Kultur. Ein Querschnitt durch die erste Homosexuellenzeitschrift der Welt*, ed. by Joachim S. Hohmann (Frankfurt: Foerster Verlag, 1981), pp. 345–73

LACAN, JACQUES, *The Four Fundamental Concepts of Psycho-Analysis* (New York: Norton, 1978)

LANDFESTER, MANFRED, 'Werner Jaegers Konzepte von Wissenschaft und Bildung als Ausdruck des Zeitgeistes' in *Werner Jaeger — Wissenschaft, Bildung, Politik*, ed. by Colin Guthrie King and Roberto Lo Presti (Berlin: De Gruyter, 2017), pp. 5–50

LANDFRIED, KLAUS, *Stefan George: Politik des Unpolitischen* (Heidelberg: Lothar Stiehm Verlag, 1975)

LANDMANN, EDITH, *Gespräche mit Stefan George* (Düsseldorf: Helmut Küpper vormals Georg Bondi, 1963)

LANDMANN, GEORG PETER, *Vorträge über Stefan George: Eine biographische Einführung in sein Werk* (Düsseldorf: H. Küpper, 1974)

LANDMANN, MICHAEL, 'Georg Simmel und Stefan George', in *Georg Simmel und die Moderne: Neue Interpretationen und Materialien*, ed. by Heinz-Jurgen Dahme, and Otthein Rammstedt (Frankfurt am Main: Suhrkamp, 1984), pp. 147–73

LANE, MELISSA S., and MARTIN RUEHL, eds, *A Poet's Reich: Politics and Culture in the George Circle* (Rochester NY: Camden House, 2011)

LAPLANCHE, JEAN, and JEAN-BERTRAND PONTALIS, *The Language of Psychoanalysis*, trans. by Donald Nicholson-Smith (London: Karnac Books, 1988)

LECK, RALPH MATTHEW, *Vita sexualis: Karl Ulrichs and the Origins of Sexual Science*. Urbana (Chicago: University of Illinois Press, 2016)

LEITAO, DAVID, 'The Legend of the Sacred Band', in *The Sleep of Reason: Erotic Experience and Sexual Ethics in Ancient Greece and Rome*, ed. by Martha Nussbaum, and Juha Sihvola (Chicago: University of Chicago Press, 2002), pp. 143–69

LEONARDI, LAURA, 'Changes in the We–I Balance and the Formation of a European Identity in the Light of Norbert Elias's Theories', *Cambio. Rivista sulle Trasformazioni Sociali*, 1.2 (2016), 168–75

LEPENIES, WOLF, *Die drei Kulturen: Soziologie zwischen Literatur und Wissenschaft* (Reinbek bei Hamburg: Rowohlt, 1988)

LEPSIUS, SABINE GRAEF, *Stefan George: Geschichte einer Freundschaft* (Berlin: Die Runde, 1935)

LINKE, HANSJÜRGEN, *Das Kultische in der Dichtung Stefan Georges und seiner Schule* (Munich: H. Küpper (vormals G. Bondi), 1960)

LUETKENS, CHARLOTTE, 'The Myth of the Small Group', in *Synopsis: Festgabe für Alfred Weber*, ed. by Edgar Salin (Heidelberg: Verlag Lambert Schneider, 1948), pp. 251–79

LUKÁCS, GEORG, *Kurze Skizze einer Geschichte der neueren deutschen Literatur* (Darmstadt: Luchterhand, 1963)

——'Die neue Einsamkeit und ihre Lyrik: Stefan George', in *Die Seele und die Formen* (Darmstadt: Luchterhand, 1971 (1908), pp. 117–32

——*Soul and Form*, trans. by Anna Bostock (London: Merlin Press, 1974)

——*Die Zerstörung der Vernunft*, in *Werke*, IX (Darmstadt: Luchterhand, 1960)

LUNBECK, ELIZABETH, 'The Narcissistic Homosexual: Genealogy of a Myth', in *History and Psyche: Culture, Psychoanalysis, and the Past*, ed. by Sally Alexander and Barbara Taylor (New York: Palgrave Macmillan, 2012), pp. 49–66

MAASEN, THIJS, 'Man–Boy Friendships on Trial: On the Shift in the Discourse on Boy Love in the Early Twentieth Century', *Journal of Homosexuality*, 20.1–2 (1990), 47–70

——*De Pedagogische Eros in het Geding: Gustav Wyneken en de Pedagogische Vriendschap in de Freie Schulgemeinde Wickersdorf Tussen 1906–1931* (Utrecht: Interfacultaire Werkgroep Homostudies, Rijksuniversiteit, Utrecht, 1988)

MANN, DOUG, *Understanding Society: A Survey of Modern Social Theory* (Oxford: Oxford University Press, 2008)

MANN, THOMAS, *Tagebücher 1918–1921*, ed. by Peter de Mendelssohn(Frankfurt a.M.: Fischer, 1979)

MATT, PETER VON, 'Der geliebte Doppelgänger: Die Struktur des Narzißmus bei Stefan George'. *Das Schicksal der Phantasie: Studien zur deutschen Literatur* (Munich: Carl Hanser, 1994), pp. 243–56

MATTENKLOTT, GERT, *Bilderdienst: Ästhetische Opposition bei Beardsley und George* (Munich: Rogner und Bernhard, 1970)

——'Die Griechen sind zu gut zum schnuppern, schmecken und beschwatzen: die Antike bei George und in seinem Kreis', in *Urgeschichten der Moderne: Die Antike im 20. Jahrhundert*, ed. by Bernd Seidensticker and Martin Vöhler (Stuttgart: Metzler, 2001), pp. 234–48

——'Walter Benjamin und Theodor W. Adorno über George', *Wissenschaftler im George-Kreis: Die Welt des Dichters und der Beruf der Wissenschaft*, ed. by Bernhard Böschenstein, Jürgen Egyptien, Bertram Schefold and Wolfgang Graf Vitzthum (Berlin: De Gruyter, 2005), pp. 277–90

MATTENKLOTT, GERT, MICHAEL PHILIPP, and JULIUS H. SCHOEPS, eds, *'Verkannte brüder'? Stefan George und das deutsch-jüdische Bürgertum zwischen Jahrhundertwende und Emigration* (Hildesheim: Georg Olms Verlag, 2001)

MCINTOSH, MARY, 'The Homosexual Role', *Social Problems*, 16.2 (1968), 182–92. Repr. Steven Seidman, ed., *Queer Theory/Sociology* (Oxford: Blackwell, 1996), 33–40

MIDGLEY, DAVID, 'The Absentee Prophet: Public Perceptions of George's Poetry in the Weimar Period', *A Poet's Reich: Politics and Culture in the George Circle*, ed. by Melissa S. Lane and Martin A. Ruehl (Rochester: Camden House, 2011), pp. 117–29

MORWITZ, ERNST, *Die Dichtung Stefan Georges* (Berlin: Bondi, 1934)

MORWITZ, ERNST, and OLGA MARX, TRANS., *The Works of Stefan George*, 2nd edn (Chapel Hill: University of North Carolina Press, 1974)

MOSSE, GEORGE L., *Germans and Jews: The Right, The Left and the Search for a 'Third Force' in Pre-Nazi Germany* (London: Orbach and Chambers, 1971)

——*The Image of Man: The Creation of Modern Masculinity* (New York: Oxford University Press, 1996)

MÜLLER, KLAUS, *Aber in meinem Herzen sprach eine Stimme so laut: Homosexuelle Autobiographien und medizinische Pathographien im neunzehnten Jahrhundert* (Berlin: Männerschwarm, 1991)

NORTON, ROBERT EDWARD, *Secret Germany: Stefan George and his Circle* (Ithaca: Cornell University Press, 2002)

OCKENDEN, RAY, 'Kingdom of the Spirit: The Secret Germany in Stefan George's Later Poems', in *A Poet's Reich: Politics and Culture in the George Circle*, ed. by Melissa S. Lane and Martin Ruehl (Rochester NY: Camden House, 2011), pp. 91–116

OELMANN, UTE, and CAROLA GROPPE, eds, *Stefan George — Ernst Morwitz: Briefwechsel (1905–1933)* (Berlin: De Gruyter 2019)

OELMANN, UTE, UND ULRICH RAULFF, eds, *Frauen um Stefan George*, Reihe: Castrum Peregrini, NF, Bd. 3 (Göttingen: Wallstein Verlag, 2010)

OESTERSANDFORT, CHRISTIAN, 'Platonisches im *Teppich des Lebens*', *George-Jahrbuch*, 7 (2008/9), 100–14

OOSTERHUIS, HARRY, 'Homosexual Emancipation in Germany before 1933: Two Traditions', *Journal of Homosexuality*, 22.1–2 (1992), 1–28

—— 'Sexual Modernity in the Works of Richard von Krafft-Ebing and Albert Moll', *Medical History*, 56.2 (2012), 133–55

—— *Stepchildren of Nature: Krafft-Ebing, Psychiatry and the Making of Sexual Identity* (Chicago: University of Chicago Press, 2000)

OSTERKAMP, ERNST, 'Die Küsse des Dichters: Versuch über ein Motiv im *Siebenten Ring*', in *Stefan George: Werk und Wirkung seit dem Siebenten Ring*, ed. by Wolfgang Braungart, Ute Oelmann and Bernhard Böschenstein (Tübingen: Niemeyer, 2001), pp. 69–86

—— 'Poesie des Interregnums: Rudolf Borchardt über Stefan George', In *Rudolf Borchardt und seine Zeitgenossen*, ed. by Osterkamp, Ernst (Berlin: Walter de Gruyter, 1997), pp. 1–26

—— *Poesie der leeren Mitte: Stefan Georges Neues Reich* (Munich: Carl Hanser Verlag, 2010)

—— *Ihr wisst nicht wer ich bin. Stefan Georges poetische Rollenspiele* (Munich, Carl Friedrich von Siemens Stiftung 2002)

OSWALD, VICTOR A., JR., 'The Historical Content of Stefan George's *Algabal*', *The Germanic Review*, 23.3 (1948), 193–205

—— 'Oscar Wilde, Stefan George, Heliogabalus', *Modern Language Quarterly*, 10.4 (1949), 517–25

PETERSDORFF, DIRK VON, 'Als der Kampf gegen die Moderne verloren war, sang Stefan George ein Lied: Zu seinem letzten Gedichtband *Das Neue Reich*', *Jahrbuch der Deutschen Schillergesellschaft*, 43 (1999), 324–52

—— *Fliehkräfte der Moderne: Zur Ich-Konstitution in der Lyrik des frühen 20 Jahrhunderts* (Tübingen: Niemeyer, 2005)

—— 'Wie viel Freiheit braucht die Dichtung? "Das Zeitgedicht" im *Siebenten Ring*', *George-Jahrbuch*, 5 (2004/5), 45–62

PETROW, MICHAEL, *Der Dichter als Führer? Zur Wirkung Stefan Georges im 'Dritten Reich'* (Marburg: Tectum, 1995)

PIEGER, BRUNO, and BERTRAM SCHEFOLD, eds, *'Kreis aus Kreisen': Der George-Kreis im Kontext deutscher und europäischer Gemeinschaftsbildung* (Hildesheim: Olms, 2016)

———, eds, *Stefan George: Dichtung — Ethos — Staat: Denkbilder für ein geheimes europäisches Deutschland* (Berlin: Verlag für Berlin-Brandenburg, 2010)

PINCUS, A. L., and M. R. LUKOWITSKY, 'Pathological Narcissism and Narcissistic Personality Disorder', *Annual Review of Clinical Psychology*, 6 (2010), 421–46

PLATO, *The Dialogues*, trans. Benjamin Jowett, 1 (Oxford: Clarendon Press, 1892)

PLESSNER, HELMUTH, *Die verspätete Nation* (Frankfurt a.M.: Suhrkamp, 2001; 1st edn 1959)

PLUMMER, KENNETH, ed., *The Making of the Modern Homosexual* (London: Hutchinson, 1981)

POST, JERROLD M., 'Narcissism and the Charismatic Leader-Follower Relationship', *Political Psychology*, 7.4 (1986), 675–88

RASCH, WOLFDIETRICH, *Die literarische Décadence um 1900* Munich: C. H. Beck, 1986)

RÄTTIG, RALF, DIR., *Stefan George: Das geheime Deutschland* (3sat, ZDF, Deutschland, 2018)

RAULFF, ULRICH, *Kreis ohne Meister: Stefan Georges Nachleben* (Munich: C. H. Beck, 2009)

REBENICH, STEFAN, ' "Dass ein strahl von Hellas auf uns fiel" ': Platon im George-Kreis', *George-Jahrbuch*, 7 (2008), 115–41

REICHARDT, SVEN, *Faschistische Kampfbünde: Gewalt und Gemeinschaft im italienischen Squadrismus und in der deutschen SA* (Cologne: Böhlau, 2002)

RENN, LUDWIG, *Meine Kindheit und Jugend* (Berlin: Aufbau Verlag, 1971)

RIECKMANN, JENS, ed., *A Companion to the Works of Stefan George* (Rochester, NY: Camden House, 2005)

——*Hugo von Hofmannsthal und Stefan George: Signifikanz einer 'Episode' aus der Jahrhundertwende* (Munich: Francke, 1997)

RIEDEL, MANFRED, *Geheimes Deutschland: Stefan George und die Brüder Stauffenberg* (Cologne: Böhlau Verlag, 2006)

RILKE, RAINER MARIA, 'Fünf Gesänge', *Kriegs-Almanach* (Leipzig: Insel-Verlag, 1915), pp. 14–19

ROBERTSON, RITCHIE, 'George, Nietzsche and Nazism', in *A Companion to the Works of Stefan George*, ed. by Jens Rieckmann (Rochester: Camden House, 2005), pp. 188–205

RONNINGSTAM, E., 'Narcissistic Personality Disorder: A Clinical Perspective', *Journal of Psychiatric Practice*, 17 (2011), 89–99

ROOS, MARTIN, *Stefan Georges Rhetorik der Selbstinszenierung* (Düsseldorf: Grupello, 2000)

ROPER, JOHN HERBERT, *The Gemeinschaft der Eigenen and the Cultural Politics of Homoeroticism in Germany, 1896 — 1933*, PhD dissertation <https://repository.upenn.edu/dissertations/AAI3635545/>

RUEHL, MARTIN A., 'Aesthetic Fundamentalism in Weimar Poetry: Stefan George and his Circle, 1918–1933', in *Weimar Thought: A Contested Legacy*, ed. by Peter E. Gordon and John P. McCormick (Princeton: Princeton University Press, 2013), pp. 240–71

SALIN, EDGAR, *Um Stefan George: Erinnerung und Zeugnis* (Düsseldorf and Munich: Helmut Küpper vormals Georg Bondi, 1948)

SANDFORT, THEO, EDWARD BRONGERSMA, and ALEX VAN NAERSSEN, 'Man–Boy Relationships: Different Concepts for a Diversity of Phenomena', *Journal of Homosexuality*, 20.1–2 (1990), 5–12

SCHÄFER, ARMIN, *Die Intensität der Form: Stefan Georges Lyrik* (Cologne: Böhlau, 2005)

SCHEFF, THOMAS J., 'Looking-Glass Self: Goffman as Symbolic Interactionist', *Symbolic Interaction*, 28.2 (2005), 147–66

SCHIRRMACHER, FRANK, 'Dies ist der Pfeil des Meisters: Der Staat des Dichters Stefan George, der Verrat und der ästhetische Fundamentalismus: Aus Anlaß der Studie von Stefan Breuer', *Frankfurter Allgemeine Zeitung*, 14 November 1995 <https://www.faz.net/aktuell/feuilleton/buecher/rezension-sachbuch-dies-ist-der-pfeil-des-meisters-1465090.html> [accessed 10 March 2020]

SCHLAYER, CLOTILDE, *Minusio: Chronik aus den letzten Lebensjahren Stefan Georges*, ed. by Maik Bozza and Ute Oelmann, Castrum Peregrini, NF, Bd. 4 (Göttingen: Wallstein 2010)

SCHMALENBACH, HERMANN, 'Die soziologischen Kategorien des Bundes', *Die Dioskuren: Jahrbuch für Geisteswissenschaften*, 1 (1922), 35–105

SEDGWICK, EVE KOSOFSKY, *Between Men: English Literature and Male Homosocial Desire* (New York: Columbia University Press, 1985)

SHILS, EDWARD, 'Primordial, Personal, Sacred and Civil Ties', *British Journal of Sociology*, 8 (1957), 130–45

SHOOKMAN, ELLIS, *Thomas Mann's Death in Venice: A Novella and its Critics* (Rochester, NY: Camden House, 2003)

SIBALIS, MICHAEL, 'The Regulation of Male Homosexuality in Revolutionary and

Napoleonic France, 1789–1815', in *Homosexuality in Modern France*, ed. by Jeffrey Merrick and Bryant T. Ragan (Oxford: Oxford University Press, 1996), pp. 80–101

SIBLEWSKI, KLAUS, '"Diesmal winkt sicher das Friedensreich": Über Stefan Georges Gedicht, "Der Krieg"', in *Stefan George*, ed. by Heinz Ludwig Arnold, Munich: text + kritik, 168 (2005), 19–34

SIMMEL, GEORG, 'Stefan George: Eine kunstphilosophische Studie', *Neue Deutsche Rundschau (Freie Bühne)*, 12.2 (1901), 207–15

SOLOMON, ANDREW, *Far from the Tree: Parents, Children and the Search for Identity* (New York: Scribner, 2012)

SOMBART, NICOLAUS, 'Männerbund und politische Kultur in Deutschland', in *Typisch deutsch: Die Jugendbewegung. Beiträge zu einer Phänomengeschichte*, ed. by Joachim H., Knoll and Julius H. Schoeps (Opladen: Leske und Budrich, 1988), pp. 155–76

SONTHEIMER, KURT, *Antidemokratisches Denken in der Weimarer Republik: Die politischen Ideen des deutschen Nationalismus zwischen 1918 und 1933* (Munich: Nymphenburger Verlags-Handlung, 1962)

STEAKLEY, JAMES D., *The Homosexual Emancipation Movement in Germany* (New York: Arno Press, 1975)

—— 'Sodomy in Enlightenment Prussia: From Execution to Suicide', *Journal of Homosexuality*, 16.1–2 (1989), 163–75

STEFAN-GEORGE-STIFTUNG, ed., *Einleitungen und Merksprüche der Blätter für die Kunst*, Vorwort von G. P. Landmann (Düsseldorf and Munich: Küpper, 1964), pp. 23–26

STEIN, ARLENE, and KEN PLUMMER, '"I Can't Even Think Straight": "Queer" Theory and the Missing Sexual Revolution in Sociology' (1994), in *Queer Theory/Sociology*, ed. by Steven Seidman (Oxford: Blackwell, 1996), pp. 129–44

STEINHAUSSEN, JAN, *'Aristokraten aus Not' und ihre 'Philosophie der zu hoch hängenden Trauben': Nietzsche-Rezeption und literarische Produktion von Homosexuellen in den ersten Jahrzehnten des 20. Jahrhunderts: Thomas Mann, Stefan George, Ernst Bertram, Hugo von Hofmannsthal u.a.* (Würzburg: Königshausen und Neumann, 2001)

STERN, J. P., *The Dear Purchase: A Theme in German Modernism* (Cambridge: Cambridge University Press, 1995)

SAUERLAND, KAROL, *Diltheys Erlebnisbegriff: Entstehung, Glanzzeit und Verkümmerung eines literaturhistorischen Begriffs* (Berlin: De Gruyter, 1972)

TAMAGNE, FLORENCE, *A History of Homosexuality in Europe*, 1 (New York: Algora Publishing, 2004)

TAYLOR, CHARLES, *Modern Social Imaginaries* (Durham, NC: Duke University Press, 2004)

—— *Sources of the Self: The Making of the Modern Identity* (Cambridge, MA: Harvard University Press, 1989)

THOMPSON, JOHN B., *Studies in the Theory of Ideology* (Cambridge: Polity Press, 1984)

THORMAEHLEN, LUDWIG, *Erinnerungen an Stefan George* (Hamburg, E. Hauswedell, 1962)

TOBIN, ROBERT DEAM, *Peripheral Desires: The German Discovery of Sex* (Philadelphia: University of Pennsylvania Press, 2015)

TRAKL, GEORG, 'Grodek', *Das dichterische Werk* (Munich: Deutscher Taschenbuch Verlag, 1972), pp. 94–95

USINGER, FRITZ, *Stefan George: Essays* (Aachen: Rimbaud, 1988)

VALLENTIN, BERTHOLD, *Gespräche mit Stefan George 1902–1931* (Amsterdam: Castrum Peregrini, 1967)

VAN KRIEKEN, ROBERT, *Norbert Elias* (London: Routledge, 1998)

VERWEY, ALBERT, *Mein Verhältnis zu Stefan George: Erinnerungen aus den Jahren 1895–1928* (Leipzig: Heitz, 1936)

VIERING, JÜRGEN, '"Nicht aus Eitelkeit — der Gesammterscheinung wegen": Zur Beziehung zwischen Stefan George und Ida Coblenz', *Euphorion*, 102.2 (2008), 203–31

VILAIN, ROBERT, 'Stefan George's Early Works, 1890–1895', in *A Companion to the Works of Stefan George*, ed. by Jens Rieckmann (Rochester: Camden House, 2005), pp. 51–78

VORDTRIEDE, WERNER, 'The Mirror as Symbol and Theme in the Works of Stéphane Mallarmé and Stefan George', *Modern Language Forum*, 32 (1947), 13–24

WÄGENBAUR, BIRGIT, and UTE OELMANN, EDS. (im Auftrag der Stefan George Stiftung). *Stefan George/Karl Wolfskehl und Hanna Wolfskehl: 'Von Menschen und Mächten'. Der Briefwechsel 1892–1933* (Munich: Beck 2015)

WASNER, ALEXANDER, DIR., *Der merkwürdige fall des stefan george* (sic) (SWR, Deutschland, 2018)

WEBER, MAX, *Wirtschaft und Gesellschaft: Grundriss der verstehenden Soziologie*, 5th edn, ed. by Johannes Winckelmann(Tübingen: Mohr, 1980)

WEEKS, JEFFREY, 'The Construction of Homosexuality' (1977), in *Queer Theory/Sociology*, ed. by Steven Seidman (Oxford: Blackwell, 1996), pp. 41–63

WHISNANT, CLAYTON J., *Queer Identities and Politics in Germany: A History, 1880–1945* (New York: Harrington Park Press, 2016)

WILLIAMS, JOHN ALEXANDER, 'Ecstasies of the Young: Sexuality, the Youth Movement, and Moral Panic in Germany on the Eve of the First World War', *Central European History*, 34.2 (2001), 163–89

WOLFSKEHL, KARL, 'Die Blätter für die Kunst und die neuste Literatur', *Jahrbuch für die geistige Bewegung*, 1 (1910), 1–18

WOLTERS, FRIEDRICH, *Stefan George und die Blätter für die Kunst: Deutsche Geistesgeschichte seit 1890* (Berlin: G. Bondi, 1930)

WOODS, GREGORY, *Articulate Flesh: Male Homo-Eroticism and Modern Poetry* (New Haven: Yale University Press, 1987)

WUTHENOW, RALF-RAINER, 'Weltverhängnis: Stefan George, der Krieg und die Krise'. Uwe Schneider, Andreas Schumann, eds. *Krieg der Geister: Erster Weltkrieg und litrarische Moderne* (Würzburg: Königshausen und Neumann, 2000), pp. 109–20

ZANUCCHI, MARIO, 'Ernst Osterkamp, *Poesie der leeren Mitte. Stefan Georges Neues Reich*' (Review), *Arbitrium*, 30.1 (2012), 107–11

ZELLER, BERNHARD, *Stefan George 1868–1968: Der Dichter und sein Kreis. Eine Ausstellung des Deutschen Literaturarchivs im Schiller-Nationalmuseum Marbach a.N., 1968*, Sonderausstellung des Schiller-Nationalmuseums, Katalog Nr. 19 (Munich: Kosel Verlag, 1968)

INDEX

Achilles and Patroclus 17, 39, 155
Adorno, Theodor 1, 32–33, 34, 93, 99–100, 128–29, 140, 142, 151
aesthetic fundamentalism 2, 35, 38, 94, 116, 142, 147, 178 n. 16
   see also Breuer, Stefan
Anderson, Benedict 10
Aurnhammer, Achim 41

Bachofen, Johann Jacob 22–23, 30
backshadowing 8, 143
Band of Chaeronea, *see* Theban Band
Baudelaire, Charles 33, 63, 76
Bebel, August 18
Benjamin, Walter 32–33, 151, 156, 181
Benn, Gottfried 104
Blüher, Hans 9, 22–25, 29, 42, 76, 103, 155, 156
Böcklin, Arnold 117, 166
Boehringer, Robert 29, 151, 161
Borchardt, Rudolf 29, 32
Borkenau, Franz 22
Brand, Adolf 8, 18–19, 22, 39, 44 n. 8, 65, 75, 134, 157
Braungart, Wolfgang 31, 36, 37, 40–41, 126
Breuer, Stefan 13, 29, 32, 35, 38, 94, 142, 143
Brooke, Rupert 136
Bund, *Männerbund* 4, 6–7, 9, 14 n. 12, 15 n. 20, 20–26, 29, 30, 35, 42, 68, 69, 70, 71, 72, 90, 91, 93, 98, 99, 100, 101, 103. 104, 106, 115, 116–17, 123, 124, 127, 131, 134–39, 141, 144, 145 n. 31, 147–49, 151–52, 153, 155, 156, 158, 161, 163, 166, 169, 171, 173, 174, 175, 179 n. 20
Butler, Judith 9
Butler, Marian Eliza 154

Castoriadis, Cornelius 10
Catullus 68, 161
charisma 4, 7, 13, 22, 24, 27, 29, 31, 34, 35, 36, 37, 90, 103–04, 107, 108, 110, 115, 119, 127, 1131, 134–35, 141, 143, 148, 151, 153, 161–63, 166, 173, 176, 178 n. 18
Coblenz, Ida 67, 68, 79, 85, 94
Cohrs, Adalbert 8, 168, 169, 180 n. 58
Cooley, Charles Horton 11

Dante 76, 117, 125, 159
David, Claude 34, 40, 63, 142, 150, 163, 175, 177 n. 10
Dilthey, Wilhelm 124, 144 n. 15

Durkheim, Emile 10, 11
Durzak, Manfred 34–36

Ebermayer, Erich 5, 8, 14 n. 13, 71, 104
   Dr. Angelo 65, 95, 111 n. 32
Egyptien, Jürgen 37, 38, 51, 122, 144
Eichendorff, Joseph Freiherr von 54
Elias, Norbert 10–12, 43
Erikson, Erik, 44 n. 10, 132, 133

First World War 4, 6, 7–8, 10, 13, 24, 25, 27, 29, 31, 32, 33. 37, 91, 93, 104, 136, 147–49, 150, 155, 157, 158–63, 165, 166, 168, 176, 177 n. 1
Foucault, Michel 9–10
Fra Angelico 108, 116
Fraenkel, Hans 22
Freud, Sigmund 23, 38, 64, 99, 125, 142–43
Fricker, Christophe 37–38, 114 n. 90
Friedemann, Heinrich 167, 168
Friedlaender, Benedict 18, 19, 44 n. 8
Friedrich II 17

Gadamer, Hans-Georg 1, 2, 150–51
Gemeinschaft 11, 13, 21, 33, 35, 70, 144
Gemeinschaft der Eigenen 8, 13 n. 4, 19, 30, 39, 42, 44 n. 8, 65, 75, 134, 156
George, Anna Maria Ottilie 79
George, Friedrich (Fritz) 67
George, Stefan:
   Blätter für die Kunst 25, 27, 28, 35, 36, 37, 40, 78, 123
   Geheimes Deutschland 2, 7, 25, 29, 34, 35, 37, 100, 115, 134, 136, 147–49, 153, 161, 162, 163, 165, 166, 169, 172, 174, 176, 178 n. 16, 180 n. 65
George-Circle 28–30
   Maximin 2, 7, 27, 29, 30, 31, 33, 37, 39, 40, 42, 43, 70, 78, 79, 90, 91, 93, 97, 108, 115, 122, 123–31, 134–35, 141–43, 145 n. 24, 147, 148, 149, 151, 153, 154–56, 162, 165–67, 171, 172–76
Secret Germany, *see* Geheimes Deutschland
'Suprasexual love' 3, 30, 42
works:
   Algabal 7, 26, 39, 40, 52, 58, 60, 63–66, 72, 73, 80, 94, 95, 110, 142, 143
   'Grosse tage' 63
   'Ihr hallen prahlend in reichem gewande' 64
   Die Aufnahme in den Orden 29, 131–34
   Die Bücher der Hirten und Preisgedichte, der Sagen

und Sänge, und der Hängenden Gärten 7, 28, 39, 58, 66, 68, 78, 80
'Das Bild' 71
'Der Ringer' 67
'Der Saitenspieler' 67
'Der Tag des Hirten' 67
'Der Waffengefährte' 69, 70, 131
'Lieblinge des Volkes' 67
'Maiwind fuhr übers brache feld' 78
'Preisgedichte' 68
'An Antinous' 68
'An Damon' 68
'An Erinna' 68
'An Isokrates' 68
'An Kallimachus' 68
'An Menippa' 68
'An Phaon' 68
'Soll nun der mund der von des eises bruch' 79, 80
'Stimmen im Strom' 74
Die Fibel & Zeichnungen in Grau 6, 26, 27, 39, 51, 56, 58, 60, 94, 142
'Abendbetrachtung' 52
'Das Bild' 55
'Der Schuler' 56, 58
'Die Schmiede' 53
'Die Sirene' 52
'Du standest in der wolken wehen' 52
'Einer sklavin' 55
'Erkenntnis' 55
'Erster frühlingstag' 55
'Frühlingswende' 56
'Gift der Nacht' 54
'Gräber' 52, 53, 54
'Herzensnacht' 52
'Ich wandelte auf öden düstren bahnen' 52
'In der galerie' 55
'Keim Monat' 53
'Legenden' 56, 67
'November-Rose' 52, 55
'Schon künden heissere sonnenstrahlen an' 52
'Seefahrt' 55
'Sei stolzer als die prunkenden Pfauen' 52
'Warum schweigst du ...' 52
'Wechsel' 54, 55, 60
Hymnen 26, 39, 58–60, 94
'Ein Hingang' 59
Das Jahr der Seele 6, 7, 27, 32, 34, 51, 66, 77–94, 98, 110, 122, 163
'Erinnerungen an einige Abende innerer Geselligkeit' 86
'Komm in den totgesagten Park' 79–81, 89, 113 n. 66, 122
'Nach der lese' 84–85
'Nachtwachen' 87
'R. P.' 88

'Sieg des Sommers' 80, 85
'Traurige Tänze' 87, 88
'Überschriften und Widmungen' 86, 89
'Waller im Schnee' 85
Maximin: ein Gedenkbuch 123
'Vorrede zu Maximin' 123
Das Neue Reich 6, 8, 27, 29, 40, 41, 42, 66, 91, 93, 98, 115, 124, 149, 150–74, 175–76, 177 n. 10 & 11, 178 n. 16 & 18
'An die Kinder des Meeres' 157
'Burg Falkenstein' 166
'Das Licht' 169, 172
'Das Lied' 169–70, 174
'Das Wort' 170–71
'Der Dichter in Zeiten der Wirren' 164
'Der Krieg' 149, 158–63, 168
'Der lezte der getreuen' 179
'Der mensch und der drud' 166
'Du schlank und rein' 66, 173, 174, 176, 179 n. 37
'Einem jungen Führer im Ersten Weltkrieg' 149, 165
'Gebete' 166
'Geheimes Deutschland' 165–66
'Goethes lezte Nacht in Italien' 19, 150, 152–56
'Hyperion I–III' 156
'In stillste ruh' 169, 172
'Nachklang' 158
'Schifferlied' 169
'Seelied' 169
'Sprüche an die Toten' 18, 29, 166, 167, 169
'Victor ★ Adalbert' 168–69
'Walter W' 167, 169
Pilgerfahrten 7, 26, 39, 58, 60, 62, 78, 94
'Gesichte I and II' 62
'Lauschest du des feuers gesange' 62
'Schweige die klage!' 61
'Siedlergang' 60
'Wir jagen über weisse steppen' 61
Der siebente Ring 27, 32, 33, 35, 36, 40, 42, 58, 70, 90, 106, 110, 115–31, 134, 142, 143, 151, 152, 153, 155, 167, 175, 178 n. 18
'Auf das Leben und den Tod Maximins' 126
'Das Zeitgedicht' 116
'Der Minner' 117
'Der Spiegel' 119
'Die Hüter des Vorhofs' 116
'Empfängnis' 129
'Gestalten' 115, 117, 119, 131
'Gezeiten' 115, 117, 119, 121, 128
'Im windes-weben' 129
'Kunfttag I' 124
'Kunfttag II' 124
'Landschaft II' 128
'Lieder' 116, 128, 129, 130, 131

'Lobgesang' 121, 122
'Manuel und Menes' 117
'Maximin' 115, 124, 128, 131
'Stern der dies jahr mir regiere!' 116
'Tafeln' 130
'Templer' 116
'Traumdunkel' 116, 128, 131
'Zeitgedichte' 115, 116, 117, 119, 131
'Zum Abschluss des VII. Rings' 130
Der Stern des Bundes 6, 27, 39, 42, 56, 102, 106,
   110, 115, 119, 123, 127, 128, 134–42, 143,
   144 n. 15, 147, 149, 150–51, 152, 153, 155,
   157–58, 159, 161, 162, 163–64, 165, 167, 171,
   173, 175, 176, 178 n. 18
Lieder an die heilige Schar 134
'Schlusschor' 140
Tage und Taten 33
Der Teppich des Lebens & Lieder von Traum und Tod
   6, 7, 27, 32, 33, 39, 41, 51, 56, 66, 81, 90,
   94–110, 115, 116, 147, 163, 172
'Das Kloster' 108, 116
'Den Brüdern' 109
'Der Jünger' 106
'Der Verworfene' 81, 106
'Ein knabe der mir von herbst und abend sang'
   109
'Fahrt-Ende' 109
'Lachende Herzen' 109
'Nacht-Gesang' 109
'Tag-Gesang' 109
'Traum und Tod' 147
'Vorspiel' 94, 96–97, 99, 100, 102, 104, 105,
   106
Gérardy, Paul 28, 68
Gesellschaft 21
Glaeser, Ernst 104
Gleichen-Rußwurm, Alexander von 19
Gleim, Johann Wilhelm Ludwig 17
Glöckner, Ernst 30, 150, 165, 168
Goethe, Johann Wolfgang, 17, 28, 29, 92, 117, 124,
   152–55, 173, 174
'Ganymed' 17, 121, 129
Italienische Reise 160
Gothein, Percy 158, 161
Groppe, Carola 36, 37
Grünewald, Eckhart 166
Gundolf, Friedrich 27, 28, 37, 74, 75, 78, 102, 108, 117,
   123, 140, 161

Habermas, Jürgen 10
Habitus 10–12
Hall, Radclyffe:
   The Well of Loneliness 5
Hamecher, Peter 2
Harden, Maximilian 13 n. 4
Harmodius and Aristogeiton 17, 19, 153, 155

Hauptmann, Gerhart 104
Heftrich, Eckhard 35, 63
Heidegger, Martin 171
Heine, Heinrich 92, 116, 174
Heliogabalus, Emperor of Rome 63, 111 n. 32
Hellingrath, Norbert von 156, 161
Herf, Jeffrey 13, 94
Hesse, Hermann:
   Unterm Rad 21
Heyer, Wolfgang 161, 167, 168
Heym, Georg 159
Hildebrandt, Kurt 151, 161, 176
Hindenburg, Paul von 160
Hirschfeld, Magnus 2, 8, 18, 22, 30, 39, 42, 75, 134,
   156
Hofmannsthal, Hugo von, 28, 30, 32, 33, 66, 77–80,
   81–83, 101–02, 107–08, 113 n. 80, 123, 131, 141,
   143
'Ballade des äußeren Lebens' 78, 82
'Der Prophet' 77, 107
'Gespräch über Gedichte' 82
'Herrn Stefan George / einem, der vorübergeht' 77
Hölderlin, Friedrich 141, 144–45 n. 15, 156
homosexual imaginary, *see* imaginary
homosexuality 1–4, 9–10, 17–20, 21, 22–26, 29, 30, 31,
   33. 34, 37, 38–40, 59, 63, 64, 74, 75, 79, 92–93,
   99, 104, 107, 110, 133–34, 143, 153, 155, 156, 157,
   166, 179 n. 20
homosociality 9, 39, 45 n. 32, 76
Horace 161
Huch, Roderich 28
Husmann, August 89
Huysmans, Joris-Karl:
   A Rebours 63

imaginary 3–8, 10, 12, 19, 26, 42, 65–66, 71, 76, 81,
   90–92, 99, 102–03, 119, 126, 133, 134, 143, 152,
   156, 157, 175–77 n. 9
Imperial Criminal Code, Paragraph 175, Imperial
   Criminal Code 2, 18

Jaeger, Werner 20, 44 n. 9, 98
Jahrbuch für sexuelle Zwischenstufen 2
Jansen, Wilhelm 19, 44 n. 8
Jünger, Ernst 13
Jungmann, Fritz 22

Kantorowicz, Ernst 27, 29, 37
Karlauf, Thomas 36, 37, 53, 57, 151, 168
Keats, John, 'negative capability' 82, 112 n. 63
Keilson-Lauritz, Marita 4, 37, 38–39, 59–60, 122
Kerr, Alfred 20
Kertbeny, Karl Maria 2
Klages, Ludwig 23, 27, 28, 68. 80
Klein, Carl August 26, 28, 102, 108
Kleist, Ewald Christian von 17

Kleist Heinrich von 17
Kohut, Heinz 143
Kolk, Rainer 36, 37, 63
Kommerell, Max 27, 37, 156
Krafft-Ebing, Richard von 18, 42
Kronberger, Maximilian 27, 29, 30, 32, 78, 108, 116,
  123–27, 135–36, 144 n. 9, 165

Landfried, Klaus 35, 63
Lechter, Melchior 27, 40, 123
Leopardi, Giacomo:
  'L'Infinito' 176
Lepenies, Wolf 35
Lepsius, Reinhold 108
Lepsius, Sabine 108, 125
Lukács, Georg 1, 32, 40–41, 74, 99, 151

Mackay, John Henry 30, 42
  Fenny Skaller 5, 14 n. 13, 76, 157
Mallarmé, Stéphane 4, 26, 58, 59. 63, 76
Mann, Klaus 8, 34, 156
Mann, Thomas 4, 5, 27, 71, 104
  Der Tod in Venedig 5, 20, 65, 76, 99, 157, 161
  Dr. Faustus 148
Männerbund, see Bund
Matt, Peter von 38
Mattenklott, Gert 13, 31, 35, 36, 103, 131, 142,
  145 n. 24, 151
McIntosh, Mary 10
Moritz, Karl Philipp 17
Morwitz, Ernst x, 27, 28, 37, 60, 119, 134, 150, 151,
  158, 161, 165
Mosse, Georg 21

Narcissus 7–8, 63, 115, 119, 131, 141, 142–44, 145 n. 24
Nazism 4, 13, 26, 28, 31–33, 34–35, 36, 37, 104,
  114 n. 190, 140, 143–44, 151–52, 155–57, 164–65
Nietzsche, Friedrich 4, 33, 102, 117
  Die Geburt der Tragödie 23, 166
  Zarathustra 160
Nordau, Max:
  Entartung 6
Norton, Robert Edward 29, 37, 40, 161

Osterkamp, Ernst 36–37, 103, 122, 125, 140, 142, 151,
  153, 154–56, 178 n. 18

paedophilia 4, 5, 34, 38, 65, 155
paideia 20, 23, 44 n. 9, 98
Patroclus 127
pederasty 17, 19–20, 23, 30–31, 38, 44 n. 8,
  45–46 n. 32, 155
Perls, Richard 28, 108, 109
Persius 161
Petersdorff, Dirk von 148, 150, 163, 166, 168, 171
Petrarch, Francesco 54

Platen, August von 17
Plato 17, 23, 30, 39, 156
  Symposium 17, 19, 41
Platonic love 3, 5, 23, 35, 39, 41–43, 62, 75, 92, 156
Propertius 68
Prott, Hans von 165

Radszuweit, Friedrich 8, 14 n. 18
Rasch, Wolfdietrich 63
Rassenfosse, Edmond 68
Rausch, Albert 5, 14, n. 13, 28, 104
reactionary modernism 13, 15 n. 20, 31, 33–36, 41, 66,
  94, 100, 104, 127, 142, 147, 151, 161, 164, 166
  see also Herf, Jeffrey
Renn, Ludwig 21
Rieckmann, Jens 4, 101, 142
Rilke Rainer Maria 32, 37, 141, 159
  Fünf Gesänge 162
Robertson, Ritchie 27–28
Rolicz-Lieder, Wacław 28, 68
Rouge, Carl 3, 62
Rust, Bernhard 27, 28

Sacred Band, see Theban Band
Saint-Paul, Albert 68
Salin, Edgar 161
Saul and David 39
Schirrmacher, Frank 1, 32
Schmalenbach, Hermann 21–22
Schmitt, Carl 13
Schmitt, Saladin 165
Schuler, Alfred 28
Schurtz, Heinrich 9
  Altersklassen und Männerbünde 24
Scott, Cyril Meir 108, 109
Sedgwick, Eve Kosofsky 9
Shakespeare, William 17, 28, 54, 76
social imaginary, see imaginary
sociogenesis 10–12, 43
Sontheimer, Kurt 13
Spengler, Oswald 13
Spohr, Max 18
Stauffenberg brothers (Alexander, Bernhard, Claus) 27,
  29, 35, 176
symbolic imaginary, see imaginary
Symonds, J(ohn) A(ddington):
  Song of Love and Death 30, 46 n. 49

Taylor, Charles 3, 6, 10, 12
Theban Band 17, 30, 39, 43 n. 1, 70, 117, 127, 135, 155
third sex 18–19, 30, 42, 44 n. 8, 134, 137
Thompson, John 10
Thormaehlen, Ludwig 151, 161, 176
Tönnies, Ferdinand 10, 11, 21
Trakl, Georg 141, 159

Ulrichs, Karl Heinrich 18
Ungern-Sternberg, Alexander von:
    Jena und Leipzig 17
Urning/Uranian 18
Usinger, Fritz 33
Uxkull-Gyllenband, Bernhard von 8, 14 n. 17, 66, 123,
    164, 168, 169, 173, 174, 176, 179 n. 37, 180 n. 50,
    180 n. 58

Vallentin, Berthold 165
van den Bruck, Moeller 13
Verwey, Albert 28, 108
Verwey, Kitty 108

Wandervogel movement 9, 13, 20–26, 28, 31, 42–43, 74,
    75–76, 103, 134, 148, 151, 155, 156
Weber, Max 4, 10, 21, 36

Wedekind, Franz:
    Frühlingserwachen 21
Weininger, Otto:
    Sex and Character 6
Wenghöfer, Walter 167, 168
Westphal, Carl 9
Wilde, Oscar:
    The Picture of Dorian Gray 5
Winckelmann, Johann Joachim 17, 19, 153, 155
wir-Gefühl 10–12, 19, 30, 43, 57, 71, 76, 91, 93, 102,
    110, 117, 133–34, 135, 176
Wissenschaftlich — humanitäres Komitee 18, 44 n. 8
Wolfskehl, Karl 23, 27, 28, 123, 131, 161, 165, 177 n. 16
Wolters, Friedrich 74, 75, 161
Wyneken, Gustav 19, 25, 44 n. 8, 155

Youth movement, *see Wandervogel* movement